MW01206211

★ **BONUS EDITION** ★

THE FINANCIAL ADVISOR'S GUIDE TO A HIGHLY PROFITABLE, HYPER-EFFICIENT PRACTICE

DELIVERING
MASSIVE
VALUE

MATTHEW JARVIS CFP®

Book Produced by Raab & Co. | Raabandco.com

RAAB&Co

Book Cover and Design by Andrew Bell | Andrewbelldesigns.co.uk

Cover Photo by Chris Rosa

For licensing or bulk pricing, email info@theperfectria.com.

Second Hardcover Edition

ISBN: 979-8-9860260-6-0

Printed in the USA

Dedication

To the real brains of this operation, my high school sweetheart and best friend, Jackie Jarvis, who never once complained during the years we were flat broke while I tried to figure out the lessons outlined in this book.

To my children, Alice, Ella, and Calvin: here's to the crazy ones.

To Michael Kitces: Having me on your podcast (episode #7) forever changed the course of my life. Thank you for all you have done for me, my family, and our industry.

To Micah Shilanski, my dear friend and The Perfect RIA co-founder: you win. :)

Last and certainly not least, to my dad, Nathaniel Jarvis, for teaching me to always, always do what's best for the client.

Note on the bonus edition:

"You just published Delivering Massive Value last year! Why the hell do you want to do a Bonus Edition?!?"
—Micah Shilanski

To answer Micah's (teasing) question, here is a partial list of the hundred-plus improvements you get in this hardcover bonus edition:

- New dedication in memory of Tom Gau, with a link to three-plus hours of never-before-seen footage of Tom's best material.
- Twenty-plus sets of training videos recorded to further illustrate the scripts and best practices used by myself and my biz partner at The Perfect RIA, Micah Shilanski, in our practices to this day (including a spicy video on knowing whom to trust for advice).
- Bonus links on how I found, hired, trained, and ultimately handed off 90 percent of my client relationships to my new lead advisor (sometimes called a "junior advisor").
- The list of my ten most important books every advisor must read (online).
- Bonus resources on tax planning courtesy of Retirement Tax Services, led by my brother, Steven Jarvis, CPA.
- A checklist of questions to separate the best coaches from the mediocre and the outright frauds (online).
- New and improved value-adds, complete with links to access PDF copies.
- And for my mother, Cindy Jarvis, who encouraged me to unschool from the sixth grade until today, we fixed a couple typos.

All of these bonuses (and a special invitation to be mentored by me) can be found at www.ThePerfectRIA.com/BookBonus.

To Head Trash:
For *almost* getting me to scrap this book

There is sometimes an illusion that successful people (however you define that term) are somehow exempt from having head trash. After all, with so much success under their belt, surely they no longer worry about failure. Right? Wrong!

Just over a year ago, my finger hovered above the "approve" button for my book, *Delivering Massive Value.* If I'm being honest with you, I was pretty sure nobody would buy it and if somebody did buy it, they'd call it a pile of crap, I'd be ostracized from the industry, all my clients would fire me, and as a result of the bankruptcy it caused, my family would leave me and I'd be pushing a shopping cart full of unsold books around town offering to financial plan for food.

Thankfully with the help of my coaches, mastermind peers, and my family, I pushed through this head trash* and sent the book to the printer. Within months and without a marketing campaign, it became a bestselling book in our industry, with near universal praise from hundreds of advisors, including from Michael Kitces, who recommended it on his summer 2022 reading list, and Nick Murray, who recommended it to his subscribers (of which I've been one nearly my entire career).

I share all this because despite my success as an advisor, author, podcaster, coach to advisors, husband, father, and friend, like you, I still struggle with head trash and my success, like yours, is totally dependent on each of our abilities to push past the monster under the bed known as head trash and do what has to be done!

Happy Planning!

---

*For a quasi-spiritual guide to head trash (though the author calls it "resistance"), *The War of Art* by Steven Pressfield is a must-read. I revisit it every year. However the one thing missing from Pressfield's book is the single most effective cure for head trash/resistance: extreme accountability (see page 134).

A Note On the Line Between
Rip-and-Deploy™ and Theft

Micah Shilanski and I famously started The Perfect RIA podcast in a bar in Boulder, Colorado, during a mastermind. Just a few years later, the podcast has resulted in multiple companies, over one million downloads, and the entire industry adapting things like Surge Meetings™, Value-Adds™, Retirement Income Guardrails™, Sleep On It™, Deliver Massive Value™, Dishwasher Rule™, Head Trash, and Extreme Accountability™ as standard best practices.

Mind Blown!

What's not cool is the self-proclaimed "experts" and a handful of advisors who are now claiming credit for what we created. The worst examples of this is a thinly veiled rip-off of "Deliver Massive Value" in the form of the dirty-sounding "Deliver Deep Value" and the unsupported claims of having invented Surge Meetings™.

Perhaps we should accept the cliché that "imitation is the sincerest form of flattery," but when we think back to the tens of thousands of hours and million-plus dollars we have invested to create these systems, it feels like outright theft.

Our egos aside, the bigger issue with this theft is that like when you played the game of Telephone as a kid, when "experts" copy our work, they always get it wrong, which results in the advisors who trusted them also doing it wrong in their practice, which results in clients getting something less than massive value.

So let's make the line really clear. If you are a financial advisor implementing these strategies to Deliver Massive Value to your clients: go in peace with our blessing. If you are using our strategies in a nonprofit setting, such as an industry conference, so long as you cite "Courtesy of The Perfect RIA" and send a copy to Lifestyle@ThePerfectRIA.com, you also have our blessing.

However, any other use of our intellectual property without permission, especially if you are a self-proclaimed "expert," will result in letters from our attorneys, followed by horrors you can't imagine.

That said, we otherwise have an abundance mentality and love collaborating. So instead of stealing, just send us an email offering to work together.

For a better understanding about why we are so passionate about our intellectual property, google Dan Sullivan *What Is Intellectual Property* (of Strategic Coach fame) to listen to his analogy about removing the label from an Apple MacBook Pro and then claiming you invented it.

Contents

Introduction

Those that can't do, teach, and those
that can't teach, teach gym.

—*Jack Black*, School of Rock

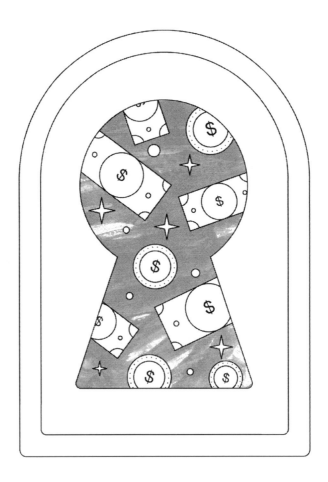

During the first five years of my career as a financial advisor, I made every possible mistake. By the time the 2008 financial crisis hit, I was making almost no money, I could hardly close any prospects, I had maxed out every possible line of credit I could find, and I felt like a total failure who was only still in the business because I was too scared to quit.

Less than ten years later, Michael Kitces described my practice on his Financial *Advisor Success Podcast* as a "highly profitable, hyper-efficient lifestyle practice." That same year (2017), my practice had a gross revenue of $1,097,000, and I took 127 days of vacation (231 if you include weekends). As I write this book, all of my numbers are far above where they were in 2017, and *The Perfect RIA Podcast* I co-host is widely regarded as one of the best advisors-training-advisors podcasts in the industry.

So what changed? How did I go from being on the brink of bankruptcy to having the practice I couldn't have even dreamed of ten years earlier? To be honest, nearly everything changed—and everything *keeps* changing.

The thing is, if you're serious about growing your financial advisor practice, it's not enough to just keep doing what you're doing and hope for the best. You need a proven system where you can set goals, measure success, and keep yourself on track. You need a foolproof way to Deliver Massive Value. That's what this book offers.

I've done my best in this book to detail my most important lessons that you can implement to transform your practice. You'll learn *proven systems* for implementing meeting surges, empowering your team, and wasting less time with clients. After all, no matter how hard you work a bad system, it will never deliver the right results. You'll learn all the ins and outs of interacting with clients and setting expectations, including the very scripts I use in my own business to set my team up for success every single day.

More than anything else, you'll learn to trust the *right people* for advice on how to run your business. The very first chapter will reveal the simple but crucial system for filtering out "big ideas" and deciding whose advice is worth trusting. (Hint: It's *not* the self-proclaimed "experts.")

The lessons in this book will give you the tools and systems you need to reclaim your time, transform your business, and Deliver Massive Value to your clients like never before. Let's begin!

Take Action
○ At the end of every chapter, you'll find a summary of the most important information you learned. You'll also find specific action steps you can use today to begin transforming your business.

○ In addition to the hundreds of changes and updates in the book, each chapter will have a series of bonuses on our website www.ThePerfectRIA.com/BookBonus. This will include PDF samples, videos, recordings, and other resources. Enjoy!

Know Whom to Trust

PROFILE OF SUCCESS

 ### "Jarvis has hit the ball out of the park with this book.

Starting with Chapter 1: Know Whom to Trust, I found actionable steps in nearly every chapter that will help me Deliver Massive Value to my clients. There are several absolute nuggets of gold in these pages that will transform my career and the financial future for my clients. I wish he would have written this guide several years ago!"

David Henderson, CFP
Aurora, CO
PlanWithDave.com

A quick Google search for "how to be a successful financial advisor" yields millions of results (243 million, the last time I checked). Along with dozens of paid results, you'll find hundreds of self-proclaimed experts and companies promising that, if purchased, their system will magically transform your practice. With so many options to choose from and wild claims of success, whose system should you follow? And more importantly, where should you invest what is likely a very limited sum of (borrowed) money you have available?

During the first five years of my career, my main sources of information and advice included self-proclaimed industry experts who had never met with a client, software developers, seminar marketers, wholesalers, branch managers, high-paid consultants, low-paid consultants, book authors, investment managers, and anyone else with an untested, unproven idea they told me would transform my business. After all, even though they wanted my money, these people all claimed to have my best interest in mind, and some of them really did stand to benefit from my success.

However, their conviction in the quality of their strategies had *no* correlation with how well the strategy would work, let alone how well it would work for me. The biggest mistake I made again and again during the first five years of my practice was incorrectly assuming that people would share with me only proven strategies for success. How wrong I was.

In this chapter, you'll learn the most important lesson of all: how to choose the right people to trust.

Listen to People with Success You Can Duplicate

I'm sure he doesn't know it, but Ray Adams was the first of a handful of real experts who changed my career forever. I don't know if it was chance, coincidence, or fate that I met Ray, who at that time was primarily a life insurance agent in Kirkland, Washington. Ray was an odd fellow whom most advisors (agents) dismissed. Perhaps because of this disapproval, Ray had a bit of a chip on his shoulder and wanted to prove he was one of the best. To do so, he was quick to show other advisors exactly how much money he was making *and* exactly how he did it.

Everyone I had met up to that point was very guarded about their income and their strategy for success. Not Ray. He laid everything out on the table, word for word, quickly acknowledging what worked and what didn't. Though I had only a dozen or so interactions with Ray, having access to his *proven strategies*—which turned out to be much more valuable than everyone else's *big ideas*—got my practice pointed in the right direction.

Even more importantly, Ray taught me the importance of trusting the people who actually had the kind of success I wanted to duplicate: successful advisors.

Ray became my hero that day. In addition to teaching me invaluable techniques that have since earned me a small fortune, Ray was the first person I had met who said, "This is how much money I made as an advisor last year, and here's how I did it." I determined that from then on, I would take advice only from people who had a level of success I wanted to duplicate.

In fact, I started to wonder about all my finance heroes, so I did some digging. Sure enough: the best I could tell, all these "experts" had made their real money on *teaching* their methods, not *using* them to make money. My attorneys have advised me not to name names, but this list includes most of the major names in our industry, each of them with a system, product, seminar, lead-generation technique, direct mail campaign, digital mail campaign, website, or service they claimed would make any advisor rich. Over the course of my professional career, I had borrowed tens of thousands to learn from these experts, and guess what? I wasn't rich. Now I knew why.

SO WHAT ABOUT ME?

You're probably asking yourself, "Hey, Matt. If you're such an expert, why have *you* taken time and energy away from seeing clients to coach other advisors? Why not just spend all that time on building your own practice?"

This is a great question to ask anyone offering advice. Good job—you're already on your way to a more successful business! Here's my story:

I wrote this book and co-founded The Perfect RIA as a way to help other advisors succeed, but also to leverage my own skills. Frankly, I was also really tired of seeing otherwise great advisors led into failure (like I almost was) by our industry "experts" with no clue how to actually build a great practice. This book is my way of, hopefully, helping other advisors avoid that fate.

To this day, I still meet with clients on a regular basis, I still run my podcast ... and I still take all the time I need for my family while making every client feel valued and Delivering Massive Value. Where's the proof? Keep reading!

The Framework for Filtering Out the Big Ideas

One day, when I was complaining to Ray about my most recent disillusionment over bad financial advice, Ray asked me one of the great rhetorical questions, one they should include in every finance and business textbook ever printed:

"If their system is so good, why haven't they used it to create a successful business?"[1]
I was stunned. There I was, chasing failures, while I had a real live success story right in front of me. His methods could have been taught in a college classroom—but he

---

1 This same logic applies to leads, seminars, direct mail, digital ads, paid appointments, and virtually any marketing product plied to advisors. If it is so good, why don't you use it?

was too busy using them to grow his business and deliver value to his clients.

Out of everything Ray taught me—and you'll find more gems in this book—his most important lesson was to give me the filter to avoid getting sucked up in other people's "big ideas." To make your own educated and informed decisions about the people trying to shape your practice, ask yourself these four key questions about any "expert" you're considering. They just may transform your business.

"If their system is so good, why haven't they used it to create a successful business?"

"If Your Ideas Are So Great, Why Are You Selling Them to Me Instead of Using Them in Your Own Practice?"

I'm embarrassed now to admit how long it took me to understand this, but back in the early days, it was a revolutionary idea to me that I should trust only the advice of people who can actually prove their ideas worked. I could finally see the ugly truth: I simply hadn't been trusting the right people.

In fact, the people I'd been handing my future potential to weren't just unqualified to advise me—they didn't have the chops for investing, period. They talked a good game and sold lots of products to advisors, but *they had never built a successful practice themselves*. At best, they were relaying what they'd seen in other practices, like a game of telephone—and at worst, they were just guessing at what would work for me.

Either way, none of what they were selling had been proven, and I was wasting thousands of dollars of hard-earned money for the privilege of learning the wrong lessons. Sound familiar?

"If Your Practice Was So Great, Why Did You Stop?"

During my hell years, I was actually impressed by self-proclaimed experts who said, "I used to have a practice just like yours, but I decided to go into consulting" (or wholesaling, products, writing, or whatever other moneymaking opportunity the person jumped into that *isn't* their chosen field). I think the reason I was impressed at that time by someone who quit our industry was that I wanted to quit so badly myself.

What I hadn't considered was that a lot of these "consultants" were really just failed practitioners: washed-up advisors who became practice consultants and authors and now speak at length about how to be successful in an industry where they totally failed … while their big ideas might have actually been copied from other, more successful practices.

I now understand that anyone who would quit this industry is a failure from whom I should take *zero* advice. Is it possible that they had an amazing practice, but it simply wasn't their life's calling to be an advisor, so they took up consulting advisors instead? I suppose it's possible (though I've yet to *ever* see that), but why would I want to take advice from someone who doesn't want to be an advisor?

"Is This How You Invest *Your* Money?

It seems obvious that any financial advisor would actually be *using* the same strategy as their clients, but here's an industry secret that might shock you (it shocked me when I first found out): not all of them do.

I once asked this question of an investment manager we were using. I had (incorrectly) assumed the investment manager was, of course, using the same investments he was recommending to clients. To my embarrassment, he answered (with the client on the phone) that no, he did not use this strategy with his own money.[2]

Why should anyone trust an advisor who doesn't practice what they preach … and why should anyone trust a consultant, author, or coach who isn't actually using the methods they're teaching you?

"Where's the Proof?"

I remember sitting in a breakout session with a renowned thought leader in our industry who was articulating a particular strategy that, on paper, sounded really great. During the Q&A, I asked how he articulated it to real clients and the exact names or providers of the products he was recommending. Without a second of hesitation or shame, he explained that he'd never met with real clients, and the products he'd been discussing were strictly academic.

WTF? Why not just tell me to offer unicorns to my clients?

Imagine going to a surgeon or getting on a commercial flight, only to have the doctor or pilot explain that they've never actually done a surgery or flown a plane, but they've read a lot about it, they've watched a lot of other people do it, and they assure you that despite having never actually done it themselves, they can coach *you* on how to do it successfully.

The big problem with these "experts" is that most of them can't prove their ideas work—because they don't, or because they've never been tested in the real world.

---

2 Asking this question may have saved my practice, as we immediately pulled all our assets from that manager, and a few years later he ended up in jail.

Unless they've recently sat across from a client or prospect, they have no idea what it takes to be successful. And if they *were* an advisor, why did they stop?

While I have no love for people claiming to be experts, this does *not* mean that you should ignore anyone who isn't an advisor. For example, I continue to learn from the greats like Michael Kitces (quasi-advisor), Jocko Willink (Navy SEAL), John Barron (coach), Joe Lukacs (coach), Tim Ferriss (life hacker), and dozens of other non-advisors.

While the self-proclaimed experts are constantly in your face, it's very difficult to find really successful advisors who are willing to share their secrets to success *and* who can actually identify what made them successful. The only way to separate the proven ideas from the big ideas is to actually see the proof. Don't be afraid to ask for it, and don't hand over a dime to the "experts" until you see it.

Action Steps

Chances are, if you're reading this book, it isn't the only resource you've considered in your quest to transform your business. Whether it's a shelf full of books, an app full of podcasts, or a calendar full of "revolutionary" seminars, this is your opportunity to hold these experts up to their own words and see if they're worth your money and your time. Take these steps today to separate the true greats from the "great ideas."

- ◯ Ask yourself: "Why did these people ever leave their practice? If their system is so good, why haven't they used it to create a successful business?"
- ◯ Take advice only from people who have a level of success you want to duplicate.
- ◯ Commit to following all of the steps and exercises in this book. You can trust *me*—and you owe it to yourself to put in the time, effort, and thought necessary for your business to reach the next level.

Bonus content available for this chapter at ThePerfectRIA.com/BookBonus:
→ My personal screening guide when selecting coaches that you can use when choosing your own coach/mentor (including if you are evaluating The Perfect RIA)
→ My most recommended books
→ Links to our most popular podcast episodes on coaching

CHAPTER 2

Implement Client Meeting Surges

PROFILE OF SUCCESS

"Implementing surge meetings saved my firm!

Before meeting Jarvis in 2017 and learning his strategy for surge meetings, I didn't think I could take on even a single additional client. I was already working around the clock, doing everything myself. Surge meetings, along with a *lot* of hard work, laid the foundation for tripling my revenue in three years and gaining control of my business."

Taylor Schulte, CFP®
San Diego, CA
www.taylorschulte.com

When I explain my schedule, specifically my vacation schedule, to other advisors, they're usually shocked. "Matthew," they say, "how can you possibly take 120 to 180 days of vacation each year? There's no way you can take that much time off and still service your clients." And those are the *polite* advisors. Many just come right out and say, "I think you're full of $#*!."

This is, essentially, an accusation that I'm either a terrible advisor or a liar, and my response depends on my mood at the time—but when I'm feeling particularly snarky, I'll toy with them. "OK," I'll say, "let's look at how much time we're both spending actually engaged with clients. Specifically, how many times are you meeting with your clients each year, and how are you delivering massive value?"

They'll then try to explain in vague terms the important, invaluable ways they're meeting *all* of their clients' needs, which usually includes being available around the clock for any inquiry and having frequent, if irregular, meetings with them. I let them get it all out of their system and then inform them: "I have meetings with my clients at least twice a year. Every calendar quarter we make sure to deliver massive value on some form of the financial planning process. They have access to my team at any time, and if it's urgent, they can reach me almost immediately. So am I really 'failing as an advisor,' or am I simply one hundred times more efficient than you?"

The thing is, we're both doing *the exact same things* (and to be honest, I'm likely doing far more), and we're spending essentially the same amount of time interacting with clients, but these other advisors are stuck to their office chair and I'm taking four to six *months* of vacation each year. (My longest stretch was living for six months on a boat in the Bahamas.) Not to pour salt in the wound, but I've also got time to co-host *The Perfect RIA Podcast*, do consulting for other entrepreneurs, organize entire conferences, and never, ever work more than forty hours a week.

THE THREE CORE TENETS OF A SUCCESSFUL BUSINESS

"The Perfect RIA" is a practice definition coined by my podcast co-host and dear friend Micah Shilanski, which adheres to three core tenets:

#1 Deliver Massive Value to clients such that you can charge a premium fee

#2 Operate at a 50 percent or better profit margin as measured by EBOC

#3 Have the ability to take up to six *months* of vacation each year, which I personally count as days I don't open my laptop for work.

So what's my secret? Well, it's several things (all outlined in this book), but more than anything, it's a form of time blocking we call "meeting surges" and I'm convinced it is the foundation of all "Perfect RIAs." Remember, only the things you implement actually count—and if you implement only *one* thing from this entire book, meeting surges will be the most transformative.

What Are Meeting Surges?

Imagine you have one hundred clients (or will someday have one hundred clients), and you want to meet with them an average of twice a year, for two hundred total meetings. Most advisors will schedule those two hundred meetings whenever it's easiest for them and/or the client, which typically looks like somewhere between two and six meetings a week, year-round.

While this approach is often justified with "I want to be available whenever clients want to meet with me," the reality is that this is just your own laziness talking. Further, it's doing both the client and the advisor a huge disservice, as it makes it difficult for the advisor to get into a meeting groove, it results in fewer vacations and higher burnout, and, ultimately, it translates into a poor client experience. So what's the alternative?

With *meeting surges*, instead of doing two to six client meetings per week, you'll see as many clients as you can in a few short weeks—ideally between 80 and 90 percent of your total client list.[1] In my office, we conduct fifteen to twenty meetings per week for three weeks with a half-hour break between each meeting. In other words, at the end of three weeks we've seen as many clients as the average advisor does in three or four *months*!

Having worked with hundreds of advisors around the world to implement surge, I can tell you from experience that not only does surging your client meetings work, but implementing surges in your own business will change your life.

Examples of Efficiency in Action

Now, let's pause here for just a minute. You might be thinking, "But Matthew, this is still the same amount of time and work, so the net benefit is zero." On paper, you are correct, but in real life, you couldn't be further from the truth. Let's look at three examples:

#1 Henry Ford's Model T

I like to use the analogy of Henry Ford and his innovative car manufacturing technique. When he first made automobiles, it took him twelve hours to assemble

---

1 My podcasting co-host Micah Shilanski can do up to forty meetings a week, and the legendary Tom Gau (who inspired me to do surges) is rumored to do as many as eighty meetings a week, but I don't have that kind of stamina and maybe my relatively light surge week of fifteen to twenty meetings is too much for you. No problem. The key is to focus on improvement, not overnight perfection.

a Model T. When he perfected the assembly line, where the system was so clearly understood and delineated that every worker could dig down on the individual element they were responsible for, Ford cut that time to roughly two hours. This is the dramatic difference you can have on your team's capacity to produce happy clients.

You may not be making cars, but the science isn't about cars: it's about the power of a good system. If you do the same task again and again and again, you're going to get better at it. If you're trying to jump between tasks, your productivity is going to go down. That's just science.

When you sit down with the fifteenth client you've talked with about the same topic, you'll have gotten *really* good at articulating your points in a way that they understand and connect with.

"Implementing surges in your own business will change your life."

#2 Cal Newport's Deep Work

One could be tempted to dismiss Henry Ford's example. After all, that was a long time ago, and it applied to factory workers and not financial planners. Fine—let's look at something a little more contemporary.

In his book *Deep Work*,[2] author Cal Newport tells us that it takes up to three hours for our brains to reach optimal performance, and every time we take an email or a phone call, that three-hour window resets. By living our scattered, unfocused lives in a state of frantic reactiveness, we simply aren't giving our brains a chance to work at maximum capacity.

#3 YOU!

Odds are we've never met, but I think more than anyone else, you can best prove my point. Imagine you get done with three weeks of surge and after recovering from the exhaustion, you look at your calendar for the next three months and it's wide open (never mind the details—we'll get to that). What could you do with that time? Work *on* your business? Travel with your family? Implement a new prospecting strategy? Pursue personal goals? Deliver Massive Value to clients? Finally, you will have time to actually *do* all of the things you've been trying (and failing) to squeeze in.

Still not sold? To be honest, neither was I when I first learned a version of this strategy from Tom Gau and Ken Unger at the Academy of Preferred Financial

---

2   Cal Newport, *Deep Work: Rules for Focused Success in a Distracted World* (New York: Grand Central Publishing, 2016).

Advisors. To this day, after years of successfully implementing surge meetings in my practice and hundreds of other practices, I'm still surprised at how well it works.

So instead of asking you to trust me, I'm going to ask you to *prove me wrong*. Pull out your calendar right now (yes, right now—it's on your phone) and pick *two* days per week and *one* week per month when you will *not* meet with or talk to any clients. (Yes, of course you'll have the occasional emergency to deal with. We'll talk about handling emergencies in a minute.)

Commit to testing this out for just one calendar quarter. If it doesn't dramatically improve your practice and your life, the next time we meet in person at an industry conference, the first round of drinks is on me. Deal? Good!

Now for the details.

Implement Meeting Surges in Three Phases

Getting surge to work is all about setting and managing expectations. In the absence of clear expectations, everyone is at the mercy of luck and the odds are definitely not in your favor. Specific to scheduling, most offices respond to a client request for a meeting with some version of "what works for you?" This is the start of a train wreck, as it tells the client that you're not very busy ... which invites the question: "If my advisor isn't busy, are they actually a good advisor?" Further, Murphy's law dictates that the client will inevitably choose a date and time when you are *not* available, which will require you to either cancel some other obligation or reject the client's offer. All of this puts you in a defensive, reactive mode—not a great mindset to be in if you're trying to Deliver Massive Value.

To mitigate this, implement your meeting surges in three phases, mastering each before moving on to the next. You and your rockstar team will be time-blocking like the pros you are in no time!

Phase One: Testing the Waters

"Which of those days work best for you?"

When you call my office for a meeting and only my office manager can schedule meetings, you will be told something like:

"Matthew is always excited to meet with you. He sees clients on Tuesdays, Wednesdays, and Thursdays. Which of those days work best for you?"

This seemingly simple script (and *all* the best scripts are simple) sets the expectations of when I *am* available and then gives the choice to the client (rather than simply saying when I'm *not* available or starting an endless back-and-forth email exchange). After the client picks a date, my team then shares the preplanned meeting blocks, which look something like this:

MONDAY			
WORKING ON BUSINESS			
	TUESDAY – THURSDAY		
	CLIENT MEETINGS		FRIDAY
			PROSPECT MEETINGS

"But what if the client can come in only on Friday?"

I hear this from advisors all the time, but we almost never hear it from clients—which means, like most things we tell ourselves to limit our own potential, that we're talking about complete and total head trash.[3] Always better to be prepared with another script, such as:

"Matthew spends Fridays with his family, but he has several times available on Tuesday, Wednesday, or Thursday."

This same logic can be applied to clients wanting times outside of your preset block, evenings, weekends, Christmas Day, or any other date or time when a professional is not available for meetings. If the client absolutely insists on a Monday or Friday, my team will respond with:

"I'm not able to schedule meetings on those days, and you will need to talk with Matthew directly to make an exception. He is available on Tuesdays, Wednesdays, and Thursdays ..."

Seeing a pattern?

CHOOSE YOUR OWN ADVENTURE	

Not seeing clients on Mondays and Fridays works best for *me*, but the magic is not in those specific days—the magic is in being intentional with your time. I have advisor friends who never come to the office before 10:00 a.m. and others who work only on the days their kids' school is in session. The key here is to be intentional about what works best for *you*.

---

3 You'll hear a lot about *head trash* in this book. What does this mean? Exactly what it sounds like: the garbage that fills your head, clutters your thoughts, and keeps you from the business—and life—you deserve. If you're like I was, you're probably carrying around a lot of it. Throughout this book, we're going to keep checking in to clear the way for you to get past your own self-imposed limitations and make the key changes necessary to transform your business. Coach Joe Lukacs, founder of the Magellan network, does great work with advisors in this area.

Phase Two: Making Changes

"I can send you a link to his calendar, or we can schedule it together right now."

After you've implemented Phase One (no client meetings on Mondays or Fridays) for a few months—no cheating!—it's time to scale up to Phase Two, where you'll carve out a few *weeks* each quarter when you will not see clients.[4]

Phases Two and Three require significantly more resetting of client expectations than did implementing Phase One. Odds are you've trained your clients to expect that they can schedule a meeting with you anytime they want, with virtually no notice. THIS HAS TO STOP! When I call any other high-level professional (doctor, accountant, attorney, or even the Tesla repair center), I have to wait days or even weeks to get an appointment.

"But Matthew!" you're probably thinking. "My clients expect white-glove service! That's why they pay me!"

Again, this is head trash, so let's work through it. When you think "white-glove service," who or what comes to mind? Let me pick two examples: Flying first-class and staying at the Ritz-Carlton. In both cases, I'm paying an incredible premium for an experience that, from a strictly utilitarian standpoint, can be had for a fraction of the price. Despite this premium, if I call to book first-class plane tickets or a room at the Ritz, I'm still at the mercy of their availability. If they have no seats/rooms, I'm out of luck. So yes, you can give the highest level of white-glove service and still not be available at a moment's notice.

"Which of those days work best for you?"

That said, a dramatic change in scheduling does require resetting expectations, often multiple times. In my office, we've been doing meeting surges for years, and yet we still reset these expectations every chance we get. This resetting of expectations happens in every client meeting, every newsletter, every discussion on scheduling, and any other chance I have.

"Matthew is scheduling client meetings in May once your tax returns for the year have been filed (or extended). I can send you a link to his calendar, or we can schedule it together right now. Which would you prefer?"

During Phase Two of surge implementation, your team's response might sound something like this:

---

4 Want to accelerate your practice transformation? While you absolutely cannot skip Phase One, you *can* skip Phase Two and proceed directly to Phase Three.

"To better serve clients, we will be doing the majority of our client meetings the second month of each calendar quarter (February, May, August, November). This way we can be sure to cover everything throughout the course of the year."

The goal with this messaging is to set expectations *and* let the clients know why it is in their best interest to do meetings this way. This is especially important in Phase Three.

ELIMINATE SCHEDULING HASSLES—FOR GOOD

"Hey, does 10:00 a.m. work?" "No, 10:00 doesn't work. How about 11:00?" "Oh, 11:00 doesn't work for me. How about 2:00?" "Nah, 2:00 doesn't work. How about Thursday?"

What a nightmare! Your office should *never* email back and forth with people about schedules. Surging your client meetings may solve a ton of productivity problems, but playing email tag to schedule those meetings is another huge waste of time and a frustration for everyone involved.

Use a Scheduling App
The easiest way to avoid the time-consuming, productivity-destroying process of scheduling client meetings is to set up some kind of link for clients to access your calendar. (In our office, we used Acuity in the past but have since switched to Calendly due to its better integration with our Salesforce platform.)

Link your calendar with a scheduling app, right now. Then, when clients call your office, your relationship manager can either email them a link to your schedule and say, "Here's my calendar" (or accept their link) or jump on a quick call to sort it out. No more email tag!

The only thing that really gets changed in this template are the key discussion items for that particular surge cycle (see Chapter 23 on value-adds). Even if my team is on the phone with a client to schedule a meeting, they will walk through this same link to ensure the meeting is scheduled within the correct time blocks and that the meeting drops into our meeting prep process.

During your first couple of surges, emails alone will not be enough, and your team will likely need to call clients directly to get them scheduled.

Never Schedule Your Own Meetings!
I know this feels like you are doing the client a favor, but you're not. "Colleen manages our calendar, so let me hand you off to her to get this scheduled."

Never, ever send emails back and forth to schedule meetings. This is an incredible waste of time and a huge source of frustration. Get a calendar link, or call the client directly!

Phase Three: Fully Committed to Surge

"I'm sorry, but this is the advisor's availability."

Phase Three is the ultimate goal, the golden ticket to delivering massive value, when 99 percent of your meetings fall during your twice annual "big" surge and your monthly two-day mini surges.[5] In our office, Phase Three looks something like this:

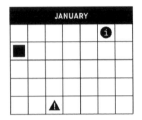
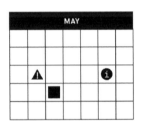
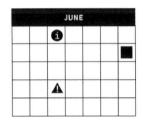
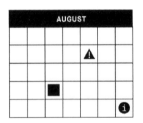

---

5 As mentioned at the beginning of Phase Two, DON'T SKIP PHASE ONE! Surge is a ton of work, and jumping in too quickly will likely bury you and your office. Ease into this one. Please.

Trouble with commitment? The best way to force yourself into these surge blocks is by taking extended vacations so you physically cannot schedule meetings during that time. (Funny how you're less likely to go running to the office when you're on a cruise somewhere.)

The other is to simply send me a check for $1,000 for every non-surge meeting you hold (see page 134 on extreme accountability). Yes, there will be a couple of true emergencies that require non-surge meetings (and you can schedule those for free)—but if you're doing more than three non-surge meetings a month, you're doing something wrong.

How to Prepare for Surge

Getting clients scheduled for surge (which mostly consists of clearing your head trash) is only half the battle. The very real other half is having streamlined systems in place for client meetings. After all, if you are going to deliver massive value in ten-plus client meetings in one week, you need a dang good system for making this a reality.

Case Prep: Team

This starts with what we call "case prep." Like a doctor's office, where the nurse takes vital signs to support the doctor's ability to diagnose, your team is there to support you. While there are things your team cannot do, there are a lot of things they can and must do if surge is going to work. Here's how I prepare my team for surge week success.

Four to six weeks before each surge meeting, I sit down with my team to review our goals and agenda for this surge, specifically what I need them to do in preparation. Here are a few of the easy things that I want for every client meeting, no matter the topic:

Checklist: There are a handful of things I need confirmed and information gathered for every meeting. This is done in the form of a checklist that I also use for taking notes and recording action items from the meeting. This form also contains notes of any outstanding action items from prior discussion, plus any questions or concerns the client had when scheduling this meeting.

Statements: Whatever financial documents you look at with clients should be printed *in advance* by your team. In our office we use a report from Orion that highlights asset allocation, account balances, and life-to-date performance. The same report is run for every client meeting, no exceptions.

Guardrails: As we talk about in Chapter 20, guardrails are the lifeblood of our practice. This report is also printed for every meeting.

Value-Add: As we'll discuss in Chapter 23, you must proactively deliver massive value every quarter. In our office, our latest value-add is printed and ready to discuss with the client.

Market Commentary/Education: For each meeting, I like to have printed some kind of illustration that provides long-term perspective for the client. This is often inspired by something I found in the *Nick Murray Interactive* newsletter, learned from Brian Wesbury at First Trust Advisors LP, or read in JP Morgan's *Guide to the Markets*. Whatever the piece, the goal is to take the focus away from today's crisis and instead focus on very, very long term.

In our office, all this information is on my desk for each client the Monday morning before the client meeting. This gives us plenty of time to make any needed adjustments and never be caught scrambling for paperwork.

Case Prep: Advisor

With so much legwork having been done by my team, I can take between five and fifteen minutes on Monday to review each client's documents, as well as my memos from prior client meetings. I add a couple of additional notes to the case prep and occasionally ask for additional resources from my team. I then review the documents again in under five minutes before walking in to meet with the client.

When designing your own case prep system, the goal is to have 70 to 90 percent streamlined for every client. This does not mean I use everything my team prepared every time, but in every meeting, I know exactly what I have and what I don't have.

Last-Minute Forms and Paperwork

A common mistake advisors make is to decide in the middle of a meeting that an action needs to be taken, and then run out and request (demand?) the team take that action on the fly. This is a recipe for failure! Now the team is rushed to complete a task that you likely did not give clear instructions for and about which they have to either guess or interrupt you (probably both). Either way, it looks like amateur hour to the client, and you'll likely make mistakes.

Instead, all paperwork and resource requests will ideally be made by Monday (or, worst case, a reasonable amount of time before the meeting starts). If you have a last-minute request for something you need before an imminent meeting—or, even worse, *during* the meeting—trust me: it can wait.

"If you're doing more than three non-surge meetings a month, you're doing something wrong."

Try this:

> "Ms. Client, we'll need to get some forms together for that, and my team will send those to you later this week. Is that OK with you?"

This same is true for questions that come up during the meeting to which you don't know the answer. Rookie advisors will do some combination of guessing, quick calculations, or—heaven forbid—opening their computer and trying to find the answer. *These are all bad ideas.*

Instead, punt:

> "That's a great question, and while I could give you a 'back of the napkin' answer, I instead want to do some research and come back with my recommendations on [date]. Is that OK with you?"

Now you can keep your meetings on track, without scrambling, while exhibiting complete professionalism to your clients at all times. Just make sure to follow through with the information you promised!

Tips for Surge Success

Make no mistake: flipping your entire client calendar on its head can be overwhelming. But the benefits you'll reap are worth the effort. Here are a few bonus tips for maximizing your surge success.

Flip the Script

"I need to talk with …"

This is likely the most common request your team receives: a request or demand to see the principal service provider—you. In most offices, the team will respond to this request with something like this:

"Let me put you on hold to see if the advisor is available."

Never do this! Never. Never. Never!

What you are really telling clients is, "Let me see if you are important enough for the advisor to talk with." Even worse, when you then pick up the phone off of hold, you've interrupted your flow (strike one). You were not expecting the call, so you're a bit flustered (strike two). And you're scrambling to find the information you need to answer the client's request (strike three!). Even worse, nine times out of ten, the client wants or needs something that your team could have handled without your involvement.

So what do you do instead? Let's look at how the scenario might unfold if your team responded a little bit differently:

THE SCRIPT: RESETTING SCHEDULING EXPECTATIONS

Client: "Hello. Can I speak with [Advisor]?"

Rockstar Team: "Hello Mr./Mrs. Client! [Advisor] would love to speak with you, but he/she is not available at this moment. Is there something I can help you with?"

Client: "I don't think you can help. When can I talk with [Advisor]?"

Rockstar Team: "[Advisor]'s next client meeting days are [date] and [date], but if this is time sensitive, I can have him/her give you a call on [date later that week, if possible]."

Client: "Great. Please schedule the call."

Rockstar Team: "Perfect! So that [Advisor] can be best prepared for your meeting, what can I tell him/her it is regarding?"

Compared with our first scenario, this one produces an infinitely better client experience. In most cases, when the client explains why they need to talk with me, it will turn out to be something my team can handle. For example:

Best Client: "I have a new bank account and need to change the link on my Fidelity accounts."

Rockstar Team: "Great News! I can take care of that for you right now. [solves the problem] Now, would you still like to meet with [Advisor]?"

Typically, if your rockstar team can solve their problem, the client won't need to see you at all! And when the team really can't handle the request, I can go into the meeting totally prepared to Deliver Massive Value to the client and potentially solve any issues before the meeting even starts.[6]

---

6 For example, your client's CPA may want to know why we did a ROTH conversion last year—something even a well-equipped team may not always be able to handle.

For any scheduled phone or zoom meetings, *always* start the call exactly on time. Try this: Five minutes before the call, stop everything else you're doing, review any call notes, and get in the zone. Then, make sure the client's phone rings at *exactly* the scheduled time.

While the difference between 10:00 sharp and 10:01 may only be a minute, it is really the difference between doing what you said you would or not.

Check In and Fine-Tune

As with every other strategy for Delivering Massive Value, surge meetings work only if you take the time to implement them—but they *improve* only if you *take the time to improve them.*

When you wrap up a surge week, quarterly value-add, or any other process, don't just file it away for next time. Systems improve by feedback loops, so it's important to review with the team what worked and didn't work so the next surge can be even more effective.

After each surge week, hold a meeting to answer the following questions about how you did and what changes you'll make next time:

- What systems worked?
- What systems failed?
- What did we learn for next time?
- How could we improve the client experience?
- How will we celebrate?

Remind yourself of your goals and objectives, and look carefully at how close you came to achieving them. What roadblocks stood in your way? What didn't flow as smoothly during that client meeting? What slide in the presentation didn't seem to connect? Take the time to reflect on these major experiences and draw specific lessons that you can apply to your business. Write down all of your objectives, and list all the ways you and your team need to improve on your process in order to better meet them next time.

Action Steps

Nothing will free up your time like implementing client meeting surges—there's simply no single more important change you can make for your business. Implement these steps to up your office's efficiency and Deliver Massive Value!

○ At a minimum, implement Phase One *right now*!

○ Work with your team (and yourself) on forcing mechanisms that will make this easy to follow. Relying on willpower in the moment will almost surely fail.

○ A system improves only if you make the effort to make it better. Continue to fine-tune your surge plans with your team so you can deliver even more value to your clients.

○ Visit www.ThePerfectRIA.com to see videos we've recorded on this topic.

Bonus content available for this chapter at ThePerfectRIA.com/BookBonus:

→ My six-week checklist leading up to surge so that you can "copy genius instead of inventing mediocrity" (Michael Henley)

→ The first video of our surge masterclass giving you actual scripts you can use with clients

→ The email we send to clients inviting them to surge

Fire PITAs (Pain in the Assets)

(and Other Clients Bringing Down Your Bottom Line)

Early in my career, I incorrectly believed that anyone willing to pay me was a client. I was so desperate to grow revenue that it was easy to accept the idea that all new revenue was good revenue. After all, "the client is always right," so even if the client was difficult to work with, abused my time, ignored my recommendations, and was generally unpleasant, their fee was paying my mortgage, so I figured this was just the price of doing business.

What I didn't understand then (and many advisors still don't understand) is that these people are not clients, but rather saboteurs who are doing everything they can to keep you from achieving success. I'm certainly not suggesting that this is a conscious or intentional desire on the part of difficult clients, nor am I such a conspiracy theorist that I think your competition has hired these people to destroy your business. Frankly, I don't care why these people abuse you. All I care about is that you understand these people are sabotaging your success and get rid of them.

Like so many advisors I've coached, you might be thinking (as I once did), "But Matthew, these are otherwise nice people and their fees feed my family ... right?" WRONG! Whatever fee they are paying, it's not worth giving up your future success. While this might sound melodramatic, it's the truth. The time, energy, and confidence these people take from you are the same time, energy, and confidence you need to catapult your practice. I'm sure you've told yourself that "when I'm successful I'll fire this person" but the hard truth is, like me, you won't become successful *until* you fire these saboteurs.

Three Clients to Send Packing

Still not convinced and/or too scared to make a change? We'll come back to this at the end of the chapter, but for now let's look at the three types of saboteurs you'll encounter in your business, how they are ruining your bottom line, and how you can "graduate" them to someone else.

Pain in the Assets

We all have (or have had) clients who make us cringe. Just seeing their name on our calendar or on the caller ID causes our mood to drop. It could be something blatant, like their consistent rudeness to our team, or something subtle, like how they talk too much during meetings. It may be them, or it may be us—but for some reason, we find no joy in working with this client.

But is this a big enough reason to let a client go?

Yes.

Why? Being a successful financial advisor who Delivers Massive Value to her clients requires a great deal of emotional energy. If all we had to do was meet with clients, this would be a relatively easy task. However, especially as we are building our dream practice, there are lots and lots of energy-draining tasks that we face daily including prospecting, compliance, bookkeeping, prospecting (yes, it's on the list twice), and anything else you don't look forward to doing. If, on top of all this, you still have a PITA client draining your energy and your confidence, this already difficult task has now become nearly impossible.

WARNING: EVEN YOUR TOP CLIENTS CAN BE PITAS!

Let me offer just one example from my practice: a saboteur disguised as a client we'll call Henry. His parents had been clients of ours for many years, and when his dad passed away, Henry took over the finances and helped care for his elderly mother. We initially dismissed Henry's PITA tendencies as misguided mourning for the loss of his father, and we told ourselves that in a few months he would get used to working with us and everything would be fine.

Two years (!) later, Henry was still a PITA of epic proportions. Each meeting was an interrogation. Henry would see a distribution from his accounts and accuse us of having stolen the money because he couldn't remember asking for a distribution. We would then show him on the statement that the funds had gone directly to his bank account or where a ROTH conversion was, to which Henry would inevitably respond, "Oh." When not interrogating us, Henry would complain endlessly about all of his personal problems. It was pure torture.

Why did we allow Henry to sabotage our practice for so long? In addition to being the child of a longtime client, Henry was one of our top ten clients in terms of the fees he paid, so firing him would be very expensive. What we only eventually realized was that keeping him as a client was costing us far more.

One day, Henry finally pushed so hard on my team that two of my most trusted rockstars came to me and practically begged that we fire him. This was not a request made lightly, as they both knew how much Henry was paying in fees, but they were willing to do whatever it took (including reducing their bonuses) to end this suffering. Their insistence *finally* had me see the light, and we promptly fired Henry.

One important note: While my team was willing to personally sacrifice to make up for the lost fees, as the business owner, it was my responsibility alone to take the entire financial hit. Take care of your rockstars, and they'll take care of you!

Some of our readers can immediately think of a client (or three) who easily meets the definition of a PITA. Those clients should receive the letter below before the end of this week. If you do not have any glaring PITAs (congratulations), I still recommend that you and ideally each member of your team complete the following exercise separately.

Take a list of all your clients in reverse-alphabetical order—a quick brain trick to cause you to look at the list differently from before. Next to each client's name, write a number between 0 and 10, with 10 being for clients with whom you absolutely love working to the point that just seeing them on your calendar lights up your day, and 5 being for clients whom you feel neither positive nor negative about. Give a 0 to any clients like Henry who are clearly giant PITAs.

Once each client has a number, compare your scores with those of your team members. For any client whose average score is less than a five, send them this letter:

Dear «firstname» and «spousefirstname»,

I'm in the process of effecting some important changes in my business and my life. To that end, I've been reviewing all my client relationships.

In thinking about our business relationship with each other this last year, I've reluctantly concluded that I will not be able to serve you in the ways you need. That being the case, it seems unfair of me to try to retain your account and I am, therefore, resigning it.

I'm sure this comes as hard news and I know that finding another advisor of our caliber will not be easy. To that end, I hope you will accept my offer to help you find another advisor whose services are better suited to your needs. If you would like, I am willing to personally introduce you to other really great advisors in the area whom you might like. I would also be glad to send you information about Fidelity's in-house advisors, or the great (and very low-cost) team of Certified Financial Planners (CFP) employed by Vanguard.

Whatever option you choose, once you have found an advisor better suited to your needs than I am, please have him or her contact me directly to facilitate the transfer of your account. I promise to give the transfer process my closest personal attention as you surely deserve.

Unless we receive other instructions from you, we will continue managing your accounts through the end of this quarter, thereby giving you several weeks to decide on how to best handle your accounts. As a gesture of good faith, we have not charged your account fees for this quarter. If by the end of the quarter you have not found a suitable replacement, I will be sending you an email with everything you need to work directly with Fidelity.

I thank you for your past business and wish you every future success.
Sincerely,

Matthew Jarvis, CFP®

Of course, that's not the only way to clear the PITAs from the client rosters. Nick Murray suggests firing one every year on your birthday. Personally, I recommend doing them all at once, but to be honest, I never had that much courage. Whatever the frequency, the faster you rip off this Band-Aid, the faster you will achieve your dream practice. Conversely, the longer you allow these PITAs to sabotage your practice, the longer it will take you to achieve success—if you ever get there at all.

Freeloaders

While the damaging efforts of PITAs are easy to spot, freeloading saboteurs often hide in plain sight. Thankfully, there is an easy way to detect them. As we did for PITAs, I want you to make a list of all your clients, but this time without names. Instead, this list, sorted smallest to largest, needs to simply display their annual fee.

This is best done in Excel, as you need to run a couple of formulas. (Alternatively, you can add your client list to the template we have at www.ThePerfectRIA.com. Here are the numbers we need:

80/20 Rule: How much of your revenue is coming from the top 20 percent of your clients, and what percentage of your clients are generating 80 percent of your revenue?
Average Revenue per Client: This is simply averaging all clients.
Target Revenue per Client: We'll look in closer detail at this important metric in the Post-it Note Business Plan you'll build in Chapter 6, but for now, let's use $6,500, which with 150 clients would give you roughly $1 million in annual revenue.

All right, time to face the truth. What do these cold, hard numbers say to you? For most advisors, just looking at this spreadsheet paints a really clear picture of who is paying for your practice and who is freeloading.

Rule Breakers

The third and final group of saboteur clients are the rule breakers. While these people often take the form of PITAs, they can sometimes be very nice people, who pay your fees but for whatever reason refuse to follow your advice. This failure to follow your advice can take lots of forms including:

- Failing to provide tax returns annually
- Failing to get the correct estate documents
- Failing to buy the insurance you recommended
- Making emotional investment decisions in the top or bottom of the market cycle
- Being non-responsive to your calls and/or emails
- Over-distributing from accounts

- Failing to save enough to meet financial goals
- Any other activity contrary to your recommendations that will potentially have significant negative impacts on their finances.

"But Matthew," you might argue, "it's their money and it's their choice." That is correct. We cannot force clients to follow our advice. But a client who does not follow your advice is not really a client—they're a walking time bomb. At some point, their failure to follow your advice will result in significant financial problems, and you will be left holding the bag.

"I fired *two hundred* freeloader 'clients,' and it laid the foundation for catapulting my practice to success."

Three Lenses for Taking Action

I get it, it's *hard* to fire a client. Not only does it always suck to be the bad guy, but even at our most successful, there's always that lingering fear that no new clients will ever replace them.

These feelings don't make you bad at business; they make you human. (You're only bad at business if you let them get the better of you!) Because we are humans and not machines, I want to offer you three lenses that will prompt you to take action.

Lens #1 You can never make it up on volume.

If your average annual client revenue is $1,000, you will *never* make it to a "highly profitable, hyper-efficient lifestyle practice." Why? Because at this average, you would need one thousand clients to get to $1 million in revenue—but serving one thousand clients would likely require a team of ten people, thus no profits.

If this lens motivates you to take action, awesome! Anyone who is less than half your target average revenue (or worse yet, less than half your average client revenue) gets graduated today. Alternatively, you might give them the opportunity to pay your average fee as detailed on page 74.

Lens #2 You are stealing from your best clients.

What if you were required to disclose to your clients how much they were paying relative to all your other clients? What would be their reaction when they discovered that some of your clients were getting the same services for a fraction of the price, or for free?

Please don't confuse this with me advocating for charging a flat fee. After all, we can easily (and accurately) make the case that the value you provide and therefore the fee you charge is directly correlated to the size and complexity of the client's situation.

However, could it not be considered unethical or (for those who insist on using the *f* word) a violation of your fiduciary duty to charge one client multiples of what you are charging another for the same services?

Don't get too hung up on the logistics of this lens, but rather, ask yourself, if a client is not paying a fee (or is paying a substantially reduced fee), are not your other clients unknowingly subsidizing this relationship? Could we not argue that the time you spend on underpaying clients is being taken (dare I say, stolen) from your other clients?

Time aside, just the emotional cost of working with people who don't value your time enough to actually pay for it is hurting all of your clients.

Lens #3 You are stealing from your family.

I'll confess that this last approach is probably unhealthy, but it worked for me, so here it goes. Anytime I found myself tempted to discount fees, or anytime I hesitated to fire a freeloader client, I imagined myself calling my family to explain that I couldn't take them to the park tonight and we had to skip our vacation next month because I would rather give someone a discount on my fees. While I never actually made this call, I would keep a picture of my family on my desk and in my conference room so that when I was too weak to hold to my fee schedule, I could take strength from the shame of having to tell my family.

Again, probably not a healthy approach and not something I'm proud to share, but it gave me the motivation to charge full price, which ultimately got me where I am today.

Whatever lens empowers you to take action, awesome. By the end of *this week*, either fire these "clients" or offer them an opportunity to pay your new minimum fee. For an email template to use for the latter, see Chapter 4.

You may be thinking, "But Matthew, I can't afford to ..." Well, in 2008 and 2009, I fired *two hundred* freeloader "clients," and it laid the foundation for catapulting my practice to success. While I can't promise you'll be a success overnight, I *can* promise that you'll never be a success if you hang on to freeloader clients.

"But Matthew, these people need my help!" Look, business is business, and charity is charity. If you want to do pro-bono financial planning, that's awesome, but don't do it at your office. Partner with your FPA chapter or some other community organization to offer pro-bono financial planning on certain days of the month at a location other than your office. This is where you can help people who can't or won't pay for your advice.

At the end of the day, these "rule breaker" clients are in fact PITAs, but we can handle them with a little more grace. When clients fail to follow your advice, channel your inner Jocko Willink by taking extreme ownership for *your* inability to effectively communicate to the client why they should follow your advice.

THE SCRIPT: LETTING PITAS DOWN GENTLY

For clients who won't stick to the program, it's time to show them the door. Try this:

"Ms. Client, I can only do my best work if [rule being broken], and I insist on only doing my best work. If you are unable to [rule being broken], I will with great sadness need to resign from your account. How would you like to proceed from here?"

Action Steps

Just as you wouldn't allow someone to physically damage your office or steal your money, you cannot continue seeing "clients" who are PITAs, freeloaders, and/or rule breakers. These imposters are the deadweight keeping you from achieving success for yourself and more importantly, keeping you from Delivering Massive Value to your real clients.

◯ Make a list of all your clients (names only) in reverse alphabetical order and have each person on your team independently rate them 0 to 10. Anyone with an average score of less than 5 (but especially less than 3) must be fired this week.

◯ Make a list of all your clients with only their annual revenue (no names) sorted from smallest to largest. Anyone paying less than half your minimum fee needs to either have their fee raised *or* be fired.

◯ Make a list of all your clients not following your rules. Give them a final opportunity to follow the rules, remembering that the reason they haven't been is that *you* haven't explained why they should. If they continue breaking the rule, follow the PITA process.

Bonus content available for this chapter at ThePerfectRIA.com/BookBonus:
→ The letter I use when I need to fire a client so that even though you are terrified to do it, you can take some peace in "If Jarvis can do it ..."
→ A video of Micah and me graduating a client in person
→ Three specific examples of clients I graduated, why, and how

Raise Your Fees and Charge What You're Worth

PROFILE OF SUCCESS ⭐

"If you are a discount advisor, providing discounted value, then by all means charge a discounted fee.

If however you are a premium advisor, providing premium value, then charge a premium fee. It's no different than the Super 8 Motel and the Ritz-Carlton charging different rates."

Micah Shilanski, CFP
Anchorage, AK
Shilanski & Associates

Second only to implementing meeting surges, charging the right level of fees is essential to your practice's success.

I know you're likely already nervous about this idea, so before we talk about raising fees, let's get really clear on fees in general. Assuming you are reading this book in a non-communist country, none of your clients are being forced to work with you. This means clients are willingly paying your fee because they feel it is worth the value you provide.

In fact, I tell every prospect and remind every client:

"It makes sense to work with our office (or any professional) only if the VALUE we provide is worth some multiple of the FEE being charged. Each quarter there will be a line item on your statement that says "Advisor Fee" and a dollar amount. You and I will both look at that number and decide if the value we provided is worth the fee. If yes, we continue another quarter. If no, then we need to have a serious discussion and possibly part ways as friends. Is that OK with you?"[1]

Sometimes advisors balk at this script, claiming it draws too much attention to your fees and sets the stage for clients to leave. News flash: Clients already know your fees, because every other article/blog post they read tells them to stop paying an advisor—and they're *already* going to leave as soon as they think you're not worth the money!

By drawing attention to fees, you are taking the high road and giving clients permission to do what they already were able to do. And by addressing the elephant in the room, you're clearing the way for the real discussions at hand.

First: Trash the Head Trash

Of course, raising fees is easier said than done. Telling your existing clients—who agreed to one set of numbers and likely won't be excited about the new one—is a difficult thing to do (or ask your team to do). And what about new clients? Will anyone ever pay your higher rates? This is, of course, only the beginning of the head trash that most advisors experience when even considering raising fees. Other variations include:

- What about fee compression? (This is a myth!)
- What about robo advisors? (They're not your competition.)

---

1 Thank you to Nick Murray for inspiring this script. It changed my life.

- What about flat-fee advisors? (They won't survive and can't Deliver Massive Value.)
- What about Jeff Bezos launching an Amazon Prime financial advisor that will not only crush our entire industry but will also force each of us to have Amazon Echos implanted in our brains? (I can't help you there …)

Here's the deal. At the end of the day, all your fears and objections to raising your fees are really some version of "If I raise my fees, all my clients will fire me, my family will leave me, my friends will hate me, and I will be left holding a 'will plan for food' sign in front of my kids' school where all the world will know I'm a complete failure." How do I know that's the core of your fears? BECAUSE IT'S MY FEAR TOO!

When I did my first round of massive fee increases years ago, it was a relatively easy decision: if we didn't raise fees, we were going out of business, so it was fear of failure behind door #1 and guaranteed failure behind door #2. At that time, we had over one hundred clients who weren't paying an AUM fee, millions of assets not being charged an AUM fee (each with a great excuse, of course), and a fee schedule that was all over the board.

Even with the threat of bankruptcy, I was still terrified each time I told a client they would have to pay a higher AUM fee (or start paying one altogether). To my surprise, almost everyone said yes, which finally gave us enough cash flow (and confidence) to focus more time and energy on Delivering Massive Value.

I have to confess, however, that no matter how successful you become, this fear never really goes away—at least it hasn't for me. We recently raised our fee on assets under $1 million from 1 percent to 1.5 percent (which you'll learn about later in this chapter). It took me *months* of coaching to get over my head trash around this fee increase, plus some serious accountability pressure to straighten me out (more on that later too), only to have my team nearly mutiny over the idea before getting on board (turns out they have similar head trash).

Let's take just a minute to tackle these fears, and then we'll jump in to logistics of how to successfully raise your fees and by how much. While I could write chapters trying to talk you out of your fear of raising fees, those fears are not rational, so no amount of reasoning will make a difference. (Remember this tidbit when talking with clients!)

Instead, I want to recommend three exercises for trashing the head trash that stands in the way of your success.

"This means clients are willingly paying your fee because they feel it is worth the value you provide."

#1 Tim Ferriss's Fear-Setting

Though I've never met Tim Ferriss, his work, starting with *The 4-Hour Workweek*, has transformed my life. Perhaps his most valuable technique is an exercise called fear-setting. He explains it nicely, so I won't repeat it here—do yourself a favor and check out his 2017 article on the topic.[2]

#2 Run the Numbers

Make a list, right now, of the clients whose fees you want or need to raise. Calculate how much more revenue you would have if they all said yes. With that number in hand, figure out how many clients would have to fire you to still break even on cash flow due to the new fee schedule the remaining clients will be paying.

Even if you only break even between the new fee schedule and the number of clients who fire you, you now have fewer clients to serve for the same income, thereby giving you more time to Deliver Massive Value to current and future clients.

#3 Get Help

Still stuck? Go back to Chapter 1 to review how to find advice you can trust, then find an advisor who has successfully done this and get their help. You can tell yourself, "If Jarvis (or some other rockstar advisor) can do it, so can I." I can't tell you the number of times I've repeated this mantra, even to this day.

#4 Shame Yourself into Raising Fees

When your head trash tells you, "It's not fair to raise fees," respond with, "No problem. I'll just tell my family we can't travel the world because I was too afraid to raise fees." Or what about this: "No problem. I'll just tell all my top clients that their high fees are subsidizing my fear of raising fees on small clients." Or even: "I'll leave instructions in my will that my tombstone say, 'Sure, he died of a heart attack caused by the stress of not having a good income, but at least he never raised fees.' "

You get the idea. Whatever you have to tell yourself to motivate this action, now is the time! Do whatever it takes. Your family and eternal reputation are at stake.

---

2 Tim Ferriss, "Fear-Setting: The Most Valuable Exercise I Do Every Month," The Blog of Author Tim Ferriss, https://tim.blog/2017/05/15/fear-setting.

#5 Find an Accountability Partner

It wasn't until I set up some *extreme* accountability with my good friend Micah that I was finally able to conquer my fears and raise my prices.

How extreme was this accountability with Micah, you ask? It involved giving Micah the following letter, addressed to my ten best clients, to be mailed if I didn't raise my fees by the time I said I would:

"Dear Best Client, this letter serves as my resignation from your account. I have discovered that I'm not serving you as well as you deserve and that you would be much better served working with perhaps the world's greatest financial advisor, Micah Shilanski. I have transferred all my personal investments to his management and I strongly recommend you do the same."

What do you think? Would you still be avoiding raising your fees if it meant losing your best clients—and a giant bet—to your best friend?

Types of Fees

Fees are a necessary part of business. I like them in theory—who doesn't like being paid?—but in practice, they're messy to deal with, and they never seem to fit every situation.

There are many ways to structure a fee schedule and plenty of examples of highly successful financial planners who use different models. There's no magic bullet; your office needs to make the best decision for your clients and financial goals.

Let's look at the main ways fees are typically structured.

AUM Fee

As you know, AUM stands for *assets under management*, and taking a percentage of it is a common fee structure in this industry.

In a perfect world, fees would always be based on complexity or time investment—but we live in this one, where one client might check in once a year and another with the same assets might take up a hefty amount of your office's time every month. And when you're first onboarding your clients, this variance is anything but predictable.

I charge an AUM fee (currently 1.5 percent annually for assets under a million dollars and 1 percent for assets over that amount). That's not because I think it's a perfect fee structure; given the unpredictable nature of clients, it's a pretty terrible model. But like Winston Churchill said about democracy, it's the least bad option, and sometimes you have to solve for the least bad option.

Hourly Fee

Hourly fees are meant to protect a service provider from scale creep, and they're great in certain situations. I charge them myself on occasion, simply because I like to give prospects who may not quite fit into my system yet but are working toward it the option to talk to me.

However, I caution against using them for all but the most straightforward of tasks, simply because they may end up creating a barrier for the client to call the office.

For example, what if a client is scared about the markets and thinking about selling something they shouldn't? If they called your office right away, you or your staff might have had the opportunity to talk the client down before they did anything drastic. But if they're worried it's going to cost them $500, they may wait to call me until they're in the process of closing their account. Your hourly rate has created a psychological barrier for your client that cost them undue stress and a pile of money.

By setting hourly rates, you're setting strong expectations, and you're protecting yourself from situations where you might be asked to give your time for free. But before you go this route, consider the signals you're sending your clients, and consider whether you can set expectations and protect yourself in other ways.

Financial Planning Fee

There's a lot of debate in our industry about whether to charge a financial planning fee to a prospective new client. Lots of places do it for free; one advisor friend of mine charges $10,000.

Personally, I do not charge financial planning fees. My office considers this part of the prospect process (which you'll learn more about in Chapter 10). I eventually want clients to appreciate the value I can bring them so much that they don't bat an eye at my fees, but I have to give them a chance to taste that value first. I want to knock down as many barriers to entry as possible when a potential client walks into my office.

However you decide to set your rates, think about your most time-consuming client, and make sure your new rate will cover you in case a new client tries to break that record.

How *Not* to Set Your Fees: Compare Yourself to the Studies

If I can get on my soapbox for one second: ignore all the industry studies about fees and the claims that AUM fees are morally wrong. These studies all tell you my practice shouldn't even exist. They say fees can only be so high before clients balk, an advisor can only make so much, that million-dollar practices need huge teams to support, that no advisor can take weeks (or, heaven forbid, months) of vacation, and lots of other fairy tales mid-level financial advisors tell themselves that keep them from making the kind of fundamental changes that really matter.

Making matters worse, these studies fail to meet even the lowest standards of statistical rigor. The participants self-select (a.k.a., volunteer themselves, often in exchange for a trivial benefit), the numbers are all self-reported (a.k.a., it's all liar's data), and successful practices don't waste their time giving practice data to vendors who are just going to sell it to solicitors.

Even if the studies could be believed, I don't care much what self-proclaimed experts think I should be doing. Instead, I rely on what is working in my practice and in the hundreds of other highly successful practices.

The second (and equally bad) place I see advisors look for direction on fees is to the lowest common denominator, a.k.a., the Walmart strategy. As of this writing, there are firms (our attorneys have advised us not to name names) who will let a client work with a CFP® for somewhere between 30bps and *free*. In fact, many firms will actually *pay* clients to transfer their accounts.

Ignoring that these firms have other revenue sources and massive economies of scale, you will never win the price war against the big-box investment firms, so don't waste your time or energy even worrying about the lowest price provider, at least not when it comes to pricing.

How to Set Your Fees: Copy Success!

You can (and many advisors do) spend a lifetime figuring out the "perfect" fee schedule—but it doesn't exist, and while you're sitting at the top of the mountain looking for divine inspiration on the perfect fee schedule, your clients and prospects will be gladly paying an imperfect fee to another advisor. Not to belabor this point, but the time you are spending figuring out a fee schedule is delivering *no* value to anyone. Not your clients, not your prospects, not your family. Nobody.

The quickest, easiest, and arguably best way to set your fee schedule is to simply copy someone else. As we discussed in Chapter 1, copy only those people whose *proven* success is as good as or better than your goals. How? Just ask, or pull their ADV. Or, really, just ask someone you admire for a copy of their fee schedule.

What's my fee schedule, you ask? Here it is, as of the time this book went to print:
- Households whose investable assets with our firm fall under $1 million pay 1.5 percent.
- Households whose investable assets with our firm are over $1 million pay 1 percent.

"But Matthew!" I can hear you scream. "With this fee schedule, a client with $900,000 pays around $13,500 annually and a client with $1.1 million pays around $11,000 annually." That is correct. I admit, my fee model is flawed. So why do I use it? That's easy to explain: it's easy for clients to understand, and I'd much, much rather spend my energy finding new ways to Deliver Massive Value and bring on new clients than sit on the mountain figuring out a better fee schedule.

If you can clear through your own personal head trash and convince yourself, "If Matthew can charge 1.5 percent under $1 million, so can I," then go in peace and raise your fees accordingly. If, however, your head trash has you thinking some version of "That might work for Matthew, but it will never work for me," don't worry—raising your fees is within your reach! Let's slow down and tackle this in phases.

Phase One: No More Freeloaders!

You are a professional. Anyone who is unwilling to pay your fee does not deserve even a minute of your time, as this is a business and not a charity. Not enough? Think of it like this: if you go out of business because you were unwilling to charge fees appropriate to the value you deliver, you won't be able to help *anyone*.

If and when you feel charitably inclined, you are welcome and encouraged to engage in pro bono financial planning *outside* of your office. You can even partner with your local FPA chapter or charity to offer free financial planning days—just *not* at your office. (Not only is this a great thing to do for your community, but it gives you an easy out next time somebody asks you for free advice!)

When I committed to being a professional, I told over one hundred "clients" that if they wanted to talk to me again, they would have to pay an hourly fee (see page 51 for a word-for-word template you can use today to tell your clients you're raising your prices). You can too.

Phase Two: Everybody Pays at Least 1 Percent

While I'm convinced that 1 percent became some kind of industry standard simply because the math is easy, no advisor who Delivers Massive Value should be charging *less* than this amount. As such, the first phase in your fee schedule progression is to create a list of all clients, their AUM, and their actual annual fee.

From there, you can quickly determine the exact percentage each person is paying. Anyone paying less than 1 percent is getting a letter *this quarter* raising their fee. No exceptions. Not for your mother, your uncle, your friend, your spiritual leader, or anyone else. Everyone pays at least 1 percent, or they're gone.

> **"If you go out of business because you were unwilling to charge fees appropriate to the value you deliver, you won't be able to help *anyone*."**

Phase Three: Raise Your Fee in Waves

It took me three tries to get to 1.5 percent for all clients under $1 million. My first round was all clients under $300,000. A couple of years later it was all clients under $500,000. Finally, it was all clients under $1 million. If you have the courage, I would do it all at once, but otherwise, do it in stages. The key is to commit to exact dates when you will do each wave of fees *and* find some form of extreme accountability to make sure you stick to the plan, like an accountability partner or a mastermind group.

Whichever phase or fee schedule you are considering, set a timer *right now* for sixty minutes. Use that time to think about your new fee schedule, and at the end of that time, lock in a fee schedule that scares you. You are welcome to revisit your fee schedules once a year, when you update your ADV. For now—stay firm!

How to Actually Raise Your Fees

When it comes right down to it, it's hard to pull the trigger on asking people who are already giving you money to give you even more of it. Here's a quick guide for making that process a little easier.

Send the Damn Letter

It's all well and good to choose a new fee structure (but seriously, congratulations on that), but at some point, you have to actually tell a client that their fee is going up.

I'll be honest that I'm a giant wimp when it comes to raising fees, and if I had to do it face to face, I'd probably chicken out. I used to really beat myself up over this, but instead I found a system that worked for me: sending a letter.

While some may consider this the "wimpy" option, sending a letter has several advantages, including the following:
- You can do an entire block of clients all at once.
- You are less likely to make exceptions than when you sit down with a longtime/favorite client in person.
- Much of the work/pain can be delegated to your team.
- Keeping things digital makes it much easier to stick to the deadline.

Here is the first letter that my office mails out to announce our fee increase. As with everything else in this book, feel free to copy it or adapt it to your own practice.

"THE TIMES THEY ARE A CHANGIN' "
–Bob Dylan, 1964

Dear «nicknamefirstname» and «spousenicknamefirstname»,

I think we can be totally certain Dylan was NOT singing about [YourCompanyName], but times have also been changing for us. What started XX years ago with [Name] offering insurance-based solutions has now become a comprehensive financial planning firm whose service to clients and resulting success has been recognized across the country. While it is our names being recognized, without YOU and YOUR confidence in our firm, none of this would be possible. For that, we will forever be in your debt.

Because of our success in serving clients, we now receive far more business opportunities than we could ever accept, which along with the ever-increasing cost of business, is requiring us to make several adjustments to ensure we can always deliver the highest levels of service to you and our other clients.

The most noticeable of these adjustments is *a change to the fees we are charging our clients*. For the better part of two decades, the fee for our services has been 0.25% of your Fidelity balance, charged quarterly for a total of 1% annually. Starting XX/XX/XXXX the new fee for our services for clients under $1,000,000 will be 0.375% quarterly for a total of 1.5% annually on Fidelity accounts. This adjustment to our fee schedule will allow us to continue providing you with our nationally recognized levels of client service. As always, our job will continue to be delivering massive value that you feel is worth multiples of the fee we are charging.

To implement this change, enclosed is our revised advisory contract that requires your signature and return no later than XX/XX/XXXX. We have included a self-addressed, postage-paid envelope for your convenience. We know that change is never easy, so our thanks in advance for your understanding.

–[Full Name]

Most (but certainly not all) of your clients will simply return the fee agreement. For those who don't, we preschedule a follow-up letter that includes a deadline for when they must return the letter, or we will resign from the account. Approximately one week before that deadline I call any remaining clients to confirm they want us to resign and to wish them all the best.

The hardest part in this process? Mailing the letters. I know it's hard. Really, really hard. But if it were easy, everyone would do it and none of us would get paid. Really, really hard moves like these are what separates the best advisors from everyone else.

BRING THE ROCKSTARS ON BOARD!

Just as you have head trash around raising fees, so too does your team. Like you, they worry that every client will leave, and they will end up unemployed. You *must* go through the same fear-setting exercises with your team. Even if they don't necessarily agree with the increase, they need to be on board with it.

The Only Exceptions: New Clients

I don't know about you, but when I'm a customer, I hate feeling like I've been given the bait-and-switch. That's something I never want to make my clients feel, especially my new clients, which is why I make one of my rare exceptions for the small percentage of clients who are new.

Exactly how you'll approach your new-client policy is up to you. In my office, we make sure everyone has been a client for a full year before asking them to pay the higher rate. We notify our new clients at the same time as the other clients, but we send them a separate letter.

Dear [client],

In order to offer you the value that we do and to stay competitive in the market, we are raising our client fees to X. Because you're a new client, we will wait to implement that fee increase for you until the end of the year.

That way, clients are aware of the shift ahead of time, and they'll appreciate being given extra time to move to the new rate or make other arrangements. And—more importantly—no one will ever walk away feeling like I gave them the bait-and-switch.

The best thing you can do to set yourself and your staff up for success is to give them a script with carefully crafted responses to the types of calls they might receive. Here are a few of the scripts I use in my office:

Client: "I'm concerned about your fee increase because … "
Advisor: "I understand that you are concerned about XYZ. This is something we thought a lot about before raising our fee, and it's one of the reasons we waited so long."

Client: "Why are you raising my fee?"
Advisor: "It was a difficult decision, but we've been charging the same fee for nearly X years. During that time, the quality of our services and the cost of doing business has increased substantially. We hope it will be another X years before we raise them again."

Client: "What if I don't want to pay more?"
Advisor: "One of the great things about our relationship is that we only continue working together if the value we provide you exceeds the fees you pay us. We think our value still far exceeds our new fee, but that's a decision you must make. While we would hate to lose you as a client, we understand that it might not be a good fit. As such, we've interviewed local advisors who are willing to work with you for the same fee you are currently paying."

Client: "What am I even paying for?"
Advisor: "Our fee increase, the first in X years, is going toward the cost of delivering our nationally recognized client service. The increase is a result of everything from postage stamps to health insurance to the cost of office space."

Client: "Why is this happening now?"
Advisor: "This is something we've been putting off for years, but we really couldn't wait any longer."

Client: "But I've been a client for XX years!"
Advisor: "And we appreciate you! That's why we waited nearly X years to raise our fees."

Client: "I heard that fees are actually going down. What gives?"
Advisor: "Like Walmart, a lot of firms try to offer the lowest fee possible. The problem is that their quality/service usually matches this fee. We offer amazing service and are still charging below-average fees for our industry."

Client: "XYZ firm will do it for less."
Advisor: "I can't speak to XYZ firm's services or policies, but I would recommend that you make sure the price they quoted includes any hidden fees, and I would look closely at what you are getting for that fee. While our fee appears higher, our service is dramatically better."

This last script is specifically for your team to use, as they should never get stuck defending your fee schedule to an upset client:

Client: "I'm upset/angry. This isn't right!"
Advisor: "I totally understand. Like you, we never like to see costs going up, which is why we waited nearly X years to increase our fee. I really think you should talk with [your name]. Can I have them return your call?"

While not directly related to raising fees, I wanted to give you a few other scripts to use when dealing with questions or concerns on this topic. As with all scripts in this book, do not use these scripts word for word, as they will sound like scripts. Instead, figure out how to say them in your own voice and practice. When someone tells you, "MY GOD! HOW CAN YOU CHARGE 1.5 percent?!?" your answer needs to be as smooth, confident, and calm as if they had asked your name or where you grew up. With that in mind, here are a few of my most common responses:

Client: "Can I get a discount?"
Advisor: "I would love to give you a discount, because I'd really like us to work together. However, if I gave you a discount, I would feel morally obligated to give all my other clients the same discount, which just wouldn't work."

Client: "I've heard/read/been told that other firms charge less than you."
Advisor: "I too have heard that, though I've yet to actually see any firms that offer our same level of service for a lower fee. If you find one, please let me know."

Client: "Do I still have to pay you when my accounts lose money?"
Advisor: "Kind of. Because our fee is tied to the value of your accounts, when (not if) they temporarily go down in value, so too does our fee."

Celebrate When Clients Walk Out on You

Not everyone wants to stay at the Four Seasons; that's what Motel 6 is for. In this industry, we have to assume that with any fee increase, some percentage of paying clients are going to change their mind and walk out the door. But what if this is a good thing?

You don't want all of them to leave, of course (and trust me, they won't). But think about it: by freeing your time up from the clients who don't support your new business goals, you're making yourself available to all the potential clients out there who will happily pay a fee that corresponds with the massive value you're preparing to deliver. In my own experience having helped dozens of advisors raise fees, I expect that about 10 percent of your clients will offer some kind of pushback, and 5 percent or so will leave. But even if 20 to 50 percent of your clients leave, the new fees paid by existing clients will offset the loss—and more importantly, you'll be a far better advisor for proving to clients (and the universe) that you are a high-caliber advisor.

It helps to look at real numbers. How many clients do you have to lose before you still break even on cash flow? If you used to have fifteen clients at the lower rate, but now you have ten at the higher rate, you're making the same amount of money, but because you're not spreading yourself so thin, you're going to do a better job serving those ten clients.

If you don't have clients leaving you because your fees are too high, then they're too low. That's just Economics 101. Say goodbye to any of the minor-league players who won't continue with you. You're in the majors now.

Action Steps

News flash: reading about fees will *not* actually cause you to make more money. Like every chapter of this book, the only things that count are the actions you take. Here are just a few action steps I recommend you take right away, without delay. Put this book down and go do them! (You can pick up this book again once you're charging the kind of fees that really give you the freedom to transform your business.)

○ Set a timer for sixty minutes and when it goes off, have in stone (or at least laminated), your fee schedule. *All* clients who join your practice from this point on pay this schedule, no exceptions.

○ Set dates on your calendar when you will implement each of the fee increase phases.

○ As necessary, find the extreme accountability *you* need to actually make this happen.

○ Visit www.ThePerfectRIA.com to get access to PDFs of the letters in this chapter.

Bonus content available for this chapter at ThePerfectRIA.com/BookBonus:

→ A video of the most brilliant script I've ever seen/used on managing client expectations on the "right" fee that you can use today in your practice

→ PDF versions of the letters in this chapter that you can Rip-and-Deploy

→ Real-world examples of other advisors using this strategy in their practice

---

Empower Your People

Cultivating a Team of Rockstars

PROFILE OF SUCCESS

"I've always had a vision for my practice, but I didn't have a road map to get there.

Jarvis's book, podcast, and Invictus Coaching Program helped me implement dozens of changes to make my practice more efficient, deliver more value to clients, and create a better work balance for my team. Knowing who I could trust to get through my head trash made all the difference."

Brian Skinner
Milford, CT
Skinner Wealth Strategies

Without a Post-it Note Business Plan, you don't have a clear direction. Without surge meetings, you have no time. Without getting rid of imposter clients, you'll never have capacity for real clients. But without a rockstar team, nothing else you do will ever matter.

No matter where you focus your business growth first, without a team you can trust, you'll never be able to consistently Deliver Massive Value to clients.

Clear the Head Trash

Going into the financial crisis of 2008, we had a five-person team on $311,000 of gross revenue. It doesn't take a rocket scientist to figure out that we were losing tons of money ($52,372 annually, to be exact). In hindsight, I can't for the life of me figure out what everyone was doing, but at that time, everyone was constantly busy, and we couldn't imagine having fewer employees.

Then, through a series of events—a family emergency and near bankruptcy—we were forced to go from a team of five to a team of just two. At first it seemed impossible to get all the work done with only two of us, but then something magical happened: Parkinson's Law, which states that an activity will take as much time as is allocated. Or said less eloquently: in an office, everyone will always be busy.

You see, once we were forced to get all the work done with two people, we became ruthless at operating at hyper-efficiency. We accidentally developed the systems that would not just save our business but help it thrive.

What I later learned is that systems could elevate our business *without* leaving us in a constant tailspin. I want to help you avoid the pain and heartache I experienced in those early days by helping you identify and correct the most common mistakes advisors make, figure out how to correct those mistakes, and learn how to ultimately create and manage a rockstar team.

Before empowering your team to help your business level up, let's clear some more head trash around ways you're limiting your own success.

Don't Try to Do Everything Yourself (Even If You Can)

Sometimes it can seem like it's easier to just do everything ourselves than teach someone else to do it. But this way lies danger—the danger of never getting out from under all the busywork that keeps you from the business of your dreams.

This mistake takes several forms, but the chronically capable among us all experience it at one time or another. You may feed yourself any number of excuses, including but not limited to:

- I can do it faster.
- I can do it better.
- I can do it cheaper.

• It will take longer to show someone else.

• Nobody else can do it but me.

These range from the irrelevant to the downright absurd. But ultimately, this mistake boils down to *you* being your own worst enemy. Time to stand out of your own way.

More Isn't Always Better

While some advisors think they can't afford to hire even a part-time virtual employee, other advisors are convinced that the only path to growth is to hire more people. Both are wrong. While you *must* have at least one team member, hiring another person will not solve your issues of poor productivity and bad leadership. As a general rule, your first team member should be hired immediately, but your second isn't needed until you pass $1 million in revenue.

Systems Simplify

Throughout this chapter and the rest of the book, I'll show you examples of systems you can put in place in your own practice. These systems are designed to keep your business operating at maximum efficiency and offering the highest-quality customer experience possible. The only way this machine is going to run smoothly is if everyone is clear on what everyone else is doing.

It sounds daunting, but it doesn't have to be. In *The Checklist Manifesto*, author Atul Gawande offers these guidelines to create a simple, easy-to-follow system.

1. Stick to one page.
2. Establish clear ownership for each task.
3. Build in clear metrics for determining when each task is complete.
4. Look for potential breakdowns.
5. Commit to the system.

And who says you have to reinvent these systems from scratch? All great artists steal; look to others in your field for inspiration.

Who in your field is already doing what you're trying to do? Why does their system work? Are competitors and colleagues in the industry using systems your own practice could benefit from? What might someone you admire change about your system to make it more effective?

Power Tips for Empowering Your Team

In your old business, the people who took care of your client scheduling, office upkeep, behind-the-scenes prep work, and client interfacing were staff doing a job. They were your employees, they looked to you for direction, and you instructed and supervised them. That's how running a business is supposed to work, right?

Not if you want to transform your practice and start Delivering Massive Value. It's time to give your employees the freedom and authority they need to help you take your practice to the next level.

These people aren't just your staff. They're your eyes and ears with clients, your arms and legs when you're not in the office. They're important cogs in a high-functioning machine, and if you want to be able to trust them to help you keep the system running, it's critical that you take care of them and empower them to work with autonomy.

Yes, you're still the boss, and ultimately, you're in charge. But in order to Deliver the Massive Value your rates stand up to, you have to stop thinking of your team as employees to manage and start thinking of them as the support system you need to transform your business.

Give Your People More Power

"May I ask what this is regarding? ... Luckily, I can help you with that right now!"

If everyone is constantly running to you to approve every little action, you'll never get out from under your workload: your team will just keep bringing you more of it. You have to stop being responsible for every decision a business makes, and that means trusting your team with more power to meet client demands.

Consider a typical client situation. A client calls your office and wants to speak with you about their account. You're on vacation with your family, so your receptionist tells them you're not available, and the client has to wait another three weeks to speak with you. The client pushes back and demands to be squeezed in. Now, your team has to decide whether to be honest with the client or pester you on your vacation. You get to be away from the office, but your relationship manager is in a tough spot, and your clients get the sneaky feeling they're being given the runaround.

Here's the thing: clients only *think* they want to speak with you. Most of the time, what they really want is a good answer to their question, a solution to their problem. Speaking with you personally is one way for them to access that solution, but it isn't the only way.

What if the conversation looked like this instead?

Your relationship manager responds to a client call with this polite request for information:

> "So that I can schedule the appointment, may I ask what this is regarding?"

When the client explains that they have a question about a section of their financial plan, your RM should have the authority to say the following:

> "Luckily, I can help you with that right now! Let's take a look."

That's it! Then, after your RM solves the client's problem and asks if they still want to go ahead with the appointment, the client will say, "Nope—you took care of it."

The client's needs are met instantly. The RM can keep your schedule clear. And the best part is, you never had to hear about the issue at all. Isn't that better than micromanaging your team?

Set Client Expectations Early

Part of empowering your team is setting client expectations and preempting as many questions and calls as possible. Don't just tell your clients they can see you only during a scheduled block of time; explain *why* this is the best time to meet, for you *and* for them.

It's easy to understand why someone might be upset when they're told, "You can't come in and see us for another two months—that's just how we do things." But as soon as you explain to a client, "Let's meet after you've filed your tax returns so that we can review tax strategies" or "We want to meet in October so we can review year-end planning before the year runs out," they'll see how this system is in place for their own best interest as much as yours, and they'll thank you for your consideration and attentiveness to their needs.

Be Transparent

Whenever you can give someone your reason for doing something, the result tends to be more successful.

One advisor I know directed his team to tell clients that he was at a conference, even if he was in Hawaii on vacation. Why lie about your values?

Make sure your team knows that you aren't trying to hide anything, and you aren't asking them to cover for your absence. When clients want to know where you are, your relationship manager should never feel like they need to fudge the truth to make your office look good.

If you're on vacation with your family, tell your clients. If you're working remotely, tell your clients. More often than not, your clients will be excited for you. (I work with retirees, and most of them are thrilled that I'm taking time to spend time with my family while I can.)

If you're not immediately available because you're traveling with your family, be proud! That's a reason clients can appreciate and respect. And if they can't, it may be time to reconsider whether they're the right client for you.

Listen to Your Team

You've just implemented a bunch of new systems to better set client expectations and streamline efficiency, and now you're living your best life somewhere in the Bahamas. No one is bothering you, because you've empowered them to the point where they can meet a majority of the incidental client needs that crop up without having to call on you at all.

But just because you're not being bothered doesn't mean everything under the surface is all hunky-dory. Does your team find themselves fielding a lot of the same questions about your latest quarterly value-add? Have they been getting a lot of calls about a recent news story? Do clients tend not to understand a form they've been asked to review? These are all opportunities to tighten your system.

When your team raises concerns or suggests a more efficient way to do things, listen—and if they're not raising concerns, ask. The people on the front lines of your business are the most equipped to give you valuable feedback on how you can make your clients' experiences even better and deliver even more value.

Give Your Team a Script

Giving employees feedback is always difficult, especially when it comes to how an employee greets clients. I once had an office manager who wasn't happy with the way our receptionist was greeting clients. She felt the receptionist could have been warmer and more conversational, but that's a tough piece of feedback to give someone. "Try harder" isn't terribly helpful, and she felt it would be patronizing to say, "Be nicer to people."

Instead of taking an uncomfortable approach that would make everyone feel terrible, we worked to create a list of conversation prompts she could draw from when greeting clients. Now, she appears comfortable and natural with everyone who walks in the door, and everyone has something to say about her smile and pleasant demeanor. It turns out she was perfectly willing to talk all along; she just didn't always know what to say.

Throughout this book, I share scripts that you can adapt for use in your own office. It's truly amazing how confident your team can be when you give them the right scaffolding, and what a difference it can make for your clients' experiences.

NEVER LEAVE YOUR TEAM HANGING: COMMIT TO YOUR CALENDAR

As an advisor, you must have total commitment to your calendar, not just for your clients, but for your team.

As you empower your team to take more responsibility for the background tasks that keep a practice running, they're going to start checking on your available time and making appointments. You *cannot* come back to your relationship manager and say, "Hey, I know you booked those meetings, but I decided I wanted to go golfing. Can you take care of rescheduling those?" It is completely unacceptable to throw your own mistakes at your clients.

How does this work in practice? On the rare occasion where I've had something come up and I need to reschedule client meetings, I call those clients myself. I say, "Hey, listen. This came up." It had better be a legitimate reason. I have, I will admit, several times told a friend, "Hey, I'll go mountain biking with you tomorrow afternoon," and then I forgot to put it on the calendar and Colleen says, "Hey, you have three appointments."

Well, that one's on me—I need to cancel my mountain biking. I absolutely *cannot* go back to my office manager and say, "Hey, listen, I wasn't responsible for my calendar, and you need to pay the price."

THE SCRIPT: SETTING YOUR TEAM UP FOR SUCCESS

To help your rockstar team field client inquiries about your whereabouts, modify the following script for your own purposes, and use it to empower your team to respond to every client inquiry.

"Where is Matthew?"

"Out of respect for the coronavirus guidelines, Matthew is working virtually. While he's not in the office, he is still working regular hours via his laptop. Would you like me to schedule a call with him?"

"Is he working from his home in Issaquah?"

"Because his kids are out of school, Matthew and his family are doing some travel, albeit within the guidelines of social distancing. Thanks to technology, he can work virtually nearly anywhere."

> "I heard Matthew is in Mexico?"
>
> "Thanks to technology, Matthew can work virtually from almost anywhere, but let me have you talk to Matthew directly about that one. Can he call you today at XX?"
>
> "I won't/can't wait to meet with Matthew."
>
> "No problem. Matthew is committed to not letting his family adventures impact clients and he's always just one red-eye flight away from the office. Let me have him call you tomorrow to figure out a solution that works for you."
>
> "What about …"
>
> "That's a great question for Matthew. Can I have him give you a call tomorrow?"

Action Steps

The only way your business can reach the heights you've been dreaming of is if you unleash the power of the talent you have on board—your rockstar team. Take these actions today to give your team the tools they need to succeed.

○ Make a list of all the most important things for *you* to handle—the things no one else can do. Keep those "core tasks" as your key role in the office.

○ Give your team a script.

○ Commit to always keeping your calendar up to date. Your team depends on it!

Bonus content available for this chapter at ThePerfectRIA.com/BookBonus:

→ A walk-through of my three times weekly team check-in that prevents 99 percent of texts, emails, IMs, or other "gong rings"

→ My process for finding, hiring, training, and ultimately handing off 90 percent of client relationships to a new advisor on my team

→ My "out of office" checklist that each team member completes before leaving on vacation

---

Post-it Note Your Business Plan

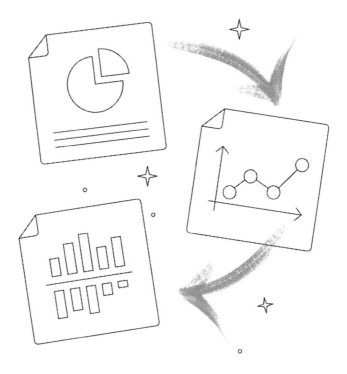

Early in my career, I spent countless hours carefully writing and rewriting business plans, comparing every KPI (key performance indicator) and industry benchmark, outlining in great detail what my revenue per employee and gross profit per relationship would be in year four of my five-year plan. After all, every self-proclaimed expert in our industry was proclaiming the importance of these business plans, and article after article was touting the KPIs of top practices.

However, as I learned from painful experience, this widely used "best practice" contains two fatal flaws. The first is that developing a detailed business plan burns up an incredible amount of time, time that would be much better spent prospecting or Delivering Massive Value to clients. After all, even the fanciest hardbound hundred-plus-page business plan is worthless if A) you go out of business because you don't have any clients or B) the few clients you have never send you referrals, because you're too busy updating your business plan to actually be a good financial advisor.

The second and more destructive flaw is that most business plans are created with the rosiest of assumptions, such as "We'll just add $25 million of new assets each year, plus a nice bull market, and in four years (maybe less) we'll easily have $100 million in assets." Never mind that your business plan doesn't actually detail *how* you will get $25 million of new assets. Never mind that you'll likely encounter a prolonged bear market. And never mind that no prospect or client cares *one bit* about your business plan. But where this plan is truly destructive to your success is that when you inevitably don't bring in the planned $25 million, your business plan reminds you of what a failure you've been.

How do I know this? Because I lived it, year after soul-crushing year. Apparently a slow learner, I would spend hours updating all of the projections each time the real world didn't match the projections (read: my pipe dream) of my business plan, carefully adjusting the numbers until on paper (and only on paper) I would reach my $1 million-of-gross-revenue goal as soon as the experts told me was humanly possible. With each update, I wasted more time, and I felt the burden of failure push me closer and closer to quitting.

This is not to say that all business planning is bad or that you should just make random business decisions. Especially for practices with north of $1 million of revenue, having a business plan with clear strategic initiatives will be critical to scaling your success. However, until you reach $1 million in revenue, your business plan should fit on just *two* pieces of paper the size of Post-it notes.

In this chapter, we'll look at incremental ways to continually improve your business's bottom line, and that starts with collecting the data you need to really understand where you are and where you want to be. As a financial advisor, you can't afford to be blind to the income needs of your practice, and you also can't sacrifice your personal desires for your life and relationships because every client is an exception. You're playing to win.

Your Post-it Note Business Plan Part One: Establish Milestones

While a traditional business plan outlines what you will do between now and your BHAG (Big Hairy Audacious Goal), as a small business, all your time and energy need to be focused just on reaching your next milestone.

As the old saying goes, anything you measure will improve. When I started to really measure the effects of the changes I was implementing in my own business, I wasn't just improving my business; I was seeing a dramatic uptick in new clients and exponentially increasing my business's effectiveness and efficiency.

If you're serious about transforming your business, you have to start treating your own business plan the way you would your very top client's account. That means looking at the data in front of you, making the best possible decisions for the continued success of your business, and following through on implementing those changes.

But just as a financial plan shouldn't take more than a page to accomplish its purpose, you shouldn't need more than a Post-it note to remind yourself of what's important to your business. In both cases, the real work happens under the surface, but you don't need to be constantly focused on the details in order to experience real insight and take strategic action.

The Post-it Note is not a metaphor. Take out your pad and writing utensil of choice, right this second. I'll wait. We're going to be talking about some very real numbers here, and you won't want to lose track of them. Keep your first Post-it note (that's all you need!) so it's always front of mind, and update it as you find ways to keep improving your systems and adding more value for your clients.

The entire process of creating your business plan should take less than one hour. Let's start by filling out the first half of your business plan, starting with the first of three important milestones to keep an eye on as you navigate your business.

Your First Milestone

The very first line in your business plan will contain a single number: your immediate income goal.

Ideally, rather than being just some random number, your first milestone will have personal meaning for you. For example, I once set the milestone of getting from my then current $30 million in assets to $50 million in assets because at that level I could spin off into my own RIA.

Using my own first milestone as an example, the first line of a business plan might look like:

Just that one line makes for a very powerful business plan, especially when you put it on your computer screen, the dashboard of your car, your bathroom mirror, and the lock screen of your cell phone. Why? Because you can now filter each of the hundreds of decisions you face as a business owner through one single lens: "Will this get me closer to my goal of $50 million AUM?" This also focuses the incredible power of your subconscious mind on this goal.

This is not your BHAG. For example, if your ultimate life goal is to reach $1 million in revenue, or $100 billion in AUM, it's often too big of a gap for your brain to cross. Instead stay focused on your next milestone, ideally one that you think you have a fifty-fifty chance of achieving.

Your Second Milestone: Incremental Goals

The next line of your business plan is to break this goal—in my case adding $20 million in new assets—into bite-size pieces. For me at that time, my average client brought $500,000 in AUM, so getting $20 million in assets required finding forty new clients.

Now my business plan has a second line:

Similar to the milestone goal, this smaller-size piece helped me direct my focus, and it gave me something I could regularly celebrate. In other words, if my only goal is $50 million in AUM, I'm a failure until I get to that number. If my subgoal is forty new clients, each time I add a client, I can celebrate!

At this point, we're maybe twenty minutes into the business plan. Right on schedule!

Your Third Milestone: How to Get There

Now comes the hardest part of the business plan: what exactly are you going to do to put this dream into action? What action or actions can you take every week to get yourself closer to your goal?

You may be thinking, "OK, Matt, I get that the high-level goals can fit onto a Post-it note, but my multipronged marketing approach fills pages of space." (Spoiler alert: this is why you don't yet have a "highly profitable, hyper-efficient lifestyle practice.")

Here's the thing: the longer and more detailed your business and/or marketing plan, the less likely it is to succeed. As such, the third and final line on your business plan is the number of people you will talk with each week. More specifically, as detailed by legendary financial planner Nick Murray in his book *The Game of Numbers*, the number of people from whom you will risk hearing "no thanks."

While the number and size of clients needed to reach a certain AUM number is easy to calculate, the math on the number of people you need to see each week is a bit vague and more importantly, very dependent on your own mental strength. I know one very successful advisor who makes ten cold calls a day. Unless you have very thick skin, this will likely be more rejection than you can handle. Instead, I suggest looking back at your past few weeks to see how many people you've risked hearing "no thanks" from (I'm guessing this is a very, very small number), and round up. Alternatively, just pick ten a week.

```
$50M OF AUM = OWN RIA

   40 NEW CLIENTS
     AT $500K

10 CONTACTS WEEKLY
```

All right! We've spent about half an hour coming up with the first half of our business plan with just three lines.[1] At the end of the day, that's really all you need to get started transforming your business—but keep reading, because the second half of the business plan will give you the additional numbers you need to keep everything in perspective.

Note: Once you get to $1 million-plus in revenue, you can expand this plan to include future hires, organizational charts, technology, and the like. Until then, put this Post-it note somewhere you can see it every single day, and use it as a filter for anything and everything that crosses your desk or mind.

ARE YOU RUNNING A BUSINESS OR A CHARITY?

One advisor I coached had built his practice around one very specific niche: people facing real money problems and debt management issues. The problem was, the people he had made it his mission to help couldn't pay the fees that would allow him to achieve his target revenue. He couldn't see the disconnect, and his emotional attachment to the status quo stood in the way of his ability to make the changes he needed to increase his income. He was floundering.

I knew he didn't want to hear it, but I sat him down and gently explained that he wasn't really running a business; he was running a charity and pretending it was a business.

Don't get me wrong: charities are important forces of social support, and if you want to run one, I fully support you. Just don't call it a business. That's a whole different ball game.

Your Post-it Note Business Plan Part Two: Key Performance Indicators

Once you've established your milestones, take out that second blank Post-it—it's time to focus on just a couple of key performance indicators (KPIs) related to your milestone goals. These KPIs can vary a bit from practice to practice depending on your milestone goals, your niche, and your business model, but ultimately, they come down to these three factors:

1. Target Revenue
2. Number of Clients
3. Average Client Size

---

1 Once you have your Post-it Note Business Plan, visit www.ThePerfectRIA.com to upload a screenshot so we can all cheer you on!

Throughout this chapter, we'll focus on a few important KPIs you'll use for your business plan. You can't skip this stuff because without a specific target in mind and clear metrics for measuring your progress toward them, you're just floundering, wondering when you'll "make it" and if change is even possible.

Let's look at the three KPIs that will help you set good parameters and make smart decisions.

Target Revenue

Start with your ideal income, the number you determined earlier in this chapter that would allow you to grow your business, free yourself from your schedule, and give your clients massive value. Now write that number on top of a fresh Post-it note.

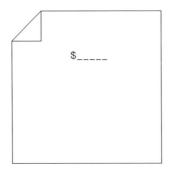

This KPI is the magic number that makes your business transformation possible. From this day forward, this is the number that guides every decision you make for your business. No exceptions! And remember to leave room—you're not finished yet. This business plan may be short, but you have a few more numbers to work through.

Number of Clients

The next important KPI in your business plan is the size of your client roster, the number of people you want as your clients each year.

Across the industry, you'll find a huge variance in the number of clients each financial advisor can comfortably and productively handle while providing customized financial advice and truly top-notch service. Not all of them calculate this successfully, and the quality of their service suffers because of it. Some advisors, myself included, handle between one hundred and one hundred and fifty clients; one I know handles around eight hundred (which I don't recommend, unless you plan to give each client only forty-five minutes a year).

Your "correct" number of clients isn't determined just by your stamina for surge week. But remember that you need to maintain your highest level of service when 80 to 90 percent of your clients all walk in the door for back-to-back meetings—use that scenario as a benchmark. There's always a temptation to take on more accounts, but to determine how many clients you can truly handle within the parameters you've set for yourself and your business, you need to know how much time you're able to invest in each one.

Use the following equation to figure out the amount of time you currently spend with each client on average.

```
number of client-facing hours / number of clients =
                    time per client
```

For example, say there are two thousand working hours in a given year. At best, one thousand of those hours are client-facing. (That's not the number I use, but it's one a lot of financial planners use.) What does the math tell you?

Example: Time Per Client
1,000 client-facing hours / 150 clients = approx. 6.5 hours per client

In the example above, you're spending an average of 6.5 hours per client. Does this fit with your schedule and your process? It does if you're making two appointments a year with half an hour of prep time each and handling four or five calls/emails a week, like we do. If you're constantly meeting your clients and spending a great deal of time preparing and fielding a great deal of calls, your time spent per client goes way up, and the number of clients you can handle per year goes way down.

When you have your ideal number of clients, add it to the next line of your second Post-it note:

Note: There's always the temptation to add more clients, but don't extend yourself beyond what you're capable of delivering at the highest possible level. Stretching yourself too thin won't help you Deliver the Massive Value your clients expect.

Average Client Size

Now, look at the amount of your income each of your clients has to represent on average in order to hit your goals. Divide your target revenue by your ideal number of clients to find the magic number: your ideal average client size.

target revenue / number of clients = average client revenue/size

For example, say your target revenue is $1 million, and you have one hundred and fifty clients. That means that on average, each of those clients needs to be earning you around $6,700.

$1,000,000 / 150 clients = $6,700 average client revenue

Now that you have the final piece of the puzzle, add that to the very end of the second part of your business plan:

That's it! Making $1 million might seem overwhelming, but breaking it into individual client goals makes everything more achievable. Even more importantly, it gives you something real to shoot for.

That's what a business plan gets you: clarity and understanding, so you can take immediate action and pivot when necessary. Keep the numbers in mind, and keep shooting higher.

> ## "It's up to you to keep that Post-it Note Business Plan in view, stay firm, and say no to the prospects who just won't help your business reach the new heights it deserves to reach."

Your business plan isn't just for keeping you focused and on track. It's also an important tool to help you answer the really big questions. Here are two examples.

"Should I get my CFP (or other designation/certification)?"

Ask yourself: Will it directly get me closer to my milestone? Will it directly get me more clients? Will it get me my ten contacts a week? If the answers to these questions are all no, then no CFP designation—at least, not yet.

This is not to say the CFP designation is not valuable. (I'm also not saying it *is* valuable, but that's a discussion for another day.) Rather, I want you to understand that anything that won't directly get you closer to your goals *must* be avoided until you reach your goals. If you are consistently contacting your ten people a week *and* steadily bringing on new clients *and* making progress toward your milestone, then maybe—and only during time you've specifically blocked out for that purpose—you can pursue your CFP designation.

"Should I start a blog (or other marketing strategy)?"

Maybe it's not a blog. Maybe it's a podcast, social media campaign, newsletter, or email campaign, or a book, or a mailing list, new ad campaign, seminar program, or any of the million other "great ideas" you might have to market your business.

Whatever it is, ask yourself the same questions: Will it directly get me closer to my milestone goal? Maybe. Will it directly get me more clients? Maybe eventually. Will it get me my ten contacts a week? If not, the answer is no.

This, too, is not to say these marketing tools are not valuable. In fact, I personally know advisors who have built wildly successful practices using each of these strategies. (Then again, for every successful one I've met, I also know hundreds who have failed.) Each of these can also be great *long-term* marketing strategies—but unless you are getting your ten contacts a week, nothing else counts. However, if you *are* getting your ten contacts a week, and you want to implement one of these strategies, great. Carve out a dedicated time on your calendar each week, and use only this time to devote to that strategy.

Business Plan Success Tips

Even with your business plan front of mind, it can be hard to stick to the plan. Here are three tips to help keep you on track and always doing what's right for your business.

Establish Hard and Soft Minimums

Once you have your average client size, you must set an asset minimum per client. (Lots of advisors argue with me about this, but just like the self-proclaimed experts, I'll start taking their "great" advice as soon as I see them running a great practice.)

Remember, this is a business, not a charity, and you can take on only so many clients without starting to lose the value you need to provide. Why make exceptions for people who won't help your business meet its goals?

At worst, I recommend that your hard minimum is fifty percent of your average client size. For example, $750,000 and $500,000 of assets under management.

Don't cheat your clients—or yourself—by making exceptions. If you have a plan in place, you'll never get caught sabotaging your business goals by cheating on your own policies.

Hold the Line

Formulating a killer business plan is not just a matter of raising fees; it's a matter of completely reinterpreting your new business goals, and then articulating those goals to the client in a way that respects them and their own goals.

Not all clients will fit into these new goals, and that's OK—you learned what to do about those clients in Chapter 3. For now, a simple word of warning:

During the course of making these changes, your resolve will be tested. Prospective clients will push back at you when you gently turn them away. Some clients will practically beg you to take them on no matter how wrong you are for their account (and how wrong they are for your system), like a fish that just keeps jumping into your boat no matter how many times you throw it back.

There's always going to be pushback. It's up to you to keep that Post-it Note Business Plan in view, stay firm, and say no to the prospects who just won't help your business reach the new heights it deserves to reach.

Establish Excuses to Celebrate Success!

Our world is so full of rejection and feelings of failure that we need to reward ourselves as well. At one point in my career, my assistant and I would go to lunch each time we added another $300,000 of AUM because it got us one step closer to our milestone goals.

Whatever makes you and your rockstar team happy, make sure to take the time to celebrate each milestone along your journey.

Action Steps

No business plan should take up more than two Post-it notes of space. By focusing exclusively on the metrics that really matter, you'll get your own Post-it Note Business Plan off to a great start.

○ Commit to your next business goal, put the key measurements on your Post-it Note Business Plan, and get to work!

○ Whatever your target revenue, calculate the number of clients and average client account size that will get your business where it needs to be. Add it to your business plan.

○ Establish hard and soft minimums and add them to your business plan. I recommend a hard minimum of 50 percent of your average client size.

Bonus content available for this chapter at ThePerfectRIA.com/BookBonus:
→ My 2010 business plan that resulted in Nick Murray telling me not to come to his conference
→ One of the spreadsheets Micah and I use to evaluate our practice annually

---

Why Investments Don't Matter

F irst, a disclaimer: I was initially hesitant to include investments in this book. This is partly because of all the compliance hassle that comes with discussing investments, but more so because nearly every advisor spends too much of their time and their client's focus on investments. What follows in this chapter is *not* investment recommendations, but rather my guide for how to discuss investments with your clients and prospects.

With that disclaimer out of the way, let's jump into how to invest money for your clients.

The Real Truth: Investment Strategy Doesn't Matter

Here's the thing the experts really, really don't want you to know (because then what would they be an expert in?): at the end of the day, it doesn't matter what investment strategy you use.

I can't tell you how many times after giving a presentation to advisors someone has come up to me to explain how their investment strategies are different (read: superior) to mine. But you know what?

It Doesn't Matter and I Don't Care!

After experiencing this dozens of times, I began to realize a startling fact: the advisors who seemed to have nothing better to do than brag to me about their superior investment strategies were typically the ones with the worst practices. As you read the following guide, don't let yourself get hung up on our differences in investing, big or small. It's not about the strategy.

To pick an extreme example, I'm a Nick Murray–style, own-equities-forever type of guy. If you think that's a totally naïve approach and you follow some other strategy instead, awesome. Remember, it doesn't matter. And I don't care.

What I *do* care about is that you can effectively communicate whatever strategy you choose to follow to your clients. After all, even *if* you found the holy grail of investing, if you can't figure out how to articulate it to clients in a way they understand, you'll still be broke.

The Only Investment Advice You'll Ever Need

If clients don't understand your recommendations, how will they decide to work with you, and how can we expect them to stick to the plan once they do?

In this section, I won't try to tell you *how* to invest. Instead, I'm going to show you precisely how to articulate your investment strategy in a way that clients understand.

"Jarvis, I get that investments 'don't matter and you don't care', but I still need to know how to invest my client's assets. Will you please show me your exact models???"

With great reservation, below you will find our current 70/30 model, which fits nicely into Retirement Income Guardrails and is used by the majority of our clients. To avoid at least some of the compliance nightmare and endless hassling from advisors convinced their models are superior, I've left off ticker symbols.

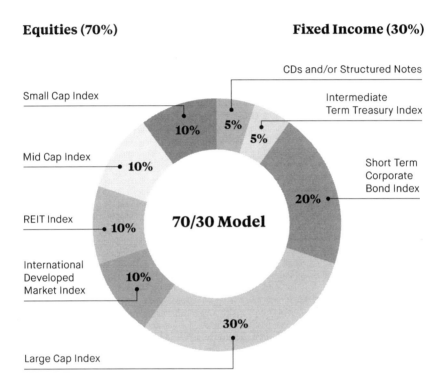

Of course past performance is no indication of future results (one of these days the sun will also quit coming up) and this is not an offer or recommendation to buy securities. More importantly, before you tell me how terrible this model is, please remember that "it doesn't matter and I don't care." :)

Marshmallow

In every discussion about investments—or really any financial planning topic—it's important to remember that while investment jargon makes sense to you, it is total Greek to the client. In other words, when you use words like *diversification, equities, large-cap, fixed income, yield curve, inflation,* or even *percentages,* you might as well be saying "marshmallow," because the client has no idea what you are saying.

This is *not* an insult to the client's intelligence! It's just the reality of a professional (you) talking to a non-professional (the client). The same holds true in every profession, from car mechanic to brain surgeon. Everything you describe to clients *must* be presented in terms they can understand.

Draw It in Crayon

I learned this strategy from a retired client who managed teams of engineers. He explained that the engineers would come into his office with complex and lengthy proposals full of endless details. Whenever this happened, he would pull from his desk a box of children's crayons and a blank sheet of paper. He would then ask the engineer to draw for him, with the crayon, whatever was being proposed. While many people were understandably confused by this request, it forced them to get past all the jargon and instead focus on only the most important parts. (This, by the way, was a major influence for my one-page financial plans.)

Please note that I am not suggesting you literally write your investment proposals in crayon. Rather, the crayon is a reminder for you to keep them as simple as possible. Yes, you need to include all the stuff required by the compliance department, but aside from that, the overall plan must be as simple as possible. In fact, I don't think you can get *too* simple here. For example, here is the exact (and only) investment detail I give to a prospect:

• Rebalance portfolio to meet long-term goals.

That's it! We'll go into greater detail on this in Chapter 10 on the prospect process and in Chapter 18 on the one-page financial plan. But for now, here's the important thing: I will not go into any more detail with a prospect on investments until after they have transferred all the money (and even then, it doesn't get much more detailed than this).

The War Chest: Tied to Goals, Not Risk Tolerance

Our industry has an obsession with risk tolerance questionnaires. This is partially a cowardly move to CYA (Cover Your Assets), but it's also an attempt to make the client do the work they are paying *you* to do. Imagine going to a doctor and having her ask you to fill out a questionnaire about how you feel in that moment about various types of medical procedures. Then, when you ask the doctor for her recommendation on what procedure you need, she says, "Well, according to your questionnaire score, your procedure will be XYZ." When you ask, "But will that solve my problem?" she keeps repeating, "Well, your score says we should do XYZ."

Sounds insane, right? It's what advisors do every day, and it's what I did before I figured out what really matters.

Yes, you need to document the client's risk tolerance, but this must be tied to their goals and not some arbitrary scorecard. How does this look in real life?

"Mr. & Mrs. Client, to achieve your goal of having the best retirement possible, we need to invest the majority of your nest egg in the world's greatest companies, sometimes known as 'equities' or 'stocks.' Over the decades you will be retired, owning these companies will give you the best ability to keep buying all the things you enjoy. While long-term owning the world's greatest companies has always worked out, there *will* be years, and even multiple years, where the price of these companies goes down a lot. For example, do you remember [recent bear market like the financial crisis or COVID-19 panic]?"

When the client responds, *listen to their answer!*

"Because we know another decline is a matter of *when*, not *if*, we need to keep a 'war chest' of cash and bonds to keep your income safe until the economy recovers. Most of my clients like to have a five-year buffer, but some like a little more and others a little less. Five years is my recommendation, because that gets us through the worst of any decline, if not the entire decline. How many years of war chest would you be most comfortable having?"

If the client responds with a number plus or minus one year, great—that's our number, and the corresponding equity/bond allocation is our target. (For example, a five-year war chest would be roughly a 75/25 allocation.) However, if the client responds with a dramatically different number, like one or ten, this means you did not do a good enough job explaining to them the importance of a five-year war chest.

If the client tells you they are interested in building a ten-year war chest, I would say something like this:

"Ten years is a great war chest buffer, as it would give us a lot of time to wait out bad markets. The only trick with ten years is that it leaves so little to invest in the world's greatest companies that we will have to reduce your income now. I'm fine either way, and we're always going to do what is best for you. I just want you to understand the long-term cost of playing it safe short-term."

If the client wanted only a one-year war chest (or worse, none at all), I would explain that while long-term this will give them incredible growth potential, any time the market dips, we'd have to cut their income, and any major life expenses would have to wait until the markets recover—which isn't always an option. This is an incredibly risky position that I don't advise, and a client who pushes back about this probably needs to be graduated out of your business.

What Works Is Better Than What's Sexy

Persuading clients to do the safe thing can be challenging—especially when everything they've seen about investments on TV or in magazines is all about the flashy accounts. Try explaining it like this:

"Mr. & Mrs. Client, there are hundreds of thousands of investment options in the world. They can be analyzed and grouped lots of ways, but every investment falls into one of two buckets: investments that are sexy and investments that work. Investments that are sexy are lots of fun. They make the covers of magazines, and they are great for bragging about to your friends. The catch is, they rarely work. Because running out of money is never an option for us, we stay entirely focused on the second bucket: investments that work. These are boring investments that rarely make headlines and they'll almost never be something to brag about. Instead, these are 'get the job done and sleep well at night' investments, which are what we rely on for our clients' investments. Is that OK with you?"

Early in my career, I was fooled by lots of sexy investments, which like bad advice from self-proclaimed experts, shall remain nameless in this book. After learning this lesson the hard way again and again, my investment models are now a collection of five to seven super-boring index funds.[1]

SEXY VS. WHAT WORKS IN REAL LIFE

One of the most financially successful advisors I've ever known personally, Tom Gau, had the ugliest website and brochures imaginable. Truly awful stuff—and yet he built multiple million-dollar practices, while also coaching hundreds of advisors to do the same. And he's not alone: my good friend and The Perfect RIA co-founder Micah Shilanski built his practice with ugly graphics, typos, misspelled words, and bad grammar, but like Gau, built a multimillion-dollar practice working just a couple of months a year. At the other extreme, I've met hundreds of advisors with fancy websites, luxury office spaces, glossy brochures, exciting social media feeds ... and no clients!

I once borrowed over $10,000 to buy a personal branding package—including fancy brochures—all of which brought in exactly zero clients. Thoughts of my business's public image were sucking up all my attention and pulling me off course. But when I stopped worrying about looking sexy and started to focus on what was really important to my bottom line—Delivering Massive Value—my practice skyrocketed.

Of course, this does not mean you should have a lousy website or a shoddy office or, worse yet, dress unprofessionally. Yes, you and your entire client experience need to look nice—but the fanciest stuff in the world will not bring you more clients. (This is a blessing, because if it did, the major companies would outspend you one hundred to one and you'd never get *any* clients.) Get yourself a decent website and a decent office, dress professionally, and focus on what really matters.

But even after you start to focus on what's truly important, you can't let your guard down: another black hole is waiting to pull you away from your carefully laid path to success.

Managing Client Expectations

Managing the money is just part of the job; the rest of it is getting your client to buy in, and that comes—as so many things do—through setting reasonable expectations about how your plans will help your clients achieve their stated and unstated goals.

---

1 I thought about publishing a list of these funds in the book, but I wanted you to always have access to our most current models. Find the most up to date list at www.ThePerfectRIA.com.

Wealth management is already an overwhelming topic to anyone who isn't trained in it; that's why you have clients in the first place. Whatever they're saying to you about their investment goals and fears, meet them on *that level* and talk through their concerns in *their terms*.

Here are a few strategies for setting the stage to communicate what really matters.

Speak Their Language

Here's one of the reasons financial advisors have such a bad rap: the lingo we use among ourselves is *so bad*. Our brains work in big numbers and percentages and data—that's why we became financial advisors, I guess.

But when we assume our clients are fluent in finance and we talk to them like they're industry insiders, we're doing them a real disservice. We are confusing them, which means their questions aren't being answered, which means they feel stupid, which makes them defensive and angry. This is not a great client experience.

It's up to you to communicate with your clients in ways that help them understand why each element of their portfolio is an important piece of their total investment picture and successful outcome. When you talk about percentages and fixed income, they won't even understand what you're saying; these are just more "finance words." Instead, talk about *years of uninterrupted income*.

Use plain English, and don't overwhelm your clients. If they remember nothing else, they'll remember how you gave them the gift of a stress-free financial meeting.

Answer the Real Question

Imagine that two clients walk into your office. They're a married couple in their early sixties with a balance of $1 million in IRAs. They want to retire as soon as possible. They aren't here to ask about your average portfolio size or what you plan to do about stock market turbulence, they have only two questions on their minds:

"How should I invest my money?"

"How much income can I get from my nest egg?"

Both of these questions can be summarized by the real question they represent:

"Am I going to run out of money and die?"

Clients don't just need answers to their questions; they need reassurance that they can confidently stop asking them altogether. They need to know their accounts are in good hands and you're making good, long-term, future-proof decisions with their money. They want to know how many years of uninterrupted cash flow they have without needing to disturb the rest of their portfolio.

Back the Least Bad Strategy

Every investment strategy poses a risk to some degree or another. It's up to you to choose the "least bad" strategy for your clients, but it's also up to you to help them understand why stable is more desirable than sexy so they can buy in.

Even the best investment advisor can't predict the future any better than a meteorologist can tell you with 100 percent certainty that it won't rain on Friday. Any financial advisor who promises they can is lying. What we *can* promise is that risks can never be eliminated, and that all it takes is a downturn in the market for a serious disruption to turn your entire financial plan upside down.

If you're setting the right expectations, your clients understand that predicting the future isn't our job; our job is to invest with confidence and give our clients the greatest chance of success for their goals. When the accounts are looking good and the clients are happy, celebrate with the client, but always use these opportunities to set expectations. During the good times, ask, "We love it when the markets go up, but what happens when they go down? Are you prepared for things to move in a different direction?"

This doesn't have to be an hour-long conversation in the weeds. In fact, it shouldn't be. That makes it a *thing*. But spending two minutes out of every meeting checking in with your client about what happens when the markets go down makes it just another expected piece of your total asset management plan.

Action Steps

As surprising as it might sound in a book about transforming your financial investment business, the investment strategy isn't what's important—it's how you communicate your strategy to clients and the integrity you display as an advisor.

- ○ Have conviction in your strategy. You know it works not because you can predict the future, but because it has always worked—and because you use it too.
- ○ Invest your own assets the same way you invest your clients' assets. This gives *you* conviction.
- ○ Be ready for the damn markets. This used to be the unsexy thing to do; these days, we all understand that there's sexy, and then there's surviving.
- ○ Speak the clients' language and really listen to what they say. If you do, you'll be able to answer the questions they're really asking.

Bonus content available for this chapter at ThePerfectRIA.com/BookBonus:

→ The exact investment allocations I currently use with clients
→ Samples of the investment recommendations I offer to prospects
→ My favorite resources for helping clients understand investments

---

Delegate Anything
< $1,000/Hour

I recently spoke with the chief marketing officer of a multibillion-dollar RIA firm. One of her first questions, which I get all the time, was, "Matthew, how do you have time to run your practice when you take like six months of vacation each year?!?" Not to be arrogant, but to drive the point home, I explained that in addition to running my practice, I also co-founded The Perfect RIA, which is now a million-dollar-plus business and I'm writing this book. But to answer her question, and yours, the way I'm able to get so much done in what seems like so little time is that I'm relentlessly focused on only doing those things that only I can do.

Conversely, early in my career I was plagued by the same limiting belief that holds back so many otherwise successful advisors: "I have to do that," a.k.a., "That can't be delegated." To build a wildly successful practice, one that allows you to make a lot of money and take a ton of vacation, while still Delivering Massive Value, requires that you do what only you can do.

Let's get a little more specific. Unless you have other client-facing advisors on your team, the jobs that only you can do likely include:

- Semi-annual meetings with clients (inside of a surge schedule)
- Responding to client questions/concerns that can't be handled by your team
- Prospecting (as part of a prospect process)
- Making strategic/visionary decisions for the firm (using your Post-it biz plan)
- Acting as CEO during scheduled blocks (e.g., HR, finances, compliance)
- Learning

That's pretty much it! For smaller practices and/or depending on your passions, your day might also include a few other tasks such as:

- Managing investments (if not outsourced)
- Marketing content creation

Because you might be thinking, "Well, Matthew forgot to list XYZ," let me take a second to list all the things a successful advisor is not doing, ever:

- Scheduling
- Answering phones or emails
- Paperwork
- Client service issues
- Making unscheduled phone calls
- Checking the mail
- Scanning documents
- Data entry
- Managing the office (e.g., ordering supplies)
- Tech support

- Ordering lunch
- Booking travel
- Anything else that can be delegated at a cost of less than $50 an hour!

In this chapter, you'll learn how to take back your time, like I did, by delegating to others all the mundane, repetitive, energy-draining, or otherwise intrusive tasks that clutter up your day, take up your time, crush your productivity, and interrupt your flow.

Why Delegate?

Delegating doesn't just free up more time. By seeing the bigger picture and focusing on what really matters, you can change the perspective of your entire team, become more efficient than the sum of your parts, and truly Deliver Massive Value to your clients on a scale you never imagined.

Remember What Your Time Is Worth

I'm sure I got this idea from Nick Murray, the preeminent author and financial advisor, but I try to value my own time at a thousand dollars an hour. If what I'm doing is worth that kind of investment, then I do it. If it's not, I delegate. That's my personal benchmark for determining whether something is truly worth my time.

This concept has brought me new perspective as to my importance in the business—and also as to where I'm *not* important. I absolutely need to be the one who makes the overall decisions about investments, clients, strategic partnerships, and changes to systems we've developed. But if I'm trying to value my own time at a thousand bucks an hour, I can't be spending it browsing Amazon for the books I want or booking travel arrangements.

This perspective makes it easy to delegate tasks I might not otherwise have considered delegating.

The same *has* to be true for your business: if you know that your time is valuable enough to charge your clients for it, it's valuable enough for you to take seriously.

For example, one of my business plan milestones was $1 million in gross firm revenue. To hit this goal—while still taking at least six weeks of vacation and never working more than forty hours a week, leaving approximately 1,760 working hours—every hour I worked had to average $500-plus of value to the practice. This is no small feat and it takes a lot of focus and intentional action.

How do you know what your own time is worth? You figured it out already back in Chapter 6, "Post-it Note Your Business Plan." To determine your own personal target hourly goal, revisit your new business plan, and establish how much your time must be worth to hit your income goals. Anything less needs to be delegated. Your business depends on it.

While it can be tempting to tell yourself, "When I earn XYZ, then I'll delegate," the reality is that without delegation, you'll never get there! If you are doing minimum wage tasks, you'll have a minimum wage practice.

Focus on the Things Only You Can Do

When you're a CEO, you need CEO-level priorities for how you spend your time. That means focusing on tasks that befit a CEO and leaving the support tasks to your support team in the office. That's what you're there for; that's what they're there for. If it's not helping you move your business forward in the way only you can, it's not worth your time or attention.

Sure, you *could* organize your own files and run your own calendar and answer your own phones. You could even wash all the windows and clean the bathrooms if you really wanted to. Those are all important jobs, and someone has to do them (especially the part about my calendar, which I am definitely *not* qualified to do). But you know that as the principal in your business—and the person responsible for everyone else's paychecks—none of those things are the best use of your time in the office.

For example, I love giving presentations and outlining talks and thinking about what my audience will need to hear and when, but I'm terrible at designing PowerPoint slides. Nothing makes me feel more useless than spending two hours trying to figure out exactly what piece of clip art to put where and whether I should use a fourteen- or sixteen-point font, then standing back and hating it all anyway.

Now, my mantra is to do only things that only I can do. Since it's best for me to just stay out of the technology trap entirely, I draw the basic concepts for my slides on paper—bullet points, suggested imagery, anything conceptual I'm trying to convey—and hand it off to a designer. Yes, I *could* have done it myself, but handing it off to someone else gets me 90 percent of what I wanted anyway in 10 percent of the time I would have spent. Now, I can take the presentation the rest of the way by tweaking what's already there and finalizing as needed.

Conserve Your Energy.

Each of us has certain activities that give us energy, that excite us and motivate us, or that fill us with dread. Understanding more about what makes you tick and what drags you down can offer valuable insight into the best tasks to free yourself from to create a more efficient workday.

Of course, if *going to work* is the thing you dread, this advice can't help you—but when it comes to individual tasks, these insights can help you design your day around a process that is more personally fulfilling to you, all while helping to clarify just where you should focus your delegating.

Look at your calendar for today, this week, or this month. What activities are you dreading? Find a way to get them off your calendar, either now or for the next time they roll around.

Whether it's PowerPoint design or planning a meeting or anything else that doesn't require your unique set of knowledge and experiences, find a way to eliminate that stress from your life. Either delegate it, change it, work around it, or eliminate it somehow, but stop trying to muscle through it. Swimming upstream and doing a task you dread is never a good use of your time.

Maximize Your Team's Skills and Talents

One of the most important changes I've ever made in my office was to ask everyone on my team to make a list of all the things they enjoyed doing, and then another list of all the tasks that sapped them of their energy and took the wind out of their sails. The illuminating results of that exercise allowed us to focus the function of our team in ways that played to our individual strengths and freed our days from tasks we found individually draining.

Acting as a more integrated team has also led to a massive boost in efficiency. Before, we would slog through tasks that drained us, people would get irritated and snippy, and the entire situation was a huge stressor for everyone. Now, because we're all so in tune with what makes us run and what slows us down, we've all gotten to the point where we have the power to step away from any task that has become really energy-draining, in any setting, and say, "I need to step away from this and come back, or we need to figure out a way to approach this differently."

Valuing your team on an individual level for the strengths they can bring to the table also empowers them to say, "Look, if you want this project to be successful, then you need to know that the system as it stands is going to sap all of my energy, and I won't have any left to call my COIs and make appointments with prospective clients and all the other things I have to do. Can we figure out a way for someone else to do some of those tasks?" This isn't complaining; it's efficiency in action.

What to Delegate?

I know it seems like you're the only person who could possibly interface with clients the way you do—and you're right. But your clients aren't necessarily looking for *you* to fix their problem; they just want their problem fixed.

This holds true across your business and personal life. Sometimes *you* don't need to do the thing; you just need a box checked.

If you stick to doing just the things that only you can do, what's left over for your team to handle? Everything else—and if you've empowered them to support you the way you learned in Chapter 5, they're ready!

Communications

Remember that study by the McKinsey Global Institute showing that office workers spend around thirteen hours a week managing their email? If you haven't yet directed the majority of your correspondence to your team, now's the time.

You've got to get out of your email. You'll never completely eliminate it—something will always require your attention—but you've got to pare it way back. Here's what we tell clients:

"Listen, I get hundreds of emails. I want to make sure your emails are never lost. Send all your emails to ACCOUNT@jarvisfinancial.com. Our whole team has access to that email, and the first person to see it responds to it."

(Spoiler alert: that person is *never* me.)

Meeting Prep

It takes quite a bit of time to prepare for every client meeting. First you have to schedule the meeting, then you have to check their files, send forms, ask for forms, prepare your own internal documents, and that doesn't even include all the tasks you'll have *after* the meeting.

If typing your meeting notes takes more of your time and attention than you feel it's worth, stop doing it! Instead, after your client leaves, record your memo into an audio program, then send it to the person on your team whose new responsibility is to have it transcribed into a memo for your client's file (by delegating the transcription, obviously). Now, almost 100 percent of your time spent dealing with client meetings is actually spent *in those meetings*.

If typing your meeting notes isn't a problem for you, great. Find something that *is* a problem for you, and fix it.

Yes, other people have to do those things—but even though you pay your people well (you want them to stick around, right?), you're not paying them $1,000/hour well. I pay my team very well, but I also know that even if it takes them three times longer than it would take me to perform a task or take an action, it's still not worth my time.

Personal Tasks

We learned in Chapter 2 about how good systems are the backbone of any business capable of delivering the kind of value you're about to start delivering. Systems for meetings, systems for scheduling, and systems for answering the phones. But the same principles that help make your office more efficient hold true when you're talking about your own personal time.

We used to live in a world where we were "at work" as soon as we stepped foot in the office and "off work" when we left at 5:00 p.m. Now, the line between business time and personal time can be harder to discern: we might just as easily do our industry research and other professional development at 2:00 on a Sunday afternoon, if that's how we've decided to allocate that time, and we could be doing it from a remote location in the world just as easily as from our home office.

There's really no reason anymore to keep personal tasks and work tasks separate; you've got the same twenty-four hours in a day, no matter how you're spending them. Further, every decision you make over those twenty-four hours drains your energy a little bit more, and the distraction of constantly having to choose which side of the line to place the many issues that bleed into both worlds is one you can't afford. Not anymore.

Once you really start to think about it, the potential for nixing time-consuming and distracting tasks is almost staggering. Why stop at emails? Scheduling dentist appointments for your family, ordering gift cards for your nephew's birthday—you could get out from under all of it, and it's as simple as writing it down.

I challenge you to make a list of all the tasks that come across your desk that you could potentially delegate. Your list will be unique to your own business and personal responsibilities, but think big! Don't stop until you've cleared your mental schedule of everything that has to be done, but not necessarily by you. (To help you brainstorm, I'm including part of the list I made the first year I really started doing it. As you'll see, no task is too small to stop focusing on!)

Delegated Tasks:

- Set up family calendar
- Cancelled subscription service
- Find a housekeeper in Issaquah, eventually ML
  - Scheduled for 11/16
- Ella's gymnastics class - Complete 10/30
- Jackie's physical therapy appointment
- Installed What's App
- Posted 11/15 Webinar info to LinkedIn
- FinCon Contacts
- FPA Connect - 84 Contacts
- FPA Connect - LinkedIN (made connections)
- Register for FPA in AZ
- Book Hotel for FPA
- Chef - sun basket - 1st order will be delivered on 11/29
  - email into Jackie
- Follow up with Jackie about holiday cards. - Jackie is managing this
- Physician for Alice, Ella and Calvin
- Paid for house cleaning
- Executive physical for Jackie and me
- Order gift card for Mary's birthday
- Respond to all emails regarding FPA in Info@jarvisfinancial
- Cooking class for Jackie and me (invite friends to join)
  - Booked, 12/15
- Property in Moses Lake - change address to office
- Updated family calendar with school vacation schedule
- Eye doctor for Ella. Scheduled 2/7
- Order new Tim Ferris book
- Order book Radical Acceptance
- Transferred December cooking class from 12/15 to 12/30
- Registered Jackie for January 11th cooking class (added 2nd ticket)
- Booked time at ski hill
- Booked rental car for Orlando
- Connect w/ coaching program clients: LinkedIn, Address
- Send Christmas Card
- Purchase 50mm lens, Lav Mic, Zoom H1, Tripod
- Ordered 2 SanDisk SD cards for camera
- Ordered Zach P. a birthday gift card
- Paid Guarav S. on Upwork
- Recommend video camera set up for recording short videos of me explaining/demonstrating topics for our coaching program. Should be nicer than an iPhone, but not much more difficult to use/upload, etc. All videos will be indoors. Include lighting & sound? Easy to travel;
- Book flight for BAM Success Summit Conference
- Ordered Colleen flowers
- Ordered Gift Card for Gwyneth's birthday
- Ordered Gift Card for Brian's Birthday
- Booked flight for Denver trip in February
- Booked hotel for California trip in May
- Booked violin lessons for Alice
- Researched mic and camera equipment for vlogging
- Paid Adam on Upwork
- Set up Alaska air mileage accounts for kids
- Find newsletter designer to improve layout
- Find technical/manual author who can convert our systems into guidebooks
- Get approved by CFP board for CE credits in 2018
- Update Freshly order, 6 meals instead of 12
- Find web person who can handle all the logistics for podcasts
- Schedule house cleaning for 2x a month
- Order camera for vlogging
- Schedule Podcast Coaching w/ Evo and Micah
- Schedule Dinner w/ John and Gina

- Booked tickets for Jazz Alley with John and Gina
- Sent in FPA Speaker Agreement and reimbursement invoice
- Completed project for Colleen for live Q&A for coaching program
- Schedule dinner w/ Monna
- Ordered Stock Images for Power Point Presentation
- Set up number to receive texts from coaching students
- Email someone on Michael Kitces's team (www.Kitces.com) to ask about permissions/licensing to use images from his site in client presentation and in teaching other advisor
- Cancelled flight from FLL to SEA, and SEA to DFW
- Booked flight from FLL (Fort Lauderdale) to DFW
- Client birthday cards - quality is key
- Organized Client Excel spreadsheet for birthday cards
- Book travel for FPA retreat in April
- Hire podcast assistant to edit files and post show notes
- Find survey program to use with clients
- Ordered Birthday Gift Card for James
- Added mileage numbers for trip to Utah in July
- Submitted CE Credits Program Approval questions to Colleen
- Called CFP to walk me through the CE Credit - program approval process
- Ordered video equipment for recording studio
- Rent a car for Florida trip in March
- Followed up with Evo about Podcast Demos
- Find survey program for Colleen and Stephanie
- Scheduled Dive Class for Jackie, Matthew and Alice
- Booked massage therapist for Boulder Trip
- Booked BlackLane pick up in Boulder
- Work with Colleen to find an office cleaner
- Updated all flights/seats out of the front row of first class
- Ordered office furniture and decor for video studio
- Booked tickets to Hawaii & Sent Micah itinerary
- Booked rental car for Hawaii
- Sent Rainmaker website template choice
- Ordered all stock images for Jenna/Power Point Presentations
- Book Hawaii flights for family – Flights booked
- Book Hotel
- Send confirmation of flights
- Confirm stock images can be used for website
- Get receipts to Colleen for Limitless Adviser Conference
- Reserve rooms for Family Adventure Summit – Awaiting the email confirmation. Paid today over the phone.
- Personal email management - see new note on subject
- ADV mailing project for Colleen - Ordered Thumb Drives
- Updated hotel reservations for April FPA retreat
- Order merchandise with new family logo. Two 2' "sticker" and a roll of 2" stickers - Ordered, Awaiting Quote, invoice, etc.
- Format and upload CE Attendance Reports
- I changed my Florida flight to the 9th. Please change my rental car location and days, and find me a hotel in St. Petersburg Florida from the 9th when I arrive to the 11th when I drive to Orlando to meet Jackie and Ella
- Research options for having Jackie and Ella fly to Tampa on the 10th (vs currently flying to Orlando on the 11th). If the cost is less than $100 per person, please make the change.
- Please start tracking time you spend working on my project with Micah (The Perfect RIA). Don't worry about looking back, just going forward. Keep a tally in the M&M show notebook. Hour increments are plenty with very brief descriptions.
- Changed Name Server for Perfect RIA
- ADV mailing project for Colleen
- Ordered Thumb Drives on 3/14
- Send Document to USB Memory Direct no later than 3/26
- Sent Nate (video guy) equipment list
- Ordered new Apple iPad for video prompter
- Set up team dropbox

Tips for Successful Delegation

Sometimes it's hard to let go of certain tasks, and some tasks are just difficult to explain to another person. That doesn't mean they aren't worth getting off your plate. Here are a few things to keep in mind as you distribute your tasks to the rest of the office.

Make Your Team Part of the Solution

Any time you can solicit the buy-in of your entire team, everybody feels valued and engaged, and it keeps morale high. This is especially true when it comes to decisions that impact the entire office.

For example, many successful business owners hire a business coach to help them maximize their efficiency and improve their processes and operations. Whatever the coach recommends will certainly have an impact on how your team does their job day to day, which can make it difficult to strike the right tone about implementing changes. Why should your team suddenly start listening to some newcomer telling them how to do their jobs?

Instead of wasting your own valuable time tracking down coaches and comparing services and building spreadsheets and then springing it all on your team, make them part of the process. Have your team interview potential coaches and make recommendations for who *they* think would be the most beneficial for what you're trying to achieve.

There are two obvious benefits for making these sorts of practice-level decisions as a team: you get automatic team buy-in, because they chose the person that's recommending these changes, and it frees up your time for the deep focus your business, clients, and family deserve.

Build Good Systems

One problem a lot of business leaders have with delegation is that they think it'll take so long to teach somebody to do something that they might as well just do the thing themselves. This might be true, if you don't have a plan, but—surprise—when you have a system that works, it works every time.

For example, when we first implemented these changes, getting incoming client calls off my schedule meant I was able to sit and focus deeply on work that demanded my full attention. But empowering my team to take more of the office responsibilities had the expected result of requiring more of my time to answer questions, which meant the problem of being interrupted while doing deep work hadn't really been solved.

To fix this problem, my team and I developed a system for scheduling time on my calendar themselves when there was something to meet about. I could still be available in an emergency, but this meant that for all the normal operations, I was able to anticipate conversations and mentally prepare for them.

These days I hardly get any unscheduled communications from my team, except for the most urgent items that require immediate action.

HOW TO DELEGATE A SYSTEM

1. Write out the instructions (one page max)
2. Have the person watch you use the system as documented
3. You watch them follow the system as documented
4. Finalize the system documentation

Use Forcing Mechanisms

One advisor I coached wasn't taking those initial basic delegation steps we were recommending, no matter how hard we pushed. He refused to get a personal assistant: "Oh no, I don't need any of that. I'm doing just fine." Nothing I was saying could get him to value his time in a way that would allow his business to run successfully.

Finally, I did what had to be done: I riled him up about his least favorite political candidate for a while, then I told him that if he didn't hire a personal assistant by the end of the month and *keep* that personal assistant for an entire month, he would have to make a sizable donation to that candidate.

I watched texts come in for the entire following week with updates on his progress to find a personal assistant. (It must have worked. The last time I called his office, someone else answered the phone.)

Forcing mechanisms work when pure logic won't.

They work for the entire office, too. It sounds scary to let everyone loose to run the office without you, even when you're right down the hall. But what if you had to be gone for a month? Would they manage without you? People would have to figure out how to do things—and they *would*. But wouldn't it be easier for them if they could rely on the systems already in place?

This kind of worst-case-scenario thinking can help you understand the importance of having systems for everything your office needs to be successful.

Action Steps

No matter how efficiently you're able to do everything, you can only do so much in a day. When you find yourself spending your time performing tasks that don't match your salary goals and income expectations, those are the perfect tasks to delegate to a member of the rockstar team you're building to help you transform your business.

- ○ Make a list of all the recurring tasks that slow you down, burn you out, or just aren't worth your time. Pick the five you hate the most, and figure out how to get them off your radar.
- ○ Build good systems for all the processes you plan to delegate to someone else.
- ○ Enlist your whole team in business decisions that affect everyone. It gives you greater buy-in when it comes to potentially altering the way they do their jobs.

Bonus content available for this chapter at ThePerfectRIA.com/BookBonus:
→ The framework for setting up extreme accountability for those tasks which you just keeping holding on to
→ My top resources for finding an assistant
→ A guide for delegating anything

Scrap Your Elevator Pitch

"Having read virtually every book on growing and leading a financial advisory practice, this one is the best I've seen.

It's clear, simple, and actionable. If you implement even one of the ideas in this book, you'll make one hundred times what it costs. I have eight young advisors in my firm and will be giving a copy to each of them."

Chip Munn
Florence, SC
Signature Wealth Strategies

Financial advisors receive a lot of terrible advice—comes with the job, I guess—but one of the most common pieces of bad advice given to financial advisors is that we need a snappy elevator pitch prepared, so we can share it with everyone we meet. It sounds like a good idea on the surface, but like most bad advice, this one almost always comes from self-proclaimed "experts" who don't even have any clients.

The exact details vary, but here's the gist: when someone casually asks you, "What do you do?" you're supposed to respond with something like this:

"I provide comprehensive wealth management services to a select group of families."

If this sounds like good advice to you, it's only because it's been shoved down your throat so many times you had no choice but to swallow the Kool-Aid. Hey, no shame: they teach this stuff in business schools all over the country. Someone, somewhere, is probably cornering an unsuspecting dinner party guest with their own elevator pitch right now, and it's probably just as mystifying as the line above.

I'll confess that I myself fell victim to this bad advice for years. In fact, the exact line above used to be my elevator pitch. (I know, right?) Sadly, I spent many years and blew many potential relationships by using elevator pitches—with *no results*. Actually, it was worse than that: it branded me as a desperate salesperson.

So how is it possible that I, a relatively personable and charming individual and objectively a very good financial advisor, came up zeroes whenever I attempted to deploy this time-tested piece of business advice?

In this chapter, you'll learn why this approach is destined for failure outside of the most narrowly defined situations. You'll learn strategies for explaining your work and your services in engaging and compelling ways that connect with new people you meet while respecting their time. You'll learn how to keep people inviting you back to dinner parties. Most importantly, you'll see how I now get the bulk of my new clients through networking—and it's *not* how the "experts" tell you to do it.

Smells Like Sales

John Barron, my friend, longtime business coach, and guest on *The Perfect RIA Podcast*, summed this up perfectly in one of our episodes (#79, if you want to track it down): "We've been, as a culture in America, pitched so many times that it's something that people will go out of the way to avoid. It's the single biggest barrier to people wanting to engage with you."

Unless you're specifically attending a networking event, which is generally a waste of time, social gatherings aren't for working. They're for unwinding. If you subject your CV to people who haven't asked for it, they'll feel like they're back at work, and you'll find yourself alone at the refreshments table, wondering if it was something you said.

(Narrator: It was.)

If you listen to the real pros as they navigate social settings, you'll find they never answer "What do you do?" with an elevator pitch. Pretty much everyone gives confident one- or two-word answers, such as *doctor, attorney, teacher, computer programmer*, or *truck driver*. (Everyone except the salespeople, that is, whom you can identify by the way everyone else in the room is edging away from them.) Very few people come out of the gate swinging with the number of ear infections they cleared up last calendar year or the curricula they specialize in or the type of cargo they cross the country with. And the ones who do aren't being invited to dinner parties.

These professionals have figured out something the "experts" still haven't managed to grasp: elevator pitches are intrusive and obnoxious, and no one wants to put someone else in an uncomfortable situation.

When you launch right into your elevator pitch, you become an anomaly, an outsider. Worse, you've now abused the relationship by offering more than you were asked. Not a great way to get invited to the next party.

What to Do Instead

So are you doomed to wander the crowd as a mystery to everyone else because you never told them your specialty or explained what makes you stand out from your competitors? No! By keeping others' comfort in mind and respecting their time, it's possible to have rewarding conversations with the people around you and even walk away a few business cards lighter.

Answer the Real Question

How should you answer "What do you do?" when a new acquaintance asks you over cocktails? Directly and to the point, without a smack of salesmanship, as if they have a plateful of meatballs they'd like to eat before they get cold. (They might.) If the longer version of your answer was like a ride in an elevator, your new answer should feel like a transporter beam.

These days, when I'm asked, I initially tell people one of these two phrases:

"I run an investment firm."
"I'm a consultant."

Yes, both versions may be more than a couple of words—you caught me!—but both are brief, accurate, to the point. There's no "pitch," and each objectively true statement rolls off my tongue as smoothly and confidently as if it were my middle name.

Doctor. Attorney. Truck driver. *Consultant*. They get the idea.

The "Extended Pitch": Tread Carefully

I've seen a few slightly longer versions work, but you have to be smooth to pull this off. As such, it's not for amateurs. Here are a few examples:

"I teach people to retire." (Benjamin Brandt, *Retirement Starts Today* podcast)

"I work with Australian expats." (Ashley Murphy)

"I help dentists buy practices." (Brian Hanks)

These slightly longer answers work only because there is no shorter way of saying it. They also work because they create a ton of curiosity in the right audience.

For example, if you say, "I work with dentists," almost everyone is going to ask, "So you are a hygienist?"

Wait for the Magic Words

After you offer your short "polite company" answer with a short, non-salesy explanation of your position, one of two things will happen.

In the first scenario, they'll smile, respond with a polite "That's nice," and then head off to finish their meatballs. In this case, you did the right thing by holding back: you answered the question they were really asking, you gave them an accurate answer that helps them place you and your work in the right context, and no one had to field any unexpected discomfort or eat cold food.

Or, if you're speaking with someone whose business interests or network might really align with yours, they'll get curious. They'll sit forward, eyebrows raised. When they lob you a follow-up question, you'll know you're home free: "What does that mean? Like hedge funds?"

There it is. Now is the time to get into the details—you're still on borrowed time, but now you've been given permission to expand a little. However, it's even more important not to blow it and say the wrong thing.

So, how should you be answering? Enter the *fast pitch*.

Throw Your Best Fast Pitch

This is your second chance, and it's where the magic can happen—but only if your message is perfectly crafted and honed to perfection. Whatever their follow-up question, you now have permission to expand on your initial answer and take up more of your company's attention.

The bottom line is this: you don't want to keep people from eating their food; you want people to be so intrigued that they forget about their food all on their own. This only happens if your answer is so smooth, so rehearsed, that it comes out like an afterthought—*not* like a trap that has been sprung.

My response—which I give only to interested parties who have given me permission to expand on the short version by saying something like "You mean like a hedge fund?"—is this:

"Hmm? Not really. When people retire, I help them not get killed in taxes."

Here is why this is pure gold. If the person is not thinking about retirement and/ or is not concerned about taxes, they say, "Oh, interesting," and we both move on. However, if they *are* thinking about retirement/taxes, they get really, really curious. Suddenly, a stream of questions comes out, which then gives me permission to expand one final time:

"You have a 401(k) or IRA, right?" (They say, "Yes ...") "Well, the IRS is patiently waiting to take somewhere up to half of your account in taxes. Part of my job is to make sure this doesn't happen."

Now the hook is set. This random person—who would have run away immediately if I had led with "I help families minimize their lifetime tax bills using a proprietary strategy," a line I've actually heard recommended by an "expert"— is instead insanely curious and practically begging me for more information. But that's it: you've played your cards, the game is over, and it's time for everyone to get back to their meatballs.

YOU'RE GETTING QUESTIONS—WHY STOP?

When you strike prospecting gold during your leisure activities, it's tempting to start them down the prospect process (Chapter 10) right then and there. But no matter how eager your audience, you must stop the conversation. Any and all future questions during this meeting need to be responded to with "I'm here to [insert activity] and not talk business. If you have questions, give my office a call to schedule a time to chat."

Why is it important to stop? Because *no other professional* will let a casual conversation turn into a business call! Need an example? Here's a true story from one of my retired doctor clients:

Random Party Guest: What do you do?

Professional: I'm a doctor. (simple answer)

Random Party Guest: Cool. What kind of doctor? (permission to expand)

Professional: I'm a heart surgeon at ... (simple response)

Random Party Guest: (lifts shirt) I have this funny heartbeat. Would you take a listen and let me know if it's serious?

Professional: WTF? Put your shirt back on and call 911 if you are having heart problems!

Don't let even the most adamant of potential clients turn your party into a consultation.

Using this approach, I've gotten clients from: boating, partying, rock climbing, dirt biking, mountain biking, charity events, my kids' schools, working out, social activities, BBQs, and most anywhere else I go.[1]

In Chapter 13, you'll learn tips for narrowing your services down into a niche. In addition to helping you identify a market to focus on dominating, having a strong niche makes it much easier to develop your fast pitch. For now, here are a few tips for developing your own fast pitch with a high success rate:

Be Sticky

One financial advisor I've coached works exclusively with dentists. While this is a fantastic niche, the elevator pitch he used for years fell a little flat:

"I help dentists retire with a bucket of tax-free money."

This may be true, but it's too long, it's confusing, and it will register as salesy or pushy. However, "Retirement Planner" is too short, isn't catchy at all, and could be just as confusing as the first version.

Instead, we cut off the second part as unnecessary. Now, when anyone asks him what he does for work, he says:

"I help dentists retire."

This is the perfect fast pitch: it's short, speaks only to his niche (dentists), and is catchy enough that it sticks in people's minds. And if it's said almost as a throwaway line—something in the same tone as "I like Miracle Whip instead of mayonnaise on my burgers"—it smooths over any hint of sleazy salesmanship, and it makes the right people very curious.

Now, the next time they hear about dentists who are approaching retirement, they'll think, "Hey, wasn't that charming guy I chatted with over meatballs into helping dentists?"

To give a personal example, an advisor I coached, Ashley Murphy, who became a good friend, when asked what he does explains, "I work with Australian expats." Having never heard that before, I was instantly intrigued and asked him several questions about his work, despite me obviously not being his target market and not even knowing any Australian expats.

Some time later, I met a prospect who happened to be an Australian expat, and I immediately thought, "You need to talk with Ashley Murphy!" I know thousands of advisors around the world, but Ashley is one of only a handful who have a permanent spot in my mind because his answer is so sticky.

---

1 Anywhere else, that is, aside from Chamber of Commerce events and other "meat markets" where intense networking is expected and encouraged. *That's* a whole different ball game.

Be Intriguing

Somewhere between an elevator ride and a transporter beam, the fast pitch should feel like a brisk drive on the Autobahn. It should be as short as possible while still expanding on the question you've been asked, and it should be so filled with excitement and intrigue that the person doesn't want to stop the ride.

This is easy for people who have jobs with titles that sound exciting and intriguing all on their own. But for those of us who aren't international spies or career athletes or professional mountain climbers, we need to think a little bit harder.

Be warned: while fast pitches might seem simple, it can take a lot of work to find the right one. My recommendation is to commit to writing down one hundred different options (yes, one hundred!) and try them out on your friends. Keep them all short, speak them out loud, and keep working on narrowing down your list until you find the perfect elevator pitch for you.

Provoke Further Questions

"But wait," you may be thinking. "How will anyone know I'm a fee-only fiduciary with proprietary investment strategies?" They won't—not at this point. That's why your fast pitch has to check all the boxes:

It has to be communicated quickly. It can't be boring. It has to stick in their minds. It has to be intriguing. And it has to be perfectly calibrated to provoke follow-up questions from just the right kind of person, so that you have the opportunity to explain in greater detail.

If you do it correctly, you'll get nearly the same response from everyone. Remember, the most common response I get to "I run an investment firm" is "like a hedge fund?" My advisor friend who "works with dentists" always gets "so like a hygienist?" The goal is for your initial answer to trigger a question, which you now have permission to answer.

Random Party Guest: "You mean like a hygienist?"

Professional: "Hmm? No, I make sure dentists don't get killed in taxes when they retire."

Random Party Guest: (slightly confused) "So you're a CPA?"

Professional: "CPAs tell dentists how much they owe. I tell them how to pay less in the future."

Random Party Guest: "Huh. Interesting"

Now, this party guest has permanently put you in the place of helping dentists pay less in taxes. Not bad for a quick chat over hors d'oeuvres.

Remember, your fast pitch must be:
- Short
- Intriguing
- Sticky

You may not be an astronaut or a Navy SEAL, but hey—financial planning is exciting stuff. And if your pitch accomplishes all of these things, you'll soon have your chance to let everyone know, and you'll be the exciting professional everyone wants to hear from instead of the guy making all the other guests uncomfortable.

I'll toast to that!

Action Steps

You may be out there to network, but most people you meet casually don't give two hoots about you or your business, much less the nuances that make your rockstar practice stand out from any old investment firm. If you ever want anyone to care, you need to stifle your inner salesperson and embrace your new networking tool, the fast pitch. Just follow these steps and you'll be delivering your strongest, most effective elevator pitch of all time.

- ◯ Develop your own answer to "What do you do?" that meets all the requirements outlined above:
  - ◯ One word or phrase
  - ◯ Creates curiosity
  - ◯ Is *not* a generic term like "financial advisor"
- ◯ Wait for permission. If you're in an investor meeting, "What do you do?" is an invitation to get into detail. If you're at a social gathering, don't take up more time than you've been given permission to take. If they're really interested, they'll let you know. (If they're not, reread this chapter to see what you missed!)
- ◯ PRACTICE, PRACTICE, PRACTICE! I'm not kidding: you need to practice your elevator pitch until it comes out as smoothly and confidently as if I asked you your name or where you went to high school. Practice out loud every time you look in the bathroom mirror so you can whip it out when it's time like it's the most natural thing in the world.
- ◯ Be ready with the answer to the questions that inevitably follow when you give your first answer. For example, if you answer, "I help women retire," be ready for "Only women? Why not men?" A great follow-up response to this might be, "The world is full of men telling women what to do. I work with successful women who want advice from other women."
- ◯ Track how many times each week you are able to answer the question, "What do you do?" and then work to increase this number.

Bonus content available for this chapter at ThePerfectRIA.com/BookBonus:

→ Videos of me giving my elevator pitch

→ Worksheet for crafting your elevator pitch

→ Interview with Coach John Barron on your pitch

Craft the Prospect Process

"Following Jarvis's processes has been a major piece that has allowed me to comfortably scale from zero to forty-six clients in eighteen months (brought in twenty-one clients in a single quarter).

I can focus on onboarding new clients throughout the year, knowing that there is also a specified time dedicated to deep-diving with existing clients."

Jim Crider, CFP
New Braunfels, TX
Intentional Living

For too many of the early years of my career, I was stuck in an epic catch-22: on one hand, I desperately wanted and needed new clients, but on the other, I was terrified of actually meeting with prospects. While I had dozens of failed prospect meetings, one in particular is seared into my memory.

After presenting my most elaborate financial plan (generated by financial planning software I had purchased with borrowed money), the prospect explained with all sincerity that while all this information looked interesting, it wasn't at all clear to him why he would hire let alone pay me.

I don't think he meant it as an insult, but it crushed my spirit. All I could think to say was, "Well, I guess I didn't do a good job explaining my value," to which he responded: "Pretty much. So please tell me why I would hire you." Still not knowing what to say, I offered to send him a letter explaining my value. Then he left. (In case you were wondering, I never sent the letter, and he never called back.)

Despite the emotional pain of this meeting, I'll forever be grateful for that experience, as it started the journey that led me to the nearly perfect prospect process I've outlined for you in this chapter. (Why only "nearly" perfect? Any system can be improved, and I'm always looking for improvements.) With the process I've perfected after hundreds of prospect meetings over the years, you will be able to land *every* qualified prospect as a client—and of equal importance, anyone who is *not* qualified will walk away still thinking you are an amazing advisor.

Perhaps most important of all, this process of helping a prospect make an educated and informed decision about your firm will eliminate nearly all of your head trash and fear of rejection that is so typically associated with prospecting.[1]

Prospect Process Mishap: Too Much or Too Little

One of the first questions I ask advisors when coaching them on prospecting is, "What is your current prospect process?"

Many advisors tell me, "I don't have a prospect process." I explain that they *do* in fact have a prospect process; it just may not be an intentional one. This "accidental" prospect process typically looks like the advisor talking at the prospect long enough, saying all the same things that every other advisor says until the prospect agrees to work with them, more out of desperation than anything else.

This approach leaves most advisors with very few clients and lots of rejection. Why? Because you are essentially relying on the prospect "liking" you more than anyone else ... which means when they say no, it's literally because they don't like you enough as a person. Ouch.

---

1 I would be remiss if I failed to credit Tom Gau as well as John Barron of Apollo Coaching. Each provided the foundation of what would become my prospect process. That said, I've invested hundreds of hours fine-tuning and perfecting this process.

On the other end of the spectrum, many advisors give me a long-winded, nonsensical explanation that I'm not sure even they understand, and I've stopped paying attention before they've finished the summary of their process. Admittedly, I have a really short attention span (ADD is a superpower, not a disease), but even the most focused prospect will lose interest when you blast them with endless jargon.

It's like your elevator pitch: if you can't explain your process in one breath, it's too long. Further, also like the standard elevator pitch, your only success will come when the prospect is so exhausted from your process that the thought of going through it again with another advisor has them signing up out of sheer desperation, which I suppose is one way to get a yes.

What Makes a Prospect Process Successful?

By now, you know why having a system is so important: by codifying every potential turning point into an easy-to-understand system, you can ensure that every last detail is focused on giving your prospect exactly the information they need, exactly when they need it. By the time they get to the end of the process, if they haven't dropped out (or been gently nudged aside), they're perfectly primed to place your services and potential benefits to them in the proper context, and they'll truly appreciate the value you bring them.

Make sure the process you develop fulfills these important criteria for prospecting success.

Establishes Value

Lots of different marketers (and a bunch of those "experts") see this as a funnel, but in my office, we see the entire prospect process as a way to help people make an educated and informed decision about our firm. Luckily, this strategy sounds amazing from a marketing standpoint, so it tends to be an easy sell!

Imagine walking into a Honda dealership to buy a car. There's not a dealership in the country where a salesperson will walk up to you and say, "Hi! I'd like to help you decide if a Honda is the right car for you. If it's not, I'll direct you across the street, where you can buy a Nissan." That's just not how it works.

But when a prospect calls my office, I say, "We follow this process to help you make an educated and informed decision about our firm or any other firm that you talk to." Everybody loves that: I'm telling them upfront that I won't give them the hard sell, which puts all of us on the same page. And the fact that I'm giving them a free education in vetting a financial advisor means I'm *already* delivering value from the moment they walk in the door.

THE **PERFECT** RIA   **GENERAL INFORMATION**

Please complete the information below and email to [insert your company contact email] or upload via our secure link, listed below my signature line. Thank you!

Name *(Last, First, MI)*

Phone *(Mobile)*

Name *(Last, First, MI)*

Phone *(Mobile)*

Address

Email

City

State

Zip

What are your biggest financial concerns?

Primary questions for our team:

Planned retirement date, or if retired, date of retirement

In order to advise you best, it is our approach to take a comprehensive look at your financial situation. This will be accomplished if you will provide complete statements (vs. screenshots) of the following documents:

• Company Plan Statements (i.e., 401(k), 403(b), 457, etc.)
• All Other Investment Account Statements
• Life Insurance and Long-Term Care Insurance Statements
• Recent Tax Returns—all pages, for two years
• Estate Documents (i.e., Will, Trust, POA)
• Social Security Statements (if available)

If you are unable to provide the above-mentioned documents before your appointment, please contact us to reschedule.

Eliminates the Fear of Rejection

As I mentioned earlier in the chapter, I created the prospect process to be more confident and effective in expressing my own value. In doing so, I found one unexpected benefit that made me even more passionate about systems than I already was, if that's possible: *I stopped worrying if people were going to say yes or no.*

At the end of the day, it didn't really matter to me if they became my client, because I knew it wasn't about me—it was the system. They either fit into it, or they don't, and if they don't, that leaves room for the next client who does. No harm, no foul.

If somebody comes in and says they want help consolidating their credit cards, or they want a highly active investment strategy with hedge funds and alternatives, or they only want to pay one tenth of a percent, there's nothing personal about it: they're just not a good fit for my services. None of those are rejections of *me*, and the fact that they aren't a good fit has nothing to do with the value I bring to my clients who are.

THE PERFECT PROSPECT PROCESS

Make sure your prospect process accomplishes these three things for your client:
- Establishes value
- Eliminates the fear of rejection
- Sets expectations

Sets Expectations

There's so much obvious value packed into this prospect process that prospects sometimes try to skip important steps and sign up right away. But by sticking to the prospect process, you're able to build in multiple points of contact where you can keep explaining what you're doing and why and reminding them what's coming next.

Throughout the prospect process, you're preempting concerns, letting prospects know what to expect, and preparing them for what it's like to be your client and follow your winning systems.

Doesn't Make It Look "Too Easy"

On our recent trip to Florida, I started getting terrible earaches. I went to the local clinic, and after the nurse had collected all my information and filled out the forms, the doctor walked in and said, "It's TMJ. You grind your teeth at night. You need surgery. Have a nice day."

Say what?

First of all, I had no idea whether I should trust this guy's assessment. He may have had a white lab coat and a stethoscope, but his answer was so immediate that it felt like he'd picked it out of a hat; he didn't even *hint* that there might have been a process behind his thinking. And even if he was right, the almost automatic ease with which he dispensed his advice made me question the value of it. It just seemed too easy, and I walked away from the encounter annoyed that I had to pay him.[2]

It's easy for financial planners to do the same thing to our prospects: we make financial planning look too easy, and then we're surprised when people don't want to hire us or pay our fees. But we know the same thing doctors know: when you know what you're doing, it's *easy* to make things look easy. The hard part is reminding people how complex the system really is (and how good we really are at our jobs!).

The Prospect Process: Six Steps to Onboarding the Perfect Client

It sounds like a lot to pack into one client onboarding system, but I'm about to show you the six steps behind the prospect process I've developed for use in my office and still use to this day. When you put them all together, you'll have a powerful system that will refocus and accelerate every step of your client onboarding and transform your business.

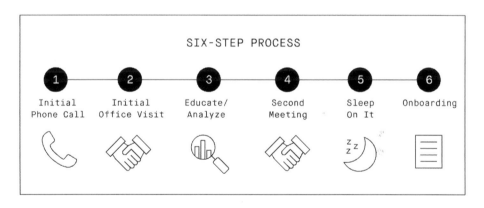

Before we begin, let me share one quick reminder about the scripts I provide throughout this chapter. As with all the scripts in this book, these are, word for word, what works for *me*, several times a week. While you *could* recite them word for word with great success, they will work much better if you rewrite them and practice them in your own words.

Now—onward!

---

2 After leaving the office, I googled "how to eliminate TMJ pain" and found a list of exercises that ended up making a huge difference. Thanks for nothing, doc!

Step 1: Initial Phone Call

Before anyone even sets foot in your office, it's a good idea to set up a fifteen-minute phone call so you can screen potential new clients and make sure you're a great fit for each other. It might seem inconsequential, but this call sets important expectations and lays the foundation for the entire prospect process: a single fifteen-minute call can save both you and your prospect from wasting a great deal of each other's time.

When prospects call for a meeting, have your team say this:

"Before having you come into the office, let's schedule a quick phone appointment to see if we are potentially a good fit for your needs and to describe our process for helping you evaluate our firm."

Then, *precisely* at the allotted time, you will call the prospect, introduce yourself, and ask:

"Is now still a good time for you?"

Then, when they tell you it is, you open by passing them the mic:

"How can I be of most assistance to you today?"

It's a small thing, but by introducing ourselves like this, we're getting their opt-in to the entire prospect process, right from the very first word. They're getting on that ride with you willingly, and they're giving you permission at every bend in the road to keep the ride going. (That's why the prospect doesn't ever feel like they're fielding a hard sell: because you're making sure they are aware of and in agreement with every step along the way.)

> **"Throughout the prospect process, you're preempting concerns, letting prospects know what to expect, and preparing them for what it's like to be your client and follow your winning systems."**

Many advisors make the mistake of jumping right in and asking sensitive questions like "What's your net worth?" and the like. I don't ever want to do that to my prospects. This isn't just about being clever or being a sly marketer—I sincerely believe that the better relationship I establish with them, the better I can serve them, and coming out of the gate with direct personal questions doesn't help me do that.

As with every step of the prospect process, think how *you* would want to be treated. Do you appreciate when a salesperson jumps right into personal questions that could potentially be used to pressure you into a decision?

The trick is to not put people on the spot but still keep the information flowing so you can figure out what side of the line they're on. To do this, I've developed a few gentle but probing phrases:

- "Please tell me a little bit about your situation."
- "What made you want to take the step of contacting a financial advisor?"
- "What are some of your financial concerns?"
- "Can you tell me in round numbers your annual income?"
- "Can you tell me the approximate balance of your retirement accounts?"

If the prospect seems like a good fit, help them be confident they are in the right place. Try a phrase such as these:

- "Many of our clients are just like you."
- "I've helped several clients in similar situations."
- "Can you tell me about your strategy for XYZ (e.g., claiming Social Security)?"

As with everything in this process, these phrases are not some kind of magic password to sales success. They will help only if you are 100 percent sincere.

Then, once I've gathered the basic information and they seem like a good fit, I'll explain like this:

> "Based on what you've described, it sounds like we could
> potentially help with your goals. If it's OK with you, I'd
> be glad to take just a minute to explain how we help potential
> clients make an educated and informed decision about our firm." ❓

I've never had someone decline this request, but I still want their permission and their buy-in to proceed, otherwise I risk raising their defenses on what could otherwise feel like a sales pitch. That's when I give them my offer:

> "Before you pay us a dollar in fees or trust us with a penny of
> your nest egg, you need to make an educated and informed decision
> if the value we can provide you is worth some multiple of our fee.
> This process starts with our phone call today, and the next step
> is a meeting together in my office. During that one-hour meeting,
> I'll answer any questions you have, and I'll also ask a lot of my
> own questions to make sure I understand your goals and financial
> situation. At the end of that meeting, the only 'hard sell' will
> be an invitation for me to do a no-cost detailed analysis of your
> situation. I don't charge for this analysis, because I want you
> to see exactly what we can do before you pay us a penny in fees.
> My analysis typically takes a few weeks, after which we will meet
> together a second time for me to present my recommendations
> and answer your questions. As with the first meeting, there is
> nothing to buy, and I will insist that you go home and sleep on it
> before deciding how to proceed. Is this OK with you?"

When they agree to this process, I explain that I'm going to transfer them over to my office manager, who handles all our scheduling and who will provide them with a list of documents to bring to our first meeting so that we can make the best use of our time together. Before transferring the call, I ask one last thing:

> "What other questions or concerns can I answer for you today?"

With that, I hand them over to my team who takes the prospect to the next phase of the process!

Let's take a look at how this conversation can go:

Advisor (at exactly the allotted time): "Mrs. Prospect? This is Advisor, is now still a good time for you?"

Prospect: "Wow, you are exactly on time. Yes."

Advisor: "Great. The purpose of this call is to see if we are potentially a fit for each other. Before I jump into my questions, let's start with any questions or concerns you have?"

Prospect: "Well, I want to retire next year and I want to make sure I have enough money."

Advisor: "Perfect. Nearly all of our clients are retired, or close to it, so one of our main jobs is finding the answer to that question. Please tell me a bit more about your planned retirement."

Prospect provides general details.

Advisor: "Sounds like you've had an interesting career and that next year would be a great time to retire. So that I can get a better feel for your situation, can you tell me a little bit about your finances and your strategy for paying for retirement?"

Prospect provides financial details.

If They Are a Good Fit

Advisor: "Great news. We specialize exclusively in clients just like you. May I take just a minute to explain how we help people make an educated and informed decision about our firm?"

Prospect: "Of course."

Advisor: "Thank you. While we help people retire all the time, this will be your only retirement so it's essential you get it right and a big part of that will be finding the right professional along the way. Because this decision is so important, we've designed a process you can use to evaluate our firm, or any other firm you are considering.

The first step is this phone call, where we do a quick assessment to make sure our specialty fits your needs, which it does.

The next step will be a meeting in our office (or on Zoom) where I'll have a lot of questions about your goals and finances. Of course, we will have plenty of time to answer all of your questions. At the end of that meeting, there will be nothing to buy, nor any paperwork to sign. The only 'hard sell' will be me asking if you want us to create a one-page executive summary of what you need to do to have the best possible retirement. There is no cost for this process as before you pay us a dollar in fees or trust us with a penny of your nest egg, we want you to see exactly how we can help. Does this process sound OK to you?"

Prospect: "Sounds great, but what are your fees?"

Advisor: "I'm glad you asked about fees as the financial world has made a science around hiding their fees. Our fee depends on the complexity of your situation, but more importantly, the value we can provide as it only makes sense to hire an advisor if the value they provide is worth some multiple of their fee. As part of doing our no-cost financial planning we will clearly detail our fees should we agree to work together. Other questions?"

Prospect: "Not right now."

Advisor: "Perfect. I'm going to pass you over to our relationship manager, who will schedule a time for us to meet and provide you with a list of documents to bring so that we can make the best use of our time together."

Follow-Up Before Initial Meeting

Making people aware of what they need to bring to the meeting in order for you to help them (and to keep them from wasting your office's time) is one thing; getting them to actually follow through is another, and it's a challenge that plagues every financial advisor.

Before any scheduled meeting, have your team make a confirmation call to clarify your expectations for the meeting and what you'll need to accomplish them. Investment statements, Social Security statements, tax returns, estate documents—clients have to bring all of it in with them in that first meeting, and they need to understand that it's serious enough to reschedule the whole meeting over.

In that call, have your team say, "We wanted to make sure you got that checklist. Will you have all of those materials ready, or do we need to reschedule this meeting for another time?" It seems obnoxious, but prospects appreciate the reminder, and it's the only way to be sure your time will be spent productively.

The Intake Form

One of the best ways to gather information about your prospect ahead of time is the intake form. However, a word of caution: keep any forms you ask your prospects to fill out very simple, and don't ask them to do a lot of work on top of gathering their statements and forms to prepare for the meeting. You don't want to make this more difficult for them than it already is.

In my office, our intake form consists of a handful of questions and a checklist: What are your top financial concerns? What's your contact information? Can you please bring these things to the meeting? If your intake form is any more complicated, spend some time simplifying it and whittling it down to just what's important for your prospect to complete. This stuff is complicated enough for your potential client; there's no reason to make it any more so.

Step 2: Initial Office Visit

The number one thing to keep in mind when your prospect walks in the door is that they're on guard. They're defensive, and they expect to be sold to. That's why this first face-to-face meeting with your prospect has nothing to do with sales. In fact, you wouldn't sign them up on the spot if they tried—which is one of the first points you should go over.

In your first meeting with a prospect, you have one goal: setting expectations (or, rather, resetting the expectations you already set on the phone). That means no selling, and no advice. You're just asking and listening, and in doing so, you're carefully laying the foundations for the client–advisor relationship you want to have in the future.

Put them at ease by reminding them they're not there for the hard sell, that today you're only talking and gathering information. By telling them what to expect, you're letting them know that between now and that point, they can talk to you freely, because you're not trying to sell them and they're not getting tricked into something. You're paving the way to have a true and sincere conversation about their goals.

Here's what I like to tell my prospects to put them at ease:

> "As I explained to you on the phone, there's nothing to buy in this meeting. There are no forms to sign; this isn't a timeshare presentation. We're not going to lock the doors until you sign up. This is just for me and you to answer questions and gather information from each other. The only 'hard sell' will be at the end of this meeting, when I'll ask you if you want me to do a more in-depth analysis of your situation at no cost and no obligation so that you can see exactly what it is we can do and exactly how we can help you, before you pay us a dollar in fees or trust us with a penny of your nest egg. Is that OK with you?"

That final question—"Is that OK with you?"—is important because it keeps people feeling like they're in charge of the situation. Keep it in mind; it's a phrase you should constantly return to with clients in other situations. Whenever you can get a client to opt in to a situation on their own, they're going to feel much more positively about it.

But even though I'm not giving advice in this meeting, I'm looking to identify problems that they're not aware of, and I'm demonstrating my credibility through the questions I ask. I want to make sure that they're at least aware of every aspect of the financial planning process, and I want them to hear how confident I am in my mastery of each one. I want every word out of my mouth to add value in their minds.

Here's the script I like to use with everything from claiming Social Security to handling the next bear market to not overpaying the IRS:

```
"What's your strategy for ____?"                        ☰
```

When they say they don't have one, I'll respond with:

```
"OK. That's something we'll look at."                   ☰
```

These simple questions and follow-up statements help set the stage for the massive value you can deliver and firmly establish you as the expert you are. Then, you'll end the meeting by setting clear expectations that they should schedule another appointment, at which point you will review your recommendations and talk next steps.

Follow-Up to First Meeting

While your prospect is waiting for their next meeting with you, this is a great time for your staff to begin assembling materials and information to send to your prospect to help preempt common questions or objections you might otherwise find yourself fielding during the second meeting.

This important step in your prospect process helps keep you from having uncomfortable conversations face-to-face, and it's another good layer of screening for your prospects to go through before they ultimately sign up. Without checking in on your prospect and preempting any questions or concerns they might have, you run the risk of having to answer uncomfortable questions face-to-face during your next meeting, and you might end up wasting each other's time.

Of course, you shouldn't send stuff just to send stuff; that wouldn't add any value. Instead, send information that's directly focused on this point in the process or that can be of direct help to that person, right now, such as the sample on page 120. And make sure to preface any information you send with why you're sending it to them and how they can benefit from investing their time, so they know it's not just more spam to contend with.

Step 3: Educate and Analyze (Behind the Scenes)

The main part of this step is creating recommendations. This is, essentially, that one-page financial plan you've been hearing so much about (sample on following pages), which we'll cover in more detail in Chapter 18. The rest of this step consists of all the things that take place behind the scenes between now and your follow-up meeting to discuss their financial plan.

One-Page Financial Plan

Name Surname XX/XX/XXXX

THE **PERFECT** RIA

Primary Goals:
- Establish financial and legacy goals?
- Maintain dignity and independence in retirement
- Minimize lifetime tax bill, preserving insurance credits as possible
- Be ready to move closer to children/grandchildren

Retirement Income
- Managed correctly, your portfolio of $1,400,000 can generate a dynamic distribution of $6,400 monthly ($8,000 gross) BEFORE estate distributions
- Defer Social Security as long as possible to maximize benefit (pending tax strategy)

Risk Management—Asset Protection
- A review of estate documents (i.e., will, power of attorney) and beneficiary agreements is needed to ensure your wishes are followed and taxes minimized
- Review property and casualty insurance for proper coverage, including "umbrella" policy
- Evaluate pros and cons of various asset protection strategies

Income Taxes
Create 10-year tax strategy incorporating inherited accounts, trust distributions, Social Security, Roth conversions, state of residency, gifting to children, and gifting to charity.

- Be prepared to lose health insurance credit due to Trust distributions
- Make gifts to children in-kind to reduce your tax burden
- Leverage tax benefits/costs of current and/or future state of residency Investment Portfolio
- Consolidate accounts to simplify tracking, improve diversification, and reduce fees
- Rebalance consolidated accounts to support income in retirement using the following framework:
  - 35% US Large Companies
  - 20% US Small Companies
  - 5% US Commercial Real Estate
  - 10% International Companies
  - 30% Cash and Bonds as a "War Chest"

Questions to Answer for a
Prospect during Your Process

THE **PERFECT** RIA

The following questions are designed to help you see "behind the curtain" of any firm to whom you might entrust your financial future.

Are your recommendations truly in my best interest?

_____

_____

_____

Will your recommendations be primarily focused in one area, or will your recommendations be comprehensive in nature? In other words, will I need to find another advisor for advice in other areas?

_____

_____

_____

Do you have the knowledge and experience necessary to successfully navigate the complicated financial planning and tax world to achieve my financial goals?

_____

_____

_____

How many clients do you serve and how does their situation compare to mine?

_____

_____

_____

How often will I hear from you?

_____

_____

_____

Pre-Appointment Email

Before they come in for their second meeting to review the financial plan you've developed, have your team check in again via email to keep your firm front of mind and remind them of the value you'll add:

> "In reviewing the information you provided, it's clear that you've been doing a great job with your finances. I did, however, find a few areas where improvements can be made, and I look forward to sharing them with you during our meeting on _____."

And of course—because you're always using every step to preempt concerns—you'll add the following statement:

> "Please let me know if you've thought of any additional questions or concerns."

Step 4: Second Meeting

Assuming you nailed it in your first meeting—and of course you did—you have three main goals for your second meeting:

1. Reset expectations
2. Deliver Massive Value
3. Set expectations for next steps

Start by checking in with how your prospect is doing. Ask,

> "What questions or concerns have you thought of since our last meeting?"

to put them at ease, make them feel in control, and flush out anything that might be on their mind.

Remind them of the purpose of this meeting: to review your recommendations and show you exactly, step-by-step, how you can improve your prospect's situation. Start with,

> "As I explained during the first meeting …"

Remind them there's nothing to buy right now: no papers to sign, no checks to write. It's just a chance for both of you to focus on how you can help them answer as many questions as you can during the hour or so you have together.

Then, pull out three copies of the one-page financial plan: one for you to look at and one for each spouse to look at, and articulate your advice in plain English. Try this script:

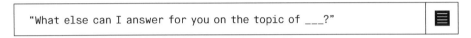

```
"To achieve your goal of _____, we need to _____,
because it will _____."
```

Go through your plan point by point, section by section, and at each step along the way, check in with the prospect: "Does that make sense to you?" "Do you understand that?" "Do you have any questions about that?" and

```
"What else can I answer for you on the topic of ___?"
```

Give them ample opportunity to ask any question they might have that hasn't been answered already, and spend the rest of your time together focusing not on signing them up, but on answering any remaining questions they may still have on their minds.

Step 5: Sleep on It

By this point, your prospects will be rifling through their pockets or purses for a pen to sign up with before you've even finished going over the one-page business plan. That's awesome! But not so fast. Didn't you have a system? Making an exception now sounds like a smart way to adapt, but this is a mistake for two reasons.

First, you've been telling your prospect all along that your process includes them going home to sleep on it. If you change your process now—even at their own request—you'll lose credibility. When people work with experts, they're used to things being nonnegotiable. The doctor won't negotiate with you on the treatment she thinks you need, and you shouldn't negotiate about your process now just because they're eager to get started.

The second reason is the one you've been giving them all along: that you truly want them to make a good decision and feel prepared for this decision. If they sign up now and they end up not being a good fit for your firm, you'll wish you had given them the space to go home and really think about it, outside of your office.

Instead, try something like this:

> "Selecting a financial advisor is a big decision. Odds are, ▤
> if you sign up with our firm, we will work together for the
> rest of your life, and I don't want you to rush into this decision.
> I'm going to insist that you go home and sleep on this information.
> And then, when you get up in the morning, you can decide if you
> think our firm can deliver value that's worth multiples of our
> fees. If the answer is yes, we can do the paperwork. If the answer
> is no, we'll part ways as friends. And if you have more questions,
> then we'll get together to answer all those questions."

By asking them to wait, you're setting yourself up as a trusted confidant, a true advisor, not a salesperson. Another benefit is that after an hour-long meeting, you're simply knackered and out of time. Getting them to go home and sleep on it also gives you time to have all the paperwork ready, and you can set up another meeting where you can focus exclusively on onboarding a client.

TO CHARGE OR NOT TO CHARGE?

Lots of advisors charge an upfront financial planning fee, and I admit, they have good reasons for that: as advisors, we spend our time looking at the prospect's situation and developing customized advice, and even with the most compelling and carefully crafted prospect process, the potential for a prospect to walk away is always looming.

Even so, I personally do not charge a financial planning fee. Part of this is legacy; about sixteen years ago, I decided not to charge for that initial financial planning session, simply because not many other advisors in my area were. ("Matt, I don't understand why I should pay you a fee for something Dave down the street says he'll do for free" is a hard point to argue.)

Instead, I simply consider my one-page financial plan part of the onboarding process, and I'm constantly delivering value by using the tips and principles throughout this chapter and the rest of the book. Clients can't help but be impressed when I tell them, "Before you pay us a dollar of fees or trust us with a penny of your nest egg, we want to show you exactly how we can help you achieve your financial goals," and they're already looking forward to the value I'll bring them once they actually start paying me.

Step 6: Onboarding

Now that you've given your prospect every opportunity to say no, it's finally time to let them say yes! The most important thing to keep in mind is that it's still about the client experience.

We talked earlier about surge week and how important it is to have every detail in order. That may be even more true of your prospect process: every single detail must be focused on the client experience and carefully tailored to the path you're leading them down. (Remember, if you're truly upholding the three goals of a prospect process, that path isn't just where you want to go—it's where your prospect wants to go as well.)

That means that every single thing you say has been rehearsed so you know you're delivering it with maximum effect, every time. It means every page in your paperwork is in order, with every signature line flagged and ready. (Please, please do not miss a line in your onboarding paperwork requiring you to contact the prospect again to sign another page.) And it means clearly articulating every section in a way that makes sense, doesn't intimidate or belittle, and helps them feel in control of the situation.

This isn't the car dealership, where you're trying to get them to sign up quickly before they realize that the price is double what you had originally quoted them.[3] You are not a car dealership. You are a trusted advisor. You're slowly and carefully walking them through the paperwork, you're never pressuring them, and you're making them comfortable about signing at the dotted line.

One thing you're probably not doing: answering a ton of questions. If the prospect isn't ready to sign, or if they want to schedule another meeting to go over even more questions you somehow haven't answered yet, take a hard look at your prospect process to see where you can add the clarity and value your prospect needs to become a client.

> ## "Now that you've given your prospect every opportunity to say no, it's finally time to let them say yes!"

Tips for Prospecting Success

Here are a handful of tips for smoothing out your system and finding even greater success with your prospecting and onboarding process.

Maintain an Environment of Success

From the moment your prospects enter to the moment they leave, everything needs to be carefully curated to best reflect the practice you want to be. There are no accidents in your office, no details that haven't been fully thought out in terms of their effects. From the reading material available in your waiting room to your nice

---

3 No disrespect intended to our friends who have car dealerships.

tailored suit, the environment you're creating for your prospects begins the second they walk in the door, and every detail matters.

For example, I have a great deal of books in my office. No cheating here; I've read every single one. (My collection hasn't always been this big; it started very small. But that's the kind of thing you have time for when you harness the power of systems.)

Almost every single time a prospect walks in, they ask someone on my team, "What's with all these books?" The response everyone on my team knows to give is, "These are all books that Matt has read." Why? So that if the prospect asks, "Why does he read so many books?" the answer is next-level: "So that you don't have to."

Always Have an Answer

Feel free to use any of the scripts I provide, here in this chapter or throughout the book. Even so, keep an eye out where you can anticipate needing to field a question again so you can write down a great answer now.

For example, when I ask people if it's OK with them if I show them a few ways to save money on their taxes, some will say, "Hey now—I want to pay all the taxes I owe." I'll respond with something cute:

> "You know what? Our philosophy is to pay the IRS all the money that you owe them, but let's not leave them a tip."

That's my line. I'm always ready with it, and it sounds as natural as can be whenever I need to pull it out and use it.

Don't Take the Wrong Clients

Not everyone will make it to the next stage of your prospect process. If they don't seem like a good fit, explain, "Based on the information that you've given me, it sounds like you might be better served by ___" and tell them whoever you think is the best fit: the attorney, the accountant, the advisor down the road.

And even in your last moments, you're adding value. Pad the rejection:

> "Just like if you needed brain surgery you would go to a neurologist, not a cardiologist, in this situation, you need a specialist for your needs, and I'm just not that specialist. However, I would be glad to personally introduce you to the person who is that specialist."

Remember, the whole point of making your business a system is that you aren't leaving any gaps for your pristine customer service to fall through. It's important to screen aggressively. When people call my office, one of the first things they are asked is, "Have you reviewed who we work with on our website?" If they haven't, we simply suggest that they take a look and then call us back.[4]

Jarvis Financial New Client Onboarding Process
"Jarvis, what happens when a prospect says YES?"

Second Prospect Meeting (presenting the plan): *"We've covered a lot today. What I want you to do next is go home and sleep on this. My team will follow up with you to schedule a time to answer any questions you need answered. If, however, after sleeping on it you don't have any questions, during that meeting we can start the paperwork."* After this meeting, I work with the team to create an account/asset tracking spreadsheet so they can have the paperwork ready for the next meeting.

First Onboarding Meeting/Q&A/Paperwork: *"Somewhat like buying a house, today we have a stack of paperwork to tackle. This isn't anyone's favorite part, but once we get it done, your life will be much easier. Please be warned, sometimes companies forget whose money this is, so our team will follow up with them and you every week until we've tracked down every penny."* After this meeting, the team follows up weekly with the client to advise them on status.

Second Onboarding Meeting/Statements/IPS (typically three to four weeks later): *"Most/all of your accounts have now been consolidated into one place for easy access and professional management. Let's take a minute to understand the statements/ log in together ... Per our executive summary, we are now going to invest the assets according to your goals (a.k.a., the models)."* In this meeting, we sign the IPS/Risk Tolerance forms. We would also follow up on other items from the one-page plan.

Normal Surge Meeting Cycle (twice annually): At this point, new clients fall into the same surge-meeting rotation as all existing clients. For the first year or two, we will revisit the one-page plan to make sure progress is being made on all tasks. We may also meet during a mini-surge to tackle any major projects, such as new estate documents.

---

4 I'm not kidding—we are *that* committed to not wasting anyone's time, whether on our end or the prospect's end, if we're not the right fit. We have a whole section on who we work with at https://www.jarvisfinancial.com/who-we-serve, and we're not afraid to use it as a screening tool.

Action Steps

To build a sustainable business, you know you have to be constantly prospecting—but this is where so many advisors fail to measure up and fail to provide the right prospect experience that translates interested parties into top clients (and spend *way* too much money in the process).

Not you—not anymore. From now on, your prospect process is based all around your potential client's needs at every stage of the way and is perfectly positioned to usher the best clients in your door. Follow these key steps to keep your prospect pipeline moving smoothly and new clients lined up waiting to sign.

○ Look at every detail of your client's experience in your office. What needs to be improved on to project an image of a highly successful business? What can you change to make the client feel even more valued?

○ Scrutinize your current intake form. If it's more complicated than a handful of questions— and if you'll just have to re-answer those questions again anyway—then reexamine your paperwork and simplify what you're asking prospects to do.

○ Be prepared. Use the scripts throughout the chapter and the rest of the book to prepare yourself for good responses to common situations you'll find yourself facing. You and your staff will never be caught scrambling again!

○ Don't be afraid to say no to prospects if they aren't right for your business. Making exceptions to your system leaves you vulnerable to dropping the ball and leaving your client with a less-than-perfect experience; stick to the clients you're best equipped to handle and keep Delivering Massive Value in your practice.

Bonus content available for this chapter at ThePerfectRIA.com/BookBonus:

→ Initial phone call video screening a prospect

→ PDFs of the resources in this chapter

→ PDF of prospect process client handout

Plan Your Marketing Calendar

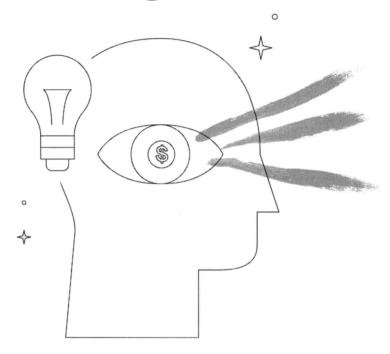

I know at least some of you are yelling at me by now, "Get to the marketing! I need more prospects to convert into clients, not some cute list of Zen practices!" I understand where you're coming from, and before I transformed my practice (read: started making money), I thought the same way. But trust me: all the marketing ideas in the world won't help you if your foundation isn't solid (see Part 1) and if your head isn't in the right place, starting with understanding what you're up against.

To say that you are a drop in the ocean of financial services is being generous. The big firms, from wire houses like Merrill Lynch to hybrid models like Edward Jones, from custodians like Fidelity to DIY platforms like Vanguard (to say nothing of the mega RIAs like Carson, Edelman, and Fisher), will *each* spend more money in your market *this month* than you will earn in your entire career. They have relatively unlimited resources; if you try to play their game, you *will* lose.

Instead of trying to beat them at their game, you need to compete at a game where not only can you win, but where the odds are dramatically in your favor. You need personal, personalized contact.

How Fast Do You Want to Grow? (Or: How Hard Are You Willing to Work?)

The beauty and curse of our industry is that your success is directly tied to the amount of effective time and energy you invest. At the same time, you also need to be realistic about how much time you can commit to marketing.

If you already have clients, you need time to deliver them massive value, and if you already have a team, you need time to work with them. And, of course, you also need time to read the latest on Kitces.com and listen to *The Perfect RIA Podcast*, so even the time you've allocated to "working" can't *all* be spent on marketing. So what to do?

Make the Time

Because it has worked so well for me and many advisors I've mentored, I strongly recommend you block out time on your calendar each week that is solely dedicated to marketing, *nothing* else. I know this isn't an original thought—the legend Nick Murray talks about this in length in his books, all of which I highly recommend— but it's a core strategy that you must follow if you want to harness the power a streamlined marketing calendar can bring to your business.

When I was in full growth mode (and not writing books), my weekly marketing calendar looked something like this:

SUNDAY: No Work
MONDAY MORNING: Study, read Kitces.com, listen to *The Perfect RIA* Podcast, CE credits, etc.
MONDAY AFTERNOON: Respond to clients, work with team
TUESDAY MORNING: Marketing Session #1 (3 hours)
TUESDAY AFTERNOON: Work ON my business (compliance, HR, tech, etc.)
WEDNESDAY MORNING: Respond to clients
WEDNESDAY AFTERNOON: Marketing Session #2 (3 hours)
THURSDAY ALL DAY: Client/prospect meetings
FRIDAY MORNING: Out-of-office marketing session (3 hours)
FRIDAY AFTERNOON: Personal R&R time
SATURDAY: No Work
1-3 EVENINGS A WEEK: Out-of-office marketing/events (2 hours each)

Using a schedule like this gave me roughly nine hours per week of dedicated marketing time. Your schedule may look totally different from mine, which is awesome. Just make sure it includes dedicated, uninterrupted prospecting time. Just to be clear, it only counts as prospecting time if that's the only thing you are doing. In other words, as soon as you start doing "research" on the internet, checking social media, reading the *Wall Street Journal,* or anything else that has no chance of you directly interacting with another human being, that time does not count.

OK, so you've got the time. Now, what to do with it?

"All the marketing ideas in the world won't help you if your foundation isn't solid and if your head isn't in the right place."

Pick the Marketing Channels You Know You Can Dominate

While there are dozens of potentially successful marketing channels (and in the following chapters, we are going to detail my four most successful marketing channels), I recommend choosing just two or three channels where you will direct essentially all of your time and energy. If I were advising my younger self or starting a new practice from scratch today, I would focus on these four main channels:

1. Networking (Chapter 12)
2. Client and Prospect Events (Chapter 14)
3. Media and Content Creation (Chapter 15)
4. COI Referrals (Chapter 16)

For each of these channels, here are the tasks I would track, focusing on what I can control and what has a high probability of me being able to invite someone to "have me take a look" at their finances:

Networking: In Chapter 12 I detail my networking strategy, but specific to this chapter, I want to focus on what you need to be counting if your networking is going to have any chance of yielding results. My ultimate KPI for this will be: number of people on my Dream 100 on whom I've attempted to leave a favorable impression (see page 143 for more on finding your Dream 100 clients). This might sound a little soft or vague, but I want to keep with what I can control. If you struggle with that KPI, then take one step back and go with: number of events I attend that my Dream 100 might also attend.

From a weekly perspective this looks like attending a minimum of one activity a week where I can cross paths with my Dream 100. This means that I need to be booked out four to six weeks in advance because if I wait till Monday morning to try to find an event this week, I will most likely fail. Because some events will cancel and others will be a bust, I want to average two scheduled events each week.

Client and Prospect Events: Spend one hour each week practicing and refining your presentation. Please note that spending time in PowerPoint does not count! Do what does count: video recording your presentation and comparing it to the best speakers you can find; fine-tuning your "close"; finding new ways to Deliver Massive Value to your audience. This is more about blocking out time than a KPI, so your KPI in this area is: number of people you personally invited to attend one of your events (target ten). On a monthly basis I would also add pitching a college to teach an adult education class.

Media and Content Creation: Spend an hour each week on media, as it is a great long-term lead source, establishes credibility, and forces you to improve your content creation. KPI: number of meaningful, value-add contacts (target five weekly). Spend one hour a week generating new content (blog, website, newsletter). Keep *The War of Art* by Steven Pressfield handy. KPI: number of paragraphs written (or minutes of podcast recorded), regardless of quality. This disclaimer is not an excuse to create bad content, but rather permission to just create.

COI Referrals: As detailed in Chapter 16, getting referrals from COIs (centers of influence) takes real work. My KPI for this strategy will be: number of COIs with whom I made meaningful personal contact (target five weekly). In a perfect world this would mean taking a COI to lunch/dinner each day, but even a personalized email or handwritten card counts if it Delivers Massive Value.

Once you have your punch list of activities, print it and keep it next to your computer for dedicated prospecting time. During this time, turn off all distractions. If that requires you to disable the internet or even work without a computer, so be it—only those activities you've established in advance count. Everything else is just playing office.

Because not everything happens the same way each week and some activities happen infrequently (e.g., client events) to this day I keep a yearlong calendar on my wall that looks something like this:

Sample Marketing Calendar

I've made several improvements since, and here is what my calendar
looks like today:

January	• Client Value-Add: 1099 Letter (RMD as applicable) • CPA/EA Networking Push • Media/Guest Blitz
February	• Client Newsletter • Surge Prep • Networking Push
March	• Client Event: Education • Pre-Surge Content Push • Spring Surge

April	• Client Value-Add: Your Choice • Create Annual Niche Content Calendar • Attorney Networking Push
May	• Client Newsletter • Media/Guest Blitz • Masterminds
June	• Networking Push • Website Updates • Refresh Office/Zoom Experience
July	• Client Value-Add: Guardrails • Finish Website Updates • Refine Niche
August	• Client Newsletter • Client Event: Appreciation • Media/Guest Blitz
September	• Networking Push • Select Next Year's Birthday Items • Surge Prep
October	• Client Value-Add: Taxes • Fall Surge • Client Event: Education
November	• Client Newsletter • CPA/EA Networking Push • Media/Guest Blitz
December	• Wrap Up Year-End Action Items • Map Out Next Year's Market Calendar • Personalize Christmas Cards

You've blocked out marketing time in your calendar. You know what you need to be doing during this time. But for some reason, at the end of the week, you keep missing your goals.

This creates two problems. First and most obvious, if you don't do these activities, your practice will never grow. Second, by not doing what you said you would do, not only have you failed to grow your practice, but you've also failed yourself. This failure of self is soul-crushing, and unlike a normal job where you would simply be fired for not doing your work, as an entrepreneur, you get to keep living in this failure until the bank forces you to stop.

Through much pain and suffering, I found a better way: extreme accountability.

Put simply, extreme accountability works like this: you do what you said you would do (e.g., make ten personal invites to your next event each week), or something extreme happens. This can be something positive or something negative. Let me offer you a couple of examples and then explain the rules:

- I once booked a nonrefundable trip to Hawaii with my wife that I could take only if I completed a major project I'd been putting off for months. Magically, it got done the day before we were scheduled to leave.
- My good friend Micah Shilanski had an operations task in his office that to him seemed impossible to delegate. He agreed to an extreme accountability that would require him giving up one third of his personal income. Magically, he got it done.
- Another advisor friend had a problem doing work at home when he should have been playing with his kids. He agreed that any time he brought his laptop home to do work, his kids would get to smash it to pieces as a science project. Magically, he hasn't brought home his laptop.
- I was once reluctant to do a fee increase, so I gave my friend Micah ten letters addressed to my ten biggest clients saying they should work with him instead of me, that Micah was to mail if I didn't increase my fee by the agreed date. Magically, I increased my fees.
- Other advisors have committed to sending a donation to their most loathed political candidate or charitable organization, along with a note: "This is the first of many donations. Please send me a bumper sticker for my car to show everyone my support."

If these seem extreme to you, good! The reasons we don't do the things we need to do is that the (imagined) pain of doing the task is more than the (imagined) pain of *not* doing it. To hack our brain, we need to reverse the balance by making the pain of not taking action so extreme that there's no way in hell you would let that happen.

To shift that balance in a way that works for us, practice these rules for extreme accountability:

Rule #1: You need an accountability partner.
This should be someone who respects you enough to hold you accountable. This cannot be someone with whom you have a romantic relationship (e.g., not your spouse) or someone with whom this level of accountability would damage the relationship. Ideally, it would be another advisor who is also having you hold them accountable.

Rule #2: It needs to scare you.
Recently, I knew I wanted to add another advisor to my team, but I was terrified to do it. As an extreme accountability, I agreed that if I didn't hire the new advisor by a certain date, I would have to take UberPool everywhere I went. There was no way in hell I was going to take UberPool, so magically I got the advisor hired. Another friend committed to driving a minivan around if she failed on her extreme accountability. When she committed to this, she said, "No way in hell I'm driving a minivan"—to which I responded, "Perfect, just get your work done!"

Rule #3: It can't hurt you or anyone else.
Sometimes advisors are tempted to pick things like "I won't golf" or "I'll skip the family vacation" or "I'll not buy any Christmas presents." While all these things are extreme, they would each cause harm to you or your family, so no deal. It has to be something that only hurts your pride or your wallet. (If you need ideas, visit ThePerfectRIA.com!)

Rule #4: It has to be 100 percent quantifiable and in your control.
Even if your goal is to bring in $$ of new AUM for the year, this is not entirely within your control, and therefore it is not a good candidate for extreme accountability. On the other hand, making ten calls a day is. With this in mind, a good goal could look like "I'll make one hundred calls to COIs by February, or I'll have to give my favorite mountain bike to charity and do all my future biking on a $20 thrift store bike.

"**Whatever strategy you embrace for your business, commit to it, and give it a chance to show results.**"

Remember: Every Marketing Strategy Will Fail If You Quit

In my mastermind groups, I know very successful advisors who have built amazing practices using every imaginable marketing strategy, from writing books, to ultra-narrow niches, to seminars, to websites and even cold-calling. If you are willing to work the strategy, it will work.

I know this is an obvious statement, but so often I meet advisors who have "tried" marketing strategies, but who gave up after the first few rejections and now blame the strategy for their failure.

Whatever strategy you embrace for your business, commit to it, and give it a chance to show results. Then, through carefully tracking the metrics you need to understand the effectiveness of your plan, you can make smart changes as necessary to hone your business.

Break it down to the very smallest action item that you can control. For example, while it's fun to say, "I want to get quoted in five publications a month," that result is largely out of your control, and choosing it as a goal sets you up for failure and rejection. Instead, choose a goal like "Make five meaningful contacts with content creators (bloggers, journalists, etc.) each week." If this is my task, then each time I get to a blocked-out marketing slot, I can focus on making these contacts.

If it were easy, everyone would do it and nobody would get paid. When explaining proven strategies like getting referrals from COIs, advisors will often complain how much work it takes. Good! That means they're sitting behind their desks, resigned to the idea that COI referrals will never work for them ... which only leaves more for you.

Don't get me wrong, it *is* a ton of work, but that's why the best practices make so much more money than everyone else.

Action Steps

When it comes to marketing, most advisors know they should do it. They just don't know how. If you're not winning the game, change your strategy, or change the game. With a marketing calendar, you'll be able to implement a system that will help you track your goals, plan your messages and materials, and get your name in front of your clients with the kind of regularity that will keep you top of mind. Follow these action steps to assemble the marketing calendar that will transform your business.

○ Make a list of all the marketing activities you know work for you. Go back through the list and write the frequency of each activity: quarterly, monthly, weekly, or daily. Now, plug those tasks into your calendar, and never worry about missing an opportunity to connect with your prospects or clients again.

○ Make a list of all the marketing activities with questionable ROI, and identify metrics for testing the effectiveness of each one. Keep returning to these metrics so you can continually refine your system.

○ Build a twelve-month marketing calendar that encompasses every marketing channel, every client holiday, every quarterly value-add, and anything else you plan to reach out to your clients about throughout the year.

Bonus content available for this chapter at ThePerfectRIA.com/BookBonus:
→ My most current twelve-month marketing plan
→ Extreme accountability worksheet
→ Worksheet for creating your marketing calendar

Getting Clients through Networking

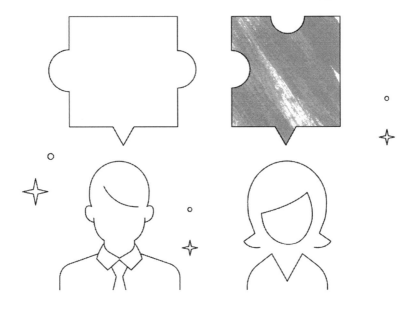

"Jarvis's book is a game-changer!

As an advisor and firm owner transitioning to this amazing profession mid-career, having a road map from someone who's already built what I want to build is of inestimable value. As Voltaire asked, 'Who is so wise to learn from the experience of others?' The answer is, anyone smart enough to read and implement Jarvis's playbook!"

Matthew Miner, CFP
Raleigh, NC
Miner Wealth Management

In 2003, when I started in the industry, I had no designations, no college degree, and only my insurance license to prove myself. I also had a crippling fear of rejection. This, coupled with zero sales skills, left me feeling unable to approach my friends or family for business: I had no confidence that anyone should work with me, because I didn't yet know how to Deliver Massive Value, and I *hated* putting people in an uncomfortable situation by asking for their business.

Desperate for clients, I decided the easiest way to find them was through networking. I did what anyone would do: I joined my local chamber of commerce. I spent the next ten years or so attending nearly every event, and guess how many clients these efforts landed me?

Zero.

I had the same results at the yacht club, the country club, and the Rotary club, and each time was even worse. Adding insult to the injury of getting zero clients, each meeting left me with a deepened sense of failure and rejection.

I spent nearly a *decade* on these networking failures, but I finally changed my strategy, and I now get roughly a third of my new clients each year from networking. But not from any of the traditional networking meat markets like the ones I've mentioned. Instead, I now network successfully through activities I love, every one of which has resulted in one or more ideal clients.

In this chapter, you will learn how to cultivate a lifestyle of connecting with people in a way that constantly generates new referrals—without ever having to ask. And you'll learn valuable networking skills, complete with plenty of scripts and examples, that you can use along the way to networking success.

Why Networking Almost Always Fails

Those pesky "self-proclaimed experts"—we've all read their networking advice.

It's all garbage.

They tell us to chase ridiculous and arbitrary metrics, like handing out five business cards a day. They tell us we have to be everywhere our clients might be. That we should offer second opinions to anyone who wants them. They throw banal statements at us as if they're supposed to be helpful:

"Broadcast your intentions." "Chase the money." "Just do it."

Seriously?

If you think about it, it's no wonder the idea of networking feels so slimy and fake. That's the way we've been taught to approach the whole topic. I didn't just spend ten years of my life chasing bad networking strategies for fun; I did it because that's what all my education, experience, and the "experts" taught me to do. I was told this was the magic formula.

Of course, as you know, it ended up being a formula for failure.

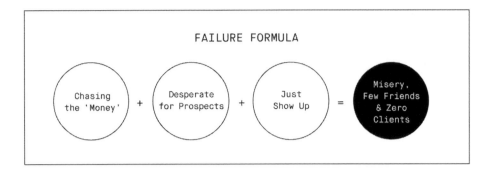

FAILURE FORMULA

Chasing the 'Money' + Desperate for Prospects + Just Show Up = Misery, Few Friends & Zero Clients

So what's really going on when we fail at traditional networking over and over? Why is this time-tested (and terrible) networking advice so broken?

Barking Up the Wrong Tree

Here's the thing: joining a yacht club to make connections and drum up new business is not a bad idea. It was just a bad idea for *me*.

When I joined the Tacoma Yacht Club, I figured, people with yachts have money, right? The problem is we only had a 21-foot boat, and the unofficial minimum was 40-foot-plus. Making matters worse, everyone else was retired, and we had three very young kids. Total nightmare! This strategy, while it sounded great on paper, yielded me exactly zero clients. It just wasn't a good match for me, so I was never able to form the trusted relationships I needed for successful networking.

When I joined the local golf club, I still hadn't learned my lesson. I was even less suited for this strategy, if possible: I hate golf. Guess how well that worked out?

On the surface, each of these strategies sounds like a good idea (and they can be). But even a basic examination shows they were obviously a bad idea for me, my personality, and my situation.

Taking the Wrong Approach

We each have different personality types, and we each have unique ways of interacting with the world around us.

Some people might find asking for referrals as natural as breathing, but for me, that's never felt like the right thing to do. I don't know if it's the fear of rejection, or just the fear of putting someone else in a situation they didn't sign up for, but I'm not comfortable with that kind of ask, in any situation. I'll never say, "Hey, John, do you know anybody I should talk to?"—I'm not going to have that discussion. It's not a bad discussion; it just doesn't work for me.

"I now network successfully through activities I love, every one of which has resulted in one or more ideal clients."

And that's really the key here. You've got to look at yourself and say,

> "What style of networking works best for me and my personality?"

Going against what we know to be best for us is never going to be a winning strategy, in life or in business.

Instead, leverage your real strengths by choosing the type of networking you'll actually enjoy—and therefore stick with—without having to maintain any arbitrary business card quotas, fake personalities, or false interest in golf.

Ten Steps to Networking Success

While my initial networking attempts were total failures, I've also had incredible success from networking. In fact, approximately one-third of my clients come from networking, now that I finally figured out how to do it.

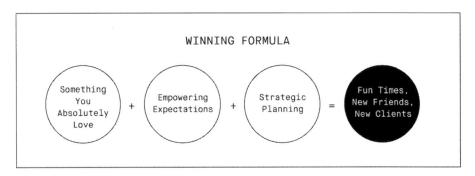

Let's learn how to implement a formula of success that you can use to steadily improve your referrals in a way that is authentic to who you are. This networking system is the strategy on which I built my very successful business, and I know it will work for you.

Step 1: Get Clear About What You Love

Before we look at networking strategies, it's important to spend time focusing on yourself and your own interests. You're going to be investing a significant amount of time in your networking strategies, and you don't want to box yourself into something that isn't right for you.

Make a list of activities you truly enjoy. (Hint: if you hate golf, *don't* write "golf.") Hobbies, causes, organizations, charities—write it all down. Once your practice is even more successful than mine, what will you do for fun?

One list of activities might look like this:

- Wake surfing
- Rock climbing
- Mountain biking
- Dirt biking
- Partying
- CrossFit
- Flying/traveling
- Volunteering at school
- Supporting favorite charities
- Writing for a newspaper

I'm sure you recognize some of these as my preferred leisure activities. In fact, this is my own list of networking events, and at some point or other, I have netted clients from every activity on that list.

Yes, I absolutely want to spend time dirt biking around with my friends and having a blast or traveling with my family and seeing the world. This *is* my leisure time. But do you know who else does those things? Other people—*people with money to manage.* People I'll naturally meet along the way, just by being out there in the world and engaging with the people around me. This, however, will not happen by accident and plenty of advisors surround themselves with ideal clients, but never get results. That's because while showing up may be half the battle, it's still only half.

Step 2: Find Your Dream 100

Like so many lessons I'm sharing in this book, success in networking comes from the very smallest of differences over other advisors. Once you've identified your favorite hobbies and/or charitable organizations and you've scheduled dedicated time for each of them, you are now going to employ the Dream 100 concept by sales legend Chet Holmes (rest in peace). In his book, *The Ultimate Sales Machine,* Chet outlines the idea that for most every business, all that is needed to achieve the highest level of success is to find 100 "dream clients." This is especially true in financial services. If you find one hundred "dream" clients who are each willing to pay you $10,000 a year in fees, combined with an efficient business, your take-home pay can be well north of $500,000. Not too shabby.

While the Dream 100 concept should be applied to all areas of your marketing, it is especially valuable in networking. Let me give you a really specific example. My wife and I have always been passionate about supporting our community. Early on in my career we spent our time and very limited money on dozens of noble organizations. Unfortunately we were spreading our efforts too thinly to be noticed and the few people who did notice, were not ideal clients. Using the Dream 100 concept, I realized that dozens of the people on my list were involved with our local hospital foundation (St. Francis Hospital of Federal Way). With this in mind, I began directing the vast majority of my charitable time and money toward this cause. Using the steps outlined below allowed me to be noticed by the people I wanted as clients. As a result, many of my Dream 100 related to the hospital foundation became clients and I was able to support a valuable cause in my community.

What If My Favorite Hobby Is Yoga?

Once when I was teaching a group of advisors about successfully networking, an advisor said, "But I love to do yoga and there's no way this strategy can work for me." I love a challenge so I jumped right in, explaining that I've gotten clients from rock climbing, dirt biking, wake surfing, and asking a random guy if I could go on a flight on his private plane. I told the yoga advisor the same thing I tell my kids: "Are you looking for problems or solutions?"

For yoga (or any hobby), I start by looking for overlap between the people who do yoga and the people I want as clients. Where do my ideal clients go for yoga? Which yoga studios and/or instructors are most popular with the kind of people I want as clients? Perfect. That's where I go. Not only that, but when do my ideal clients go to yoga? For example, on the evenings and weekends the rock climbing areas and gyms are full of stinky rock climbing bums. However, weekdays during normal business hours the bums are replaced by retired or semi-retired successful individuals.

In addition to enjoying my hobby while getting in front of ideal clients, these same people also make great friends and hobby partners, so no matter what, you win.

Step 3: Find Your People

Once you've listed a few hobbies and cross-referenced them with your Dream 100 list, it's time to find out where these people can be found. I like to use the following resources in my quest:

- Meetup
- Google search/alert
- Community calendars
- Forums
- Local clubs

Some potential clients are easier than others to track down, even when you're right in the middle of your activity. For example, plenty of people who cycle or rock climb are broke. (To be fair, plenty of people with boats are also broke.)

Be strategic about the times and locations best suited for engaging with the people you might want as clients. For example, back when I used to focus on cycling as a potential networking activity, I was more interested in the daytime rides, as the other cyclists were mostly retirees. I stood out, and I was surrounded by people I wanted as clients.

Another easy place to look is the higher-dollar activities in each hobby. Using our yoga example from earlier, once you've found the yoga studio with the highest odds of having your Dream 100, approach the studio owner about organizing a trip to a well-known yoga retreat. This will naturally draw out the most dedicated (and most financially well-off) people from this group.

Step 4: Have a Community-First Mindset

Mindset is the foundation of everything. When networking, make your primary mindset goal strengthening your community.

For example, when I was cycling, I didn't just go on group rides; I led them. I won't say this wasn't terrifying, because it was: I had anywhere from ten to fifty people counting on me to not make a single mistake. Because of this pressure, there were, understandably, very few volunteers for these positions.

But it was my way to support the community. I would be double prepared with extra maps, I'd have the entire route mapped out on Google Maps and programmed into my phone, and I would carefully set expectations. People were impressed with my preparedness, and the casual conversations I had with others occasionally turned into a client or referral.

The same is true of charities or any other group: people are drawn to those who get things done, who go above and beyond. Just be sure to stay out of politics, be careful about getting too high in the leadership (you have a practice to run, after all!), and avoid situations that could trigger resentment. Keep your eye on the prize, and stay focused.

> **"Mindset is the foundation of everything. When networking, make your primary mindset goal strengthening your community."**

Step 5: Develop an Energy Mindset

This might sound like an easy one, but you'd be surprised how difficult it can be for some people:

Be focused on having fun and building your energy.

This way, even if it takes months or years to develop clients from this hobby, you are still getting a benefit right away. This is especially true for charitable volunteering, but really in every group or hobby, we can all spot the salesperson in the group, and they get branded as such immediately.

Don't be that person! This is a long game. It is, first and foremost, about living the life you want to live; the networking part happens naturally.

Step 6: Be Curious

I know it's hard to resist the urge to spread the word about your fantastic company, but at first, the best strategy is keeping your mouth shut and listening.

Go into every event assuming that nobody wants to hear about you, and especially not about your work. Instead, focus on learning about them. What do *they* do? What do *they* love? How can you acknowledge *their* success?

Once you have some information, do your research. How can you carry on an intelligent discussion about a topic important to them?

Try some of these conversation starters to get warmed up:

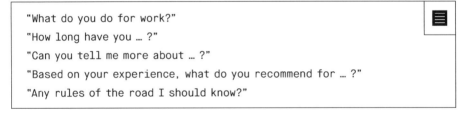

```
"What do you do for work?"
"How long have you … ?"
"Can you tell me more about … ?"
"Based on your experience, what do you recommend for … ?"
"Any rules of the road I should know?"
```

The number-one rule to this approach is this: *be humble.* No one wants to talk to a know-it-all or end up being lectured about their own experiences.

Step 7: Drop Subtle Hints

How do we let people know we're looking for clients when we never actually ask them to become clients or refer us to potential clients?

It takes a bit of practice, but here's the trick: be very subtle when talking about what you do. Always downplay; you're shooting for an air of mystery that invites further questions, not a full-on presentation.

In the example of organizing group rides, when setting expectations about the ride, I'd say things like "I'm better with money than directions."

Here are a few versions of phrases you can use with your own marketing strategy

> "I'm a money guy, not a … "
> "Guess I'll stick to my day job of … "
> "Lots of my clients … "
> "I spend a little too much time at my desk, so forgive me on … "
> "I've helped lots of clients … "
> "I'm sure you know about … "

Remember: keep it subtle, and you'll always have them wanting more.

Step 8: Get Permission First

We've all been victims of the guy trying to give everyone a second opinion. This is an immediate turnoff, and it burns important bridges. I used to sit on the yacht club board, and the members who were judged to only be there to sell their product/services were a regular topic of discussion.

Instead, make sure people are always aware that the ball is in their court.

> "Let me know if you ever want help with … "
> "How can I be most helpful with … "
> "I do a lot of that at work, please let me know if I can help with … "
> "If you ever want, let's grab a cup of coffee and talk about … "

Give them an opening, then back off gracefully—zero pressure, zero sales.

Step 9: LinkedIn

With no exception, you need to track down on LinkedIn anyone and everyone you meet. I use this strategy extensively inside the industry. It's a bit of a back door for business contacts who don't want to escalate to emails right away.

If you meet someone and start emailing them, it might feel pushy or even inappropriate. (Remember, everyone spends too much time managing their emails.) If instead you message them on LinkedIn, it feels less like an intrusion, and it's a subtle way of getting permission. And by being aware of their updates and accomplishments, you'll regularly find valuable opening points for starting a discussion.

Step 10: Be Aware (Not Scared!) of Competition

As you scout out various groups, you will quickly discover if there is any competition wading in their waters. If you do encounter other professionals in your field, you have a couple of options.

First, become friends! If they have an abundance mindset, they'll understand there's plenty out there for everyone, and every conversation with someone else in your field is an opportunity to learn another perspective. Or you might choose to keep a professional distance, remembering your own abundance mindset, or find another group.

However you approach spotting your competition in the field, you have one job: outwork them like crazy! When I started volunteering at the hospital foundation, I won tons of referrals, simply by outworking everyone else. Hard work really works.

How to Measure Networking Success

How will you know when your networking program is a success? When you do it over and over again.

Too many of us define success in a way that we have no control over. We have this number in our mind of how many referrals is "successful," or if we don't have a number in mind, we second-guess even our most referral-heavy months. We'll think, "Oh, man, we haven't gotten referrals in a long time," and then we'll look and say, "Oh—the last $10 million we brought in was from referrals!"

We need to define success and referrals as a repeatable process, a standard operating procedure that we follow. When you have a good networking system in place, you can look back and say, "Hey, I'm consistently following that system. And if I do it long enough, it's going to work." That's where you should pin your success; don't pin it on things outside of your control. *That* would be a formula for failure.

Action Steps

Just like "playing office" isn't the same as doing client surge meetings, simply spending time on the golf course does not count as networking. On the other hand, like client surge meetings, being intentional about networking can transform your business. Remember that everybody can spot a salesperson from a mile away. True networking success comes from contributing to the community and *not* giving your elevator pitch.

○ Identify your Dream 100 prospects and find places where their interests and yours intersect

○ Go to every networking opportunity (but never "networking events") with a quantifiable plan for success. This could be as simple as "introduce myself to five people."

Bonus content available for this chapter at ThePerfectRIA.com/BookBonus:
→ Worksheet for getting clients from any hobby/passion
→ Real-world examples of successful network marketing

Choose Your Niche: Picking a Battle You Can Win

"The most significant lesson I learned from Jarvis is to be hyper-focused on being the best advisor possible for a particular clientele and then be dedicated to only working with that clientele. Become the expert on their pain points and offer superlative service."

Cathy Curtis, CFP
San Francisco, CA
Curtis Financial Planning

As with all the best parts of my practice, it took me many years of painful mistakes to realize that I will never be able to beat the major financial firms on their terms. No matter how much time, energy, and money I spend on websites, brochures, advertisements, email campaigns, or any other form of marketing, it will only be a drop in the ocean compared to the resources being allocated by just *one* of the big firms. Put another way, the big firms will spend more money marketing to my area in a month than I'll earn in my entire career.

Let's do some quick math from Chapter 6 (the Post-it note business plan). To have the practice of your dreams—and earn the ~$750,000-plus annually to put you in the top 1 percent of Americans—you need 150 clients at most, each paying you an average of $10,000 a year ($1,500,000 of gross revenue). In other words, while big firms need to bring on hundreds of clients every month and take anyone who has a buck, you only need 150 top clients in your entire career.

In this chapter, I'm going to show you why narrowing your prospecting to the people you're truly best equipped to advise can help you not just position yourself as the best in your space but actually *be the best* in that space. And we'll learn how to stack the deck in your favor so you're always playing a game you can win.

Be a Specialist

Trying to be all things to all people—a generalist—is a near guaranteed path to mediocrity. So what's the alternative? What is a game you and I can win against the big firms, while also being able to Deliver Massive Value to a select group of clients?

Like essentially every other profession, the financial advisors with the most successful, profitable, and rewarding practices are those who are laser-focused specialists. Now, if you are as jaded and cynical as me, you might be thinking, "Gee, Jarvis, your 'specialty' is retirees, which narrows it down to just 60,000,000 people or so. That's hardly a specialty!"

At first glance, I'd acknowledge you are correct, but retirees are only the first layer of my specialty. While my website talks about a rather generic specialty of "retirees" (though even that is dramatically more specialized than most advisors, who, like the big firms, will work with anyone with a buck), all of my efforts are focused on people retiring within thirty-six months, with investment assets between $500,000 and $3 million and who live within a thirty-minute drive of my office. This narrows my niche of retirees from the 60,000,000 or so baby boomers to fewer than 3,000 people.

Why Niche?

The old saying is true: sometimes it *is* better to be a big fish in a small pond. Especially when the alternative is being lost in the ocean with all the sharks.

But choosing a narrow field of interest and doubling down on that through who you accept as clients has benefits far beyond the numbers. Sure, anyone can rise to the top if the circle you draw around your competition is small enough—but the process of defining and dominating your unique niche has its own unexpected returns.

> # "The financial advisors with the most successful, profitable, and rewarding practices are those who are laser-focused specialists."

You Can Be the Best

It's easy to think, "Wait a minute. I know I'm *good*, but how can I possibly be the *best*?" I used to think that way too. Now, after I chose a niche, my attitude about my market, my clients, and my ability to dominate my market space has changed.

It's not a sales pitch when I tell you I have zero doubt that no one in my area can serve my clients better than me. Is this arrogance? Maybe. If so, it's a healthy level of arrogance. How can I expect clients to trust me with their life savings if I don't trust myself?

It's also *true*—and I make sure it's true because of who I include in "my clients." For the narrow slice of people I serve, I truly *am* the best, and it's not because of any complicated gerrymandering of my client list.

It's because of everything you've learned in this book so far: my ability to Deliver Massive Value by streamlining all of my business operations, aligning our marketing calendar and every other activity with the tax calendar, building a powerful team I can trust with my business's day-to-day processes, empowering them to act on their own by giving them systems to follow, having a well-designed client experience, and always anticipating their questions and needs.

For all the other people I *don't* serve, who *don't* fit into that winning system, I'm not trying to be the best. There's no point: someone else is always going to win, and that's the way it should be.

Higher Earning Potential

Just like in medicine, where a family doctor earns a fraction of a specialist, the same is true in financial services. Since this is so commonly misunderstood, I really want to drive this point home.

I know you're going to punch me in the face if you hear me say the word *system* one more time, but it truly is the key to being able to deliver top-notch service. Every principle behind what we do during surge week—putting the office in a singular mindset to get the job done, structuring all of our client contact around our quarterly messaging, doing whatever we need to do to put our best faces forward—all of that reasoning applies to why choosing a niche you can excel in is a winning strategy and your very best bet for transforming your business.

For my practice, this is retirees, or those within thirty-six months of retirement. This is a narrow group where I can really specialize, and with only 150 clients, I can offer white-glove service. By carefully designing my client experience and truly excelling at what I do, I can be the best. I'm continually narrowing my niche by virtue of raising my minimums.

And, of course, by offering the highest level of service, you don't need a massive client list to stick to the numbers on that Post-it note business plan staring you in the face. By charging a premium, you only need one or two hundred clients to have a rockstar practice, which means your niche can be just about as narrow as you need it to be to really own it.

Stop Being Everything to Everybody

It's not just that trying to be all things to all people is playing a game you can't win. Wherever you set your benchmarks, even *attempting* to cover all the bases on your own is an uphill battle. We all know the arguments against multitasking and in favor of setting aside time for deep work: when we're pulling in all different directions at once, we're working against ourselves. And we start getting nervous as soon as we spot competition on the horizon.

Choosing a single direction to focus on and pursuing it with all of your intention and efforts makes everything you do so much more effective, and the transformation you're trying to achieve with your business will happen even faster. And you won't be afraid of competition anymore; on the contrary, you'll welcome it, because you have so much experience in your space that you've had a chance to truly excel at it, in a way the jacks- and jills-of-all-trades never could ... and since chances are you're not after the same clients anyway, anyone else you meet has the potential to become a valuable source of referrals.

"How can I expect clients to trust me with their life savings if I don't trust myself?"

THEN	NOW
No confidence	100% confident
"Smell" of fear/doubt	Project confidence
Endless objections	Minimal objections
Dismal close rate	90%+ close rate
Fear competition	LOVE competition
"We help everyone"	"We ONLY help..."
"I need you to be a client"	"You need me"
"I can figure that out"	"I don't do that, but..."

Be the Right Tool for the Job

If you needed surgery on your knee, you'd want a doctor who specializes in orthopedics, not one who does knees one day and backs the next. And you sure wouldn't expect your family doctor to be the one performing the surgery.

When I work directly with advisors on their messaging, one of the power tools I have them use with the prospects they're trying to win over is this:

> "Does the advisor you're using/considering specialize in [your type of client], or do they also work with [your type of client]?"

This reminds them why specialists exist in the first place, and it helps frame their decision in terms of what's truly best for their account in the long run, not just the immediate costs—and sets the advisor up as the smart, obvious solution.

Nearly every advisor's website includes a laundry list of "specialties," revealing that they're really just casting into the sea and hoping they net something they can land. Helping your clients understand what they need lets them come to their own realization that you're not just *a* solution, you're *the* solution. The choice is obvious; no hard sell necessary.

How to Choose a Niche

From this day forward, every aspect of your business—every marketing communication, every client outreach, every event—will be laser-focused on the niche you're choosing. It is, obviously, therefore important to make a good decision about where to aim that focus.

To make the best strategic decision that will set you up for the future you want, ask yourself these four questions. Write down a few options for each one. Don't skip this step, and don't be shy. This is just brainstorming—no wrong answers.

Where are you the absolute best?

Now's not the time to be humble. What areas of financial investment do you truly excel in? What are you good at?

I knew I was good at speaking to people about their retirement—and more importantly, I knew that with my one-page business plan, I had reinvented the possibilities for how we could speak with clients about their finances. It didn't take much of a stretch to identify the demographic of people whom I could best reach with this targeted, actionable information.

Where do you want to be the absolute best?

Thanks to surge week and other systems to keep you productive and efficient, you've blocked out time in your calendar for professional development and other high-level tasks. Don't let a lack of knowledge or experience in one area keep you from exploring that or a related area for your new focus. Are there certifications you can acquire, people you can talk to you, courses you can take?

Whatever it is, focus on the things you need to do to get there. Enhancing your public perception is your responsibility, and it's within your grasp. Make a plan, follow through, and reap the benefits of your hard work.

With whom do you most enjoy working?

One of the best things about being an independent advisor (other than the vacations) is truly being able to help the people you're most passionate about. This is a business, but it's not *all* about the numbers. Yes, you know you need to work hard to play hard. Think about surge week—you'll be working really hard, and on your fifth day of five of the exact same meetings a day, if you're not working with people you actually like, you're seriously going to regret it.

You know by now that I work with retirees. I have family and loved ones, and I want to see them all retire with dignity and financial viability. I don't want anyone, or their parents or grandparents, being left out in the cold because they didn't trust the right person to manage their money. I'm passionate about that, and it shows in the way I engage with my clients, even if I don't do it often.

Who best fits your business model?

Remember that Post-it note business plan. Those numbers are important to get clear on where your business needs to be, but they're just as important as you grow and acquire new clients, because they will help keep you moving toward that ultimate goal.

I'm passionate about helping retirees; that doesn't mean I can help *all* retirees. I choose to deliver the highest-quality white-glove service my office and I possibly can, which means keeping my client list low and charging a premium.

Your business model will demand its own set of onboarding parameters. Don't ignore them. They're there to keep you focused and on track.

Find the Sweet Spot

Now, look at the list you've made and see if any threads or patterns emerge. (Remember, you're running a business, not a charity: it's important to follow your passions in life, but you *have* to keep an eye on the bottom line. That guy with a soft spot for working with people who are down on their luck? He hasn't found the sweet spot yet.)

One advisor I worked with lives near a Google campus, and about half of his clients work for Google. His niche was obvious: everything that advisor looked at—everything that comes across his desk—has to be through the lens of how it will work for Google employees.

Once this advisor really understood the type of clients he was best situated to serve, he was able to tailor his entire practice toward that specific experience, which only better situated him to meet that narrow demographic's needs. By asking himself, "What are their personalities? What are their likes and dislikes? Are they going to be more responsive to email or physical mail?" he was able to position himself as the best in his space *and truly become* the best in his space.

Client Experience: The Key to Niche Domination

Once you've made your way to the top of your market space, the instinct is to lie back and enjoy your new batch of clients—but this is no time to be complacent. You have to work to maintain your seat at the top.

I highly recommend *The Ultimate Sales Machine* by Chet Holmes. He talks about the Dream 100 concept: if you had just a hundred people as clients, that would be all the clients you needed. So, instead of focusing on 1,000, or 10,000, or 10 million, or 300 million, focus on that 100. Remember, in this room, none of us can compete with the big advisory firms on spend.

Of the group you've identified, constantly ask yourself,

> "How can I serve this group better than anyone else in my market?"

Keeping that net small lets us really understand the needs of that particular subset of clients. As soon as you start trying to please people outside of that narrowly defined group, you're not going to be delivering as much value as possible to that core group of clients. Now you're just noise.

Action Steps

When you're in growth mode, it can be tempting to accept anyone as your client who has a checkbook and money to manage, but you know better—you know how important it is to specialize in the areas you're best at. After all, you can make the same amount of money (or more!) with just 150 high-earning clients. If you've ever found yourself wishing you had better clients (and don't we all?), drop everything and complete these brief action steps. Then take the time to sit with your results. They may just transform your business.

○ Don't be a generalist—specialize! Write down all the areas of your field in which you excel, the types of work and experience you'd like to have, and the clients you most want to help and will most benefit from your services.

○ Keep narrowing your circle until you've found the clients who best fit your business plan and personal goals. *Those* are your ideal clients, and those are the ones you should be laser-focused on. Everything else is just noise.

○ Never lose sight of the client experience as your most powerful tool to Deliver Massive Value to new prospects and continue doing so for your most valued clients.

Bonus content available for this chapter at ThePerfectRIA.com/BookBonus:
→ Interview with top advisors on their niches
→ Discover your niche worksheet
→ List of obscure yet proven niches

Prospecting Events

I once held a client and prospect event where we mailed out 10,000 postcards and budgeted for thirty meals at a fancy restaurant, and a *single person* showed up. The restaurant made me pay for all the meals, and for the next two weeks, every Styrofoam container my wife and I pulled out of the fridge for dinner was another punch to my gut.

Making matters worse, I was paying thousands of dollars to buy the best seminar presentations and thousands more to advertise for these events (all from "experts" who claimed guaranteed results, despite never having used the presentations themselves). Not only did I have a giant credit card bill for the fridge full of leftovers, but I owed thousands more for the invitations and presentations that yielded no results.[1]

I finally realized this wasn't a game I could win. I had to find a new game to play.

(I wish I could say this was because I finally learned, but if I'm honest, it was mostly because I had run out of money for seminars.)

This chapter will give you real, tested-in-the-trenches strategies for increasing your attendance and upgrading the quality of your client and prospect events. Even if seminars or other events are not part of your marketing plan, the lessons here are universal and can be applied to any marketing channel you engage with.

EXCEPTIONS DON'T MAKE THE RULE

Sure, there are exceptions. It's not that bulk-mail cold invitations will *never* work; it's just that it's going to take a *lot* to get to the attendance you want, and your success is going to depend a great deal on your unique situation. An advisor I know in an affluent metropolitan area gets all his new business from public seminars, and he mails out *one hundred thousand* invitations per month to get about twenty people to each event. If you have that kind of budget and the right demographics, maybe it will work for you, but if you're like me, this isn't an option.

Even if I wanted to play that game, I live in the Seattle area, where people won't drive ten miles to get to the nearest town, which means there aren't even that many people to whom I can send those useless invites. What works for one advisor doesn't always work for another. That's why you can't simply look for a magic marketing bullet to keep your prospecting pipeline fed with promising leads. You need a winning strategy—one that works every time.

---

1 Correction: They yielded results, but instead of the promised hordes of new clients, all I got was soul-crushing defeat. And the credit card bills.

Why Client and Prospect Events Rock

At some point on this long journey of failure, I decided I would never again buy dinner for random strangers in some misguided hope that they would feel obligated to meet with me. I also realized that most of the people who were successful in the free-dinner sales game were selling high-pressure timeshares. Ever since this realization, I've only ever bought dinner for clients, their friends, and qualified prospects, including COIs.

I love client events, which is why they're a consistent part of my marketing strategy. We try to do two to three per year—it's easy to fill the seats, and the potential returns on our investment reach far beyond their direct effects. Most importantly, I can never fail buying dinner for clients. After all, these clients are paying thousands of dollars a year and if all they do is come to dinner alone, thinking what a great guy I am for buying dinner: awesome! However what tends to happen is that clients bring their friends, who quickly become clients.

If you're new to client and prospect events and ready to get your feet wet, the simplest way to get started—and the one with the highest success rate—is by holding client education events. I know it can sound intimidating, so before I get into the nuts and bolts of putting your own client and prospect events together, let's counter any head trash you might be carrying around with a good look at the potential benefits.

Opportunity to Engage with Clients

Client education events are a great opportunity to get yourself in the same room with your clients, have a good time, bring them value, and make them better clients and better stewards of their own wealth.

Even if there's no prospects to convert because you're speaking only to your existing clients, the event is a success as long as you have clients in seats, because you're educating them; you're delivering value. And by sending a list of takeaways to all of your clients, you'll have the opportunity to connect with people even if prospects are nowhere near your seats.

Identity Theft Avoidance and Recovery: Still a Victim?

THE **PERFECT** RIA

File a Police Report
Non-emergency number

File an FTC Complaint
FTC.gov or 877-438-4338

Request a fraud alert good for 90 days
7-year fraud alert with police report
Equifax 1-800-525-6285
Experian 1-888-397-3742
TransUnion 1-800-680-7289

Expands Your Network

Hosting valuable client education events does more than just educate the people who show up. By specifically inviting your clients to bring a friend, you're expanding your list to include people who are so ready to listen to your message that they'll accompany their friend to a *financial investment* event. We call this the "warm list": a crowd full of friendly, eager faces, willing to engage and enjoy themselves and open to the message you're there to deliver (and, hopefully, to ultimately accepting your offer).

It also gives your clients another great reason to recommend you to their friends—and those referrals don't always come from the clients you might expect.

I've had referrals say to me, "I'm here because my buddy said you do these great client education events," but their buddy has never even *been* to one. Even so, he must have been reading his invitations, and even though he hasn't witnessed them firsthand, he understood the value of what those events might offer his friends. These events are also a great opportunity for reaching out to COIs who might be interested in joining.

Streamlines Your Message

Whatever value-adds you put on your marketing calendar in Chapter 11, whatever the topic, this is another opportunity to deepen that value. Choosing a theme for your event that supports or complements that value-add, whether it's about guardrails or retirement or identity theft, increases the chances that your clients will spread the word about your valuable events.

It also keeps your office focused entirely on one area. Instead of focusing on long-term care and strategic investments while adding a little bit of reallocation focus for whoever wants to talk about it, your team can steamroll your entire calendar, solving for that singular issue with ultimate effectiveness.

What Are Your Goals?

The first thing to establish when doing any kind of client and prospect event is to get really clear about your goals *and* your system for achieving them. For example, if your goal for an event is to have half the people sign up to be clients, then you need a system of incredibly hard sales, like those found in timeshare presentations.

I'm not a fan of this approach, nor do I have the emotional strength for that level of rejection, so this goal/system won't work for me. So what's a more realistic expectation or goal for client and prospect events?

After years of defeat, I decided that my primary goal for events would be to Deliver Massive Value, primarily to people who were already paying me: clients. While this goal will not directly lead to new business, it does let me approach each event with a high expectation of success. Pre-COVID-19, our office would hold two to three client education dinners a year, each with forty to fifty people in attendance, a few of whom would be prospects. Even if no prospects attended, I still had a successful evening sharing dinner with clients while Delivering Massive Value on a topic important to them.

Size Doesn't Matter (But Expectations Do)

For whatever reason, I used to think my events had to fill the room. (Thank goodness that the only restaurant in town that could host our events had a limit of thirty, or I might not have survived to write this book.) While today I can easily fill rooms of fifty people, earlier in my career, I would work to fill a room with four to ten.

Whatever size room you can fill, the key is to manage expectations. If your client/prospect arrives expecting a room of one hundred people and only ten arrive, you lose. The same is true if you hold your meeting in a room for one hundred, with only ten attendees. Whatever size group you can get, make sure attendees know what to expect and the room matches the group size. Managing these expectations looks something like:

"Mrs. Client, I'm getting together a group of [XX] friends and clients to enjoy dinner and talk just for a minute about [TOPIC]. As you know, there is never anything sold at these events, just an opportunity for professional friends to enjoy an evening of learning."

If dinner isn't your thing (or if there isn't a good option for this in your town), I've seen this strategy work successfully with wine tastings, golf pros, private chefs, paint classes, local artists, museums, cigars, cocktail hour, minor league sports, exotic car dealerships, racetracks, and really anything else you can imagine. The key is to create an event where it's incredibly easy to say yes, without the risk that they'll be sold to death.

Filling the Seats

Make sure to throw a client and prospect event that *you* want to attend, so even if nobody shows up, you can still have a good time. If at all possible, you want an event that your existing clients would want to attend (automatic win), your COIs might want to attend (another win), and ideally even your Dream 100 people. By having multiple levels of possible wins, you set yourself up for success no matter what.

Any time I'm doing a client and prospect event, I'll start by inviting all my clients. These people already pay me and equally importantly, their presence as clients creates an implied endorsement. It also gives you a chance to have them bring friends (see Chapter 17 on referrals). Each of my clients will get an invitation, along with a handwritten note. (Yes, this takes more effort, but it has much better results.)

"Nancy, I'd love to have you join us for this event. Please let me know if I can save a seat for you. Of course, we always have an extra seat for any of your friends."

The next round of invites goes to COIs. From there, target any friends who might be a good fit. Then, include your prospects, followed by every person on your Dream 100 list. And if you are still unable to fill the event after personally contacting all of these groups, try a different style of event, but don't give up until you've done at least four.

Types of Prospecting Events

Every event you do, whether it's overtly a prospecting event or not, is an opportunity for you to get in front of people and demonstrate your grasp of the topic at hand. Luckily for all of us, but especially me, seminars aren't the only way to share your expertise and experience with a crowd.

While your options are practically limitless, let's take a look at three types of client and prospect events you can throw to increase your stream of prospects.

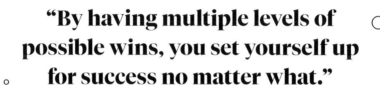

"By having multiple levels of possible wins, you set yourself up for success no matter what."

Educational Events for Professionals

The rules on these types of events vary dramatically from profession to profession and from state to state, so it's up to *you* to figure out the legalities in your area. Here's a quick shortcut: ask your COIs where they go for continuing education, specifically their favorite places for CE. If at all possible, seek to become (or hire) their favorite sources.

The key with these client and prospect events is to *not* act like an investment wholesaler who paid for the opportunity to harass COIs. Instead, focus exclusively on Delivering Massive Value so that whenever they think about a financial planner, you're the one who comes to mind.

As we discuss in Chapter 16, asking COIs for referrals, whether directly or indirectly, will fail! Simply host the event and, when asked, explain, "My clients keep asking for referrals in your line of work, and these events help me find the best ones in town. Plus, I learn a lot, which is an added bonus for me."

Client Appreciation Events

To be honest, I've never had much luck with client appreciation events. In addition to being expensive to host, for whatever reason, it's always a struggle to get clients to attend. And in the rare case they bring a friend—the real goal, after all—there seems to be a disconnect between why I would host the event and why their friend would want to hire our firm.

That said, I know plenty of firms who successfully host these types of events, so I won't tell you it can't work for you. If this feels like the right way to focus your energy and time, just make sure to have clear goals in mind and metrics you can measure so you can make smart decisions and pivot when necessary.

Teaching Paid College Classes

One way to reach prospective clients while impacting your community is by teaching a course through your local school's continuing ed program. Nearly every college and university offer these classes in the form of art, cooking, yoga, foreign language, and other such courses: taught at the campus, but open for anyone (and not for college credit).

This isn't for everyone. But if you are good at public speaking, teaching for college could be a great source of new clients for you, and even small student groups of five to ten students can bring in a steady stream of new clients.

Rather than teaching credit classes for typical college students—a difficult path, not to mention college students have no money—you want to teach non-credit classes, sometimes known as adult education classes. In my experience, the best format for these classes is a single class, either 90 or 120 minutes, taught on a variety of days and times during the semester. For example, you might schedule a Monday and Thursday night and a Saturday morning.

Typically these kinds of classes have a relatively nominal fee of $40. But your real goal is to absolutely drown them in information during the class, so that at the end, they realize there is so much you know that they don't. At the end of the class (which they paid to attend, so no selling), announce:

> "Wow, that time went fast! I'm worried I didn't have time to answer everyone's questions. I can schedule you a thirty-minute call to answer your questions. During that call, if you'd like, I can explain how to make an educated and informed decision about hiring a financial advisor."

Community colleges tend to be a little bit more approachable than universities, but if you've got a good angle, you could land a class anywhere. If you want to teach at your local college, here are a couple of hints.

1. Research what they're already doing. Look through their class list and find out what classes similar to yours they're already offering.

2. Don't be daunted. Remember, the person whose job it is to organize all the courses is just doing their job; if they see a financial planner already teaching a course, they may not see the need for your class.

3. Attend at least one class. This doesn't have to be the other financial planner's class; I've gone to painting classes before. It's simply an opportunity to see how a class goes and talk shop with the instructor about how they got started there and how it all works.

4. Ask what the college is trying to solve for. Colleges want to fill their space, they want the class to pay for itself, and they don't want a headache.

5. Spin as needed. Get specific about the value you can add to the college and your community, and explain how your class can help add that value.

Try these phrases:

- "I've taught a lot of classes, and I know you already have a class on ABC, but I believe you could benefit from a class on XYZ because…"

- "I'm doing this as a community service, so whatever you might pay an instructor for this course, just donate that back to the college."

- "I plan to invite my network to this course to help fill the seats."

- "Let's do a trial run. I'll teach one class, and if no one shows up, or if you don't think I can bring value to your students and your school, we can part ways as friends."

Six Steps to Event Success

There's no secretly brilliant newspaper ad or mailing list or marketing idea that you can use as a magic bullet to achieve certain marketing success. It's on you to make your own client and prospect events a giant success—or a giant failure.

No matter what kind of event you're holding, and whatever your unique strategy, there are six steps to making it successful. Whatever type of event you're working on, whether you're just putting it together or you've hosted it twenty times before, if you find you're missing any of these steps, there's room to improve!

And what if you don't follow these steps? The ROI you expected won't coalesce, and you'll be left with that dismal sense of rejection (not to mention a fridge full of fancy dinners). These rejections add up, making every following event harder and harder to muster the energy for. This isn't a trap you can afford to be sucked into.

Step 1: Determine the Goal

As with any effective business decision, it's important to get clear about how you measure success going in. With every event, ask yourself: what are we trying to accomplish?

Your approach to a client appreciation event where you hope they bring friends who become new prospects will be different from an event where you just want to have a good time with your clients. You may be serving the same menu, but there's a different underlying formula for the event, and the only way to achieve your goals is to be clear on what those goals are.

Whatever your main goal for the outcome of the client and prospect event, it must also do the following:

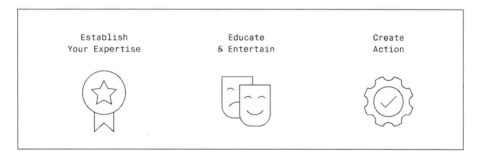

Establish Your Expertise

Educate & Entertain

Create Action

Establish and confirm your expertise. Any opportunity to get in front of a crowd is a good one; any client and prospect event you host should include time for you to have this connection with attendees. Remind them of how good you are at what you do. Without this step, no amount of marketing will help you expand your client base and telling people about your services will fall on deaf ears.

Educate and entertain. You're not hosting an event—you're creating an experience. Just like any other part of your prospecting process other than the very end of it, a prospecting event isn't focused on the sell; it's focused on helping your prospect make an educated and informed decision about your business. And, of course, they can use that knowledge to vet any other business (a comparison you welcome, since you dominate your market space).

Create action. This is where all your pre-event strategic planning either falls short or succeeds wildly. Many a presentation has gone nowhere because the call to action—the thing you hope your audience will do next—either is missing or fails to connect with the steps that happened previously.

If you have a clear direction for your presentation that sets you up as an expert in the problem they're trying to solve, has tangible value for its participants, and offers a clear follow-up action to help them get even more specific about solving their problems, that action becomes such an obvious next step that they can't help but take it.

Step 2: Deliver Like a Rockstar

Whatever type of client and prospect event you choose, there's one main characteristic to all public speaking events: eventually, you're going to have to speak in public.

Some of us were blessed with charisma and ease in front of a crowd, but that's definitely not true for all of us. Here are a few ideas for developing or enhancing your public speaking skills.

Practice, practice, practice! Bands rehearse, candidates rehearse, actors rehearse—anyone whose performance is going to be seen and judged by others should respect their audience enough to give them the best performance possible. That includes any speaker for any presentation, and it is crucial for any part of your prospect process.

Find professional training. Many local and national professional organizations exist to help untrained speakers learn to be comfortable and entertaining on a stage, and plenty of CEOs and high-level organizational leaders use these organizations to help them succeed in public. Look online and in your area to find an opportunity near you; you'll be in good company.

Take a comedy class. Because comedy is the highest and most difficult form of public speaking, with the best comics spending months and even years building new "sets." Most large cities have a comedy club that offers some kind of class. While you will have fun building your five-minute set, the real benefit is dramatically improving your stage presence.

Record and review. Have you ever had that weird experience where you hear yourself in a recording and barely recognize your own voice? Sometimes, what we hear in our head doesn't quite match what we are projecting to the rest of the world. The best way to know what you really sound like when you're giving that rockstar presentation is to film yourself and watch it with a critical eye.

Consider a personal coach. Personal coaches exist to help people get over all sorts of personal challenges, and public speaking is no exception. Look for someone in your area who specializes in professional or corporate environments, and soon you'll be speaking naturally to large crowds, entertaining them, and moving them to the next stage of your prospecting process with the best of them.

Step 3: Support the Goal with Logistics

Whatever you're planning to do, it *has* to run smoothly. Remember, it's all about the client experience; you can't let anything slip through the cracks, or you'll be known as the advisor who lets things slip through the cracks.

When my office put together our last client and prospect event, we didn't leave anything to chance. My office manager visited the site by herself to check things out in person, to walk through the venue and make sure it would work for what we needed it to work.

When you're considering a venue, tour multiple options where you plan on holding your event. We used to do ours at the country club, but the food was mediocre, and the service was slow. We ended up finding a hotel that did a buffet dinner.

A buffet may not be the classiest-sounding meal, but remember the goal you're really trying to solve for. Are you trying to give them an amazing meal? Not really. You don't want to give them a terrible meal—I've done this once before, and I'm still having twitches because of it—but you're not there to win their food business. With a buffet, they can show up, get their food, eat, and it's cleared before you start your presentation, so no one's attention is competing with the dinner service.

Think everything through, and keep in mind what you're trying to solve for. Depending on your goals for the event, the room logistics might be very different. If you're holding a social event, you don't need to worry about a stage, lighting, a microphone, or any of that. But if you're delivering a speech or addressing the group, you'll need lighting and a PA system, and you may want to consider a stage or riser.

Event Checklist

THE **PERFECT** RIA

Choose your date and topic **Choose your venue and contact them for availability** **and contract**	Min. 8 wks. prior

• Review the contract for max capacity, due dates, cancellation
   policy
 • Confirm whatever vendors will be renting space in the same
   facility during your event
 • State your preference on setup, e.g., table configuration
 • Review the menus and make choices. Check for food allergies.
   Communicate your A/V needs	

Create classy invitations using online source like **Vistaprint & include the following:**	8 wks. prior
• Date and time of event • Invite them to bring a guest • Short summary of presentation and why they should attend • RSVP deadline and how to RSVP (QR code, email, phone) • Inform guests of what to bring & what is provided	
• Mail out invitations	6 wks. prior
• Create RSVP tracking for confirmed attendance	6 wks. prior
• Develop presentation and have two other people proofread it for accuracy	4 wks. prior
• Practice your presentation	2 wks. prior
• Reminder email only to those who have not responded	1 wk. prior
• Order flowers for tables and have them delivered to venue	4 days prior
• Reminder calls or email to those who are scheduled to attend	4 days prior
• Practice and time your presentation, making sure to leave time for Q&A	1 day prior

• Have a dedicated event container w/lid. Gather handouts,
   name tags, pens, pads, business cards, A/V equipment,
   signage to direct people to the meeting
	1 day prior

• Arrive at the venue 1 hour in advance of dinner to set
   up registration table that includes the handouts, name tags,
   pens, paper, etc.
	1 hour prior

• Set up your presentation and do a mic and power check	1 hour prior

Step 4: Fill the Seats

It may seem like the number of attendees is the mark of a successful event, but that's actually not the goal. You can have a fantastic event with just five people. Somewhere between giving a presentation to an audience of one (yes, this happened to me) and attracting a crowd of people who will never convert, there's the sweet spot: valuable client and prospect events that offer you a return on investment.

Not only are fancy dinners expensive, but they have a habit of bringing in the wrong types of clients. Instead, focus on these groups of people to hold events for:

1. Clients
2. Clients' friends
3. Personal network
4. Prospects
5. Centers of Influence

Anything beyond this—and that includes mass mailings—is very expensive and has a low ROI. Don't waste your energy.

Step 5: Showtime

Time for the event! If you're prepared, you're going to do just fine, as long as you follow these rules for running a successful event without a hitch:

Start and end on time. Getting someone to take time out of their busy day and attend your event—no matter how good the food is—is a huge ask. Be respectful, and don't keep anyone waiting.

Eat first so you can focus. The last thing you need is to be distracted!

Arrive early. Make sure you're onsite an hour before the start time to account for any setup issues with pre-event music or slides.

Now, sit back, relax, and enjoy the party! You've done all of your planning, you know how to speak in a relaxed manner and engage the audience, you know your material. You've got this.

Step 6: Follow Up to Leverage Success

This is why it's so important that you, not some third party, are the keeper of all of this data. You need to be able to follow up with every attendee of your event.

This is easy if your events are for clients, but even so, have a good strategy in place for gathering contact information, because it is absolutely crucial that you follow up with your sincere gratitude and next steps.

Send a thank-you note to everyone who attended; bonus points if you follow up with a phone call. Also make sure to send bullet points to everyone, whether they attended or not, so no one misses out and everyone has access to the resources and information from the event.

Types of Client Education Events

Not sure where to start? Try one of these topics:

- Local Real Estate Trends
- Reverse Mortgages
- Long-Term Care
- Estate Planning w/Attorney
- College Planning
- F.I.R.E.(Financial Independence, Retire Early)
- Economic Update
- Understanding Social Security
- Guide to Medicare
- Understanding Tax Law
- Retirement Income
- ID Theft
- Investment Selection
- Guest Speakers

Any one of these topics has the potential to draw a crowd. Now it's up to you to do what's best for your business, your clients, and your goals!

Action Steps

Events could be an opportunity to open the floodgates to reliable prospects ... or they could leave you with a fridge full of leftovers and demoralizing credit card debt. Which will you choose?

If you're committed to putting in the time, making smart decisions, and doing whatever it takes to Deliver Massive Value through your prospecting events, you'll be able to fill seats and convert prospects like you never thought possible. Just follow these action steps and watch your attendance and conversions soar.

○ Consider all the different ways that you could be in front of a crowd that might help bring you new business. Whether that crowd is filled with your own clients or perfect strangers, any opportunity to speak is an opportunity to show or remind others that you're on top of your game—and can Deliver Massive Value.

○ Make sure that every client and prospect event has a clearly stated goal. Without knowing where you're going, your event *will* flounder, and you'll be dumping your time, effort, and marketing dollars right down the drain.

○ Take ownership of your public performance. Record yourself speaking; practice, practice, practice; and if you can't correct any issues on your own, get whatever professional help you need to succeed.

Bonus content available for this chapter at ThePerfectRIA.com/BookBonus:

→ PDF of samples in this chapter

→ Sample client event invitation

→ PDF of a JFS identity theft event slide deck

Working with the Media

"After thirteen years of building my practice, I still struggled with achieving my personal and professional goals *until* I read Jarvis's book and tuned in to his podcast!

Together they gave me pretty much every answer I'd been looking for. From scheduling to COIs, every chapter gave me a plan to put in place. I'd been burned so many times by 'experts' that being able to learn real strategies from a real advisor was a dream come true."

Dan Boorse, QAFP™
Alberta, Canada
Red Tree Financial Strategies

F or most advisors, trying to work with the media to gain awareness for your business is some kind of combination of a pipe dream and a giant waste of time. More often than not, it's just an excuse to not do real prospecting. The few advisors who do get traction with the media can measure their success only in "likes" and not clients.

That said, the few advisors who do it right are crushing it. In addition to being the source of several great clients, the media strategy that follows is the same one I employed myself, and it completely transformed my life in ways I could have never imagined.

MEDIA CASE STUDY: ME

On February 14, 2017, industry thought leader and legend Michael Kitces had me as the seventh guest on his newly launched *Financial Advisor Success* podcast. While I was honored to be on his show and flattered that it became his top episode that year (and remains one of his most popular of all time, not that I'm bragging), it did so much more: this experience launched the creation of The Perfect RIA platform, multiple mastermind groups, a series of amazing friendships—including with my RIA brother from another mother, Micah Shilanski—and this book you are reading.

Without that podcast, which was a result of the strategy that follows, I'd still have my amazing practice, but my life would be just a fraction of what it is today.

That's why, for most advisors who won't take the time to do it right, media is a terrible idea. But if you do it right, work your butt off, and have some good luck, it can be life-changing.

This is the power of media.

But—just like everything else—this game as it's traditionally played is completely rigged in favor of the biggest players. To be successful as an independent advisor, you need a better approach.

This chapter will show you that even media outreach is a game that you can win. We'll look at the types of news outlets you'll have a great shot with, plus outlets that probably aren't worth your effort.[1] We'll look at how to focus on your niche. And I'll share the winning formula I use to approach reporters, bloggers, and other broadcasters so that you, too, can find huge success with your media outreach in a

---

1 Throughout this chapter, I'm going to be showing my age by lumping all content channels (e.g., magazines, blogs, podcasts, social media, television, and all other forms of communication) into the terms "media" and/or "paper." If that's not where you plan to focus your youthful energies, that's fine; apply these lessons to your own situation and go digital if that's your thing.

way that continues to bring in clients, provide opportunities to educate and inform the public, and solidify your reputation as a thought leader.

What's Really Worth Your Time?

Measuring success with media outreach, like anything else, requires establishing clear goals. Before getting ahead of yourself, ask yourself one key question:

> `"What am I really trying to accomplish through the media?"`

Sure, a byline in a fancy newspaper would be cool—but you're not doing this to be cool. You're doing this to get your voice out there establishing you as a leader, to bring in new clients, and to do both efficiently and systematically. Everything else is just window dressing. Put another way: likes and follows, while an important piece of the funnel, don't count unless you can track them to actual fee-paying clients.

It's easy to spin your wheels at something that will never work, but that's not the habit of businesses focused on Delivering Massive Value. Let's look at a few different options that work—and don't work—for your goals when it comes to getting your name and expertise in front of someone else's willing audience.

> # "For most advisors who won't take the time to do it right, media is a terrible idea. But if you do it right, work your butt off, and have some good luck, it can be life-changing."

The Wrong Way to Approach the Media

What most advisors do to approach members of the media—which has never worked for me and I believe is a mistake—is write unsolicited articles and then submit them pre-written to the newspaper or magazine or blog or online contact they're targeting. And then they're shocked when it's not published.

Well, of course it's not published. First of all, you're not a journalist. I know that you think your writing is of the highest caliber, but unless you have an English degree or journalism background or some other experience or training, the quality of your writing is not going to be there, and the paper isn't going to invest its resources in editing a piece by a relative unknown (sorry).

The second issue is that the blogger or reporter is getting paid to write those columns—that's *their job*. If they start publishing your columns, you are essentially taking their job away from them. That's why most reporters are not inclined to publish a bunch of guest columns, especially by someone they've never heard of.

The third and most important issue is that your target clients might be reading the *Wall Street Journal*, but so are a ton of other service providers and salespeople. Do you know how many op eds the *WSJ* and other large publications receive every day? These are shark-infested waters.

That doesn't mean you shouldn't try to swim in them, and it doesn't mean that advisors haven't done it successfully. It's just that it's a tough road to go down, and it's best to approach the situation with healthy expectations.

The other reason that this traditional approach is flawed is that it takes a *ton* of time. To pick a personal example, I had an entire team help me write this book, and it still took hundreds of hours of my time. Even if you did get a spot as a guest columnist (something I once had), are you really willing to commit that much time to something that isn't your core business?

What if there was a better way?

A Better Way: Niche Media Marketing

The reason we chose a niche back in Chapter 13 is that it's much easier to dominate a smaller market space than to conquer an ocean of big-name competitors, and that same principle holds true when it comes to approaching media outlets.

The approach I've found the most success with is by picking the publications that target your audience the most narrowly. I've worked hard (and been lucky enough) to be quoted in the *Wall Street Journal* and other national publications, but as you'll see on the following pages, I've also been quoted in all sorts of local publications as well. Both categories of publications stroked my ego, but which one of them do you think is easier to land (and, more importantly, resulted in new clients?)

If all the clients you could ever need are hanging out in the treetops, why bother shooting for the moon? Instead, consider more "nontraditional" niche media outlets like these:
- Podcasts
- Blogs
- Local business journals
- Trade publications
- Newsletters of related professional organizations

The possibilities are practically endless—the smaller the market, the better luck you're going to have. Remember, the big media outlets are getting endlessly bombarded with content; they have no shortage of it, whereas smaller trade magazines and hobby podcasts are constantly struggling for good content to offer their listeners.

How to Get Quoted by the Media: The System

Everyone wants to put the media to work for them to spread the word to a wider audience than they could ever reach on their own, but few know what it takes to be successful. When approached correctly, it's not a long shot: *it works.*

Now, you can learn the system I've developed to get the respect and attention of the people in the media who can best help elevate my reputation with potential clients. Just follow this five-step system to achieving your own brand of media success!

Step 1: Know Your Audience

It is crucially important to know who your niche is and who your audience is. The wider you cast your net, the harder it's going to be to land a meaningful connection that benefits everyone.

For example, as a financial advisor yourself, you're no doubt aware of the Bogleheads® website. This wiki-style forum is a place for people who follow Jack Bogle (founder of Vanguard) and his teachings to congregate. You might think that's a great place to find people interested in finance management, and it is—but it's not a site I would target, because that audience consists of big Vanguard users who are strictly do-it-yourself. While they may want to quote you, they're not ever going to become clients.

And the tighter you make your niche, the easier this strategy becomes. One advisor I know who works only with optometrists implemented this strategy by writing to the *National Optometry Magazine*. Because the value he could provide was uniquely suited to the magazine's regular readers, they started quoting him extensively—and eventually offered him his own column in the *Review of Optometric Business*.

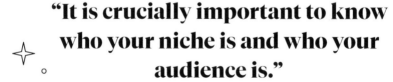

"It is crucially important to know who your niche is and who your audience is."

Step 2: Consider Your Options

Once you've identified your target audience—your people—make a list of the print and digital resources those people are visiting to solve their financial management problems. These, not the national print media conglomerates, are the first places you should consider reaching out to for your niche media marketing campaign.

Still looking for more resources? Tap your audience! Whether you're speaking with clients or potential clients, ask, "What websites do you visit when you're making important financial decisions? What blogs or books do you read? What podcasts do you listen to?" Whatever your niche and whatever your topic, this is a surefire way to focus your aim on the right kind of places.

Step 3: Monitor the Media

Once you have a good list of target publications, really get to know who they are and what they're doing for your people. Start by reading all of the content they've already published on your topic. Familiarize yourself with the types of material they provide, the columns they run, and the ways your unique experience might complement their typical material and benefit their audience.

Keep these publications on your radar and watch for new articles, blog posts, whatever they publish on topics that you can offer intelligent insight on. Forget wasting your time drafting articles and sending blind emails—don't try to do the journalist's job for them. Just reach out with compliments on a job well done, give your honest feedback, and offer a few related points to consider.

We used this exact strategy for *The Perfect RIA*. We found fifty or sixty podcasts that speak to our industry, because that's who we're focusing on in *The Perfect RIA*. We listened to their podcasts and made notes of which ones best suited our own target audience, and we closely follow their every move.

Step 4: Deliver Massive Value!

What's the approach most professionals take when they reach out to the media? It's always me, me, me. "Hey, you should talk to me. You should interview me. You should quote me. You should let me write for your organization." But why should they? What's in it for them? They get a thousand of those solicitations a day; they're not interested in yours.

Instead, remember your number-one goal for growing your business: Delivering Massive Value. This doesn't stop at clients; it's true for everyone you deal with in your business. This is your ticket for slipping in the back door.

For example, I once wrote to a journalist at *Kiplinger's Personal Finance* magazine after reading her article on long-term care, something that speaks to my audience. I said, "Hey, this was really a great article. I especially enjoyed points A, B, and C. I'm going to pass this article on to my clients. Next time you write about this topic, you may consider including the following points ..."

The journalist called me right away—the same day—and said, "Oh, I really appreciate this feedback. I'm going to write a second article. Can I interview you about it?" She ended up quoting me extensively. There I was, in a national publication: "Financial planner Matthew Jarvis, in Seattle, Washington." It really worked!

This approach works so well because you're showing reporters that you're paying attention to their stuff. You're flattering their ego. And you're offering to help them do their job without trying to take their job away. In other words, you're Delivering Massive Value!

And this approach works even better for the smaller, "nichier" podcasts, journals, and the like. I find that many of the more narrowly targeted publications are run by people who do it more as a hobby than a job—and who aren't getting pitched nearly as often as their national counterparts—so they're never insulted when I get in touch and offer to help.

(Might the same thing work for the *WSJ*? It could—but a good analogy would be calling your doctor and saying, "Hey, I read this thing about medicine. You should incorporate this in your practice." Seems pretty arrogant, huh?)

When I find an episode I particularly like of one of the podcasts I had targeted for *The Perfect RIA*, I'll give it five stars on iTunes. Then I'll take a screenshot of the five-star review and email them to say:

"Wow, I was listening to your podcast on [date] about [topic]. I really enjoyed [points two, three, and four]. I'm going to implement that in my own practice. In fact, I liked it so much that I went online and gave your podcast a five-star review—here's a screenshot of it. Keep up the good work!

As a side note, I also host a podcast called [name], and I know how hard it can be to generate content. If you're ever looking for a guest or a topic to cover, maybe we could chat about [topics A, B, or C]."

After I send that email, they almost always respond with, "Wow, you made my day! Thanks so much for your review. I can't believe anybody actually listens to my podcast. I'd love to have you on the show to talk about ..." And off we go.

All of these tactics work because you're actually giving them value. Whether you're saying you left a review or offering some content they could include next time, you're inserting yourself nicely and then giving them the opportunity to say, "All right, let's talk."

Treat media contacts the same way you would treat any networking prospect, and be humble and respectful. And always focus on the value you can deliver for them.

Step 5: Don't Give Up

Here's what happens with these strategies: the advisor decides they're going to implement one of these strategies, they do it for a couple hours, quit for long stretches at a time, and think, "Well, I really put a lot of work into it—guess it's just not for me"

RE: Enjoyed your piece on TOPIC

Name,

I really enjoyed your piece on TOPIC, so much so that I shared it with my audience on PLATFORM.

(Insert Screenshot)

(If applicable) I also took a second to add another five-star review so that more people can discover your content

(Insert Screenshot)

Next time this topic comes up, you might consider mentioning:
• Interesting Point #1
• Interesting Point #2
• Interesting Point #3

Please don't hesitate to reach out if you have questions about these points, or really anytime you are writing pieces for NICHE. Email is great, but we could also schedule a quick Zoom meeting via my calendar LINK.

Thanks again for your great content. Excited to see what you come up with next.

Rockstar Advisor

*Mad Props to Podcasting Legend John Lee Dumas of EO Fire for coaching me on this one.

Spoiler alert: that's not what "a lot of work" looks like. If you think sending out four emails is going to do it, I'm sorry to say that it's not.

Any of these marketing strategies are a long-term play that require a long-term commitment. You need to make regular time to cultivate this knowledge and awareness and these relationships.

To accomplish this, time block it. For me, every Thursday from 8:00 a.m. to 10:00 a.m., all I work on is my media strategy, and all I read or listen to are publications and podcasts strictly for the purpose of finding stories I can respond to. It's all about putting in consistent effort over time.

Choose Wisely!

You know how some actors tend to pop up as the same kind of character in the same kind of movie, over and over? It isn't always because they chose that path. For some people, their first breakout role defines how audiences see them and influences the types of roles they will be offered in the future. And when you see them acting outside that narrow box we've placed them in, it takes some getting used to.

Imagine that every podcast appearance will take off in the same way mine did, that every interview you give will be the hit blockbuster that defines how the public views your entire body of work. If you're going to be cast in the same movie over and over again, shouldn't you choose a role you enjoy playing?

WHAT IF IT WORKS?

Here are a few ideas for making the most of every media appearance you wrangle up.

- **Send it to your clients and network.** This will vary depending on the type of content, but if there's any crossover at all, make sure to share your media appearance. It isn't *just* about showing them you have sought-after opinions—but also giving them a chance to brag to their friends about you.
- **Post to your social media.** It's easy to retweet or reshare, and people love to celebrate a win. Wherever your business has a presence, share the good news and give others the opportunity to share it too!
- **Thank the author.** A quick note, especially a handwritten note, will go a long, long way to getting quoted or featured again. My thank-you notes look something like this:

"It was an honor to be quoted/featured in your article and a lot of fun working together to deliver massive value to your readers. I've selfishly directed everyone in my audience to take a look at it, which hopefully resulted in more subscribers to your work. Thanks again."

Action Steps

Getting quoted by the media is a massive level-up for your business: once you figure it out and you're in the game, this system will keep working to bring you opportunities to set yourself up as a thought leader, and it will only get easier to keep that system going.

But this happens only at the end of a carefully planned process and a *lot* of hard work. Follow these action steps to begin building your media strategy today!

○ Decide if media is a prospect channel you are willing to work. If so, commit two hours a week, every week (outside of surge), for a minimum of six months. At least initially, measure your success not by the number of times you are quoted/featured, but by the number of personalized outreaches you make.

○ Ask your clients and other people in your target client base where they get their financial information. This will give you a great starting point for publications and other media to keep track of.

○ Get to know the types of articles your target publications are already posting and look for ways to add value to their readers by sharing your own experience.

○ Keep adding value! Don't focus on yourself and your needs, and don't try to take the reporter's job away.

Bonus content available for this chapter at ThePerfectRIA.com/BookBonus:

→ Media success worksheet

→ Examples of articles I've had published

→ My scripts for being a guest

Leverage Your Centers of Influence

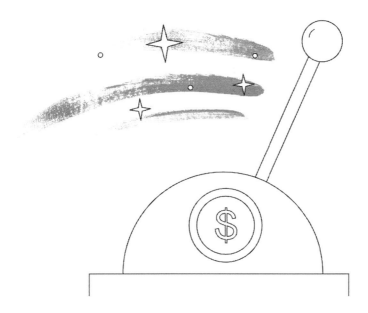

PROFILE OF SUCCESS

"I started meeting with CPAs one month ago using Jarvis's meeting process.
The first CPA who I had a meeting with referred a prospect to me a week after meeting with her. The prospect signed up yesterday and is an ideal client. Additionally, I have created five other CPA connections. I wish I would have started doing this four years ago!"

Nestor Vargas, CFP
Lakewood, CO
Green Mountain Planning

In the wide world of finance, there's this accepted wisdom that other professionals in your industry are the best source of new leads. This might include tax professionals, other advisors, and anyone else in a position to refer potential clients to you: we call these people "centers of influence," or COIs. But when was the last time you met an advisor who was actually *getting* these COI referrals? Better yet, when have you met a self-proclaimed expert promoting COI referrals who had ever even *met* with a COI?

Occasionally, I do meet an advisor who claims to be getting COI referrals. However, in most cases, it turns out they're exaggerating (a.k.a., *lying*). Or they're related to the COI (which is difficult to replicate) or paying for their referrals (not allowed in all states, logistically tricky, and generally not a great business decision).

Setting aside these less-than-honest statistics, I've never met an advisor who gets anywhere close to my referral level. Most get zero (and are quick to complain that they "always send referrals to CPAs and attorneys and never get any referrals back"). This is an absolute shame, because I know through my own experience of getting a steady stream of COI referrals every year that leveraging your centers of influence can transform the way your business runs. *If* you do it right.

In this chapter, you'll learn how to approach, cultivate, and enjoy continuous high-quality referrals from centers of influence. It requires a relatively small amount of time or money to implement, but it does require determination, consistency, a focus on the long game, and the right approach. Let's get started!

Why COIs Will Never *Give* You a Referral

Advisors love to complain about how COIs don't send referrals because they are lazy, bad businesspeople, greedy, or simply "don't appreciate how many referrals I send them." But the reality is much simpler: *you don't deserve any referrals*—yet. The one and only reason COIs don't send referrals is because those referrals haven't been earned.

"But Matthew," I can hear you object, "I send them referrals and I'm special and ..."

Yawn. None of it counts, and the longer you hide behind excuses, the longer it will take you to actually get the referrals you need.

Still skeptical? To be more specific:
- You look and sound like every other advisor.
- You have not demonstrated how you will deliver value to the COI's clients.
- The COI isn't sure if you will try to hard sell their clients.
- The COI is busy running their own business and has no reason to care about yours.
- The COI is likely being solicited by dozens, possibly hundreds of advisors, all of whom want referrals.
- The COI, especially if they are a CPA or attorney, likely does not view you as a real professional.

No wonder your calls aren't being answered!

It's true: COI marketing doesn't work out for everyone. But that's because people don't always follow the rules. They can be forgiven for this: I only figured them out through trial-and-error—more than my fair share of error—but now that I've done it, you don't have to.

Just like anything else, this is a system. Follow the rules and you'll be on your way to connecting with centers of influence who are best positioned to help your business grow.

How to *Earn* Referrals

While it's gotten better over time, I have a very high level of fear of rejection. Even the idea of asking a COI to "write down five names" makes my palms sweat and my heart pound. This is probably a good thing; while I've heard this strategy advocated dozens of times, I've never seen it actually work, so perhaps my fear saved me from repeating the same mistake made by everyone else—which seems to guarantee you will never get referrals.

So what to do instead? The first step is to create a system where you always win and, therefore, can never be rejected.

When my clients ask *me* for a referral to a COI, I want to be able to give them something better than "google it." While having a list of vetted COIs is a valuable way to Deliver Massive Value to your clients, it also lets you approach COIs as a buyer and not a seller.

Think about it: everyone, including COIs, knows when you're trying to sell something, if only because our default as American consumers is to assume that we're always being sold to. As such, if they even *suspect* you of selling something (e.g., give me referrals), they will be guarded, defensive, and generally nonresponsive.

So how do you rise to the top of a busy professional's priority list and become a main target for their referrals?

Respect Their Time: Pay for It

I'm not exaggerating when I tell you that my office gets somewhere around twenty phone calls and a hundred emails a week from people who want my time and don't want to pay for it. How many of them do you think actually make it onto my schedule? Centers of influence experience the same thing, only worse. They're *constantly* being bombarded by people in our line of work who want their time, and almost to a person, they want it for free. It's easy to get so wrapped up in our own needs and the needs of our clients that we forget the golden rule of COIs: we have to treat them as the valued professionals that they are.

I've figured out the secret to getting your foot in the door. For this strategy to work effectively, you *must* be willing to pay for an hour of their time. They are skilled professionals who live and die by hourly billing. If you are asking for an hour of their time, pay for it.

Here's the secret: to show right away that I'm a good guy and someone who respects their time, especially at the beginning of a new relationship, I offer to pay their hourly rate for any time I take up.

Setting aside this professional courtesy, the bigger reason you pay for the hour is it makes you unlike anyone else they have met. Now, we are instantly distinguished as a trustworthy person and a wise use of the professional's time. Instead of competing with every other solicitor, we come in as a *buyer*. For all but the most successful (or jaded) COI, this is welcomed with open arms.

Here's the script I use to reach out to COIs with whom I want to cultivate a relationship:

> "Ms. COI. My clients are often asking for a referral to a [whatever their profession]. So that I can give them more than a random name, I'm interviewing all the professionals in the area to find the best fit for each client. Because I can't promise you any referrals, I will be paying for this hour of your time. So that I can be prepared for our meeting with a check, what is your hourly rate?"

Even if everyone reading this book starts paying COIs for their time, doing so will still put you in the top tier in your own market—unlike the *hundreds* of other freeloaders who will call the same COI this year.

This also gives you total control of the conversation: you can talk about whatever you want, because *you're* paying the fee. This gets you the most valuable use of their time because you don't have to feel like you're intruding on them; that's why you're there, and that's what you're paying for. Now, you're at the top of their list because you're not trying to freeload off them. Remember, they live and die on hourly fees. Respect their time by offering to pay for it and watch what goodwill you generate.

Now, you're the only advisor she knows that's paid her for her time. When someone needs a financial advisor, who do you think that COI is going to refer? She knows that you're not going to hit her up and waste her time, so there's no reason for her to ever look elsewhere. You're getting her referrals for *life*.

WHO FOOTS THE BILL?

If it's tax time, and you need some information that your client just isn't getting you, and you eventually have to go over your client's head and work directly with other professionals involved in their finances, it makes sense on paper that the client should eat that cost. But before you send the bill, consider all the goodwill you could buy by spending the money yourself.

It also helps your relationship with the client. If the CPA spends an hour on a tax projection at your request and then sends the client a bill for $500, the client's going to be irate. For whatever reason, there's some behavioral psychology there. You can deduct huge fees out of a client's account, but they won't like to see a few hundred dollars as a line item that helped you get your job done. That's not their problem, not really.

Instead, by picking up the tab, your client is happy. The CPA or other professional is happy. And by being the generous one, you've increased that intangible relationship return on investment.

Bridge the Gap: Add Value First

Especially when we're talking about accountants and attorneys, we have to remember that they live in a different world than we do. They don't have the same respect for us that our clients do because they aren't the ones utilizing our services; they don't see the value we can bring to the table, because they aren't primed to look for it or receiving an immediate benefit from it.

I want to make sure to bridge that gap by being the most valuable planner they've ever seen. For example, take a look back at the value-add from Chapter 11 that we do every January: it shows the client which accounts they'll get a 1099 on and which ones they won't. We send our clients two copies: one for them, one to give to their CPA.

The CPAs *love* this. I'm not only preempting calls from the client, which is efficient for me; I'm also preempting questions the CPA might have for the client, which is efficient for them. Nothing makes the CPA angrier than having to refile a tax return because nobody told them some key piece of information, like that the required minimum distribution was going to charity. I include that in my 1099 letter:

"RMD to charity. Have your CPA give me a call."

CPAs say to me, "Wow, I wish every advisor would do this, because it's such a pain for me to track down." There's no way for the CPA to know that's happened unless someone tells them, and because I am proactive about anticipating everyone's needs, no one has to pester the client about it.

Keep the Pressure Off: Ask Without Asking

There's a reason for such low *actual* COI success rates among my esteemed colleagues: this is a long-term strategy that can take years to develop, and not everyone considers these relationships worth developing or thinks they have the time to reach out to centers of influence around them.

All this despite the fact that every industry publication you read, every wholesaler you meet with, will say, "You should talk to your centers of influence to get referrals." Perfect. You and every single other advisor on the planet Earth, plus every copy machine salesperson, every HR vendor, everyone.

In fact, this is one of those "self-proclaimed experts" things where the people who tell you to get referrals from COIs are the people who have never actually sat in front of one. They don't know what they want to hear.

Instead, ask about them. The strategy takes a page from your prospect process: people are immediately on guard against being sold to, and by putting the ball firmly in their court, you take that edge off and pave the way for a much smoother conversation.

Then, don't ask them to refer clients to you. There's no need, and it makes people uncomfortable. Instead, ask what you can do for them. Can you refer clients to them, can you connect them with some strategic business partner you know? By making yourself valuable first and foremost, you're getting all those relationship points. Because you've taken the time to explain the type of clients you serve (and paid for that time), they know exactly who you are and what you do, and they'll jump at a way to return the favor and keep the relationship going.

My Five-Step System to Actually Getting COI Referrals

Forming new business relationships can be a difficult skill to master. Before you run out and start writing checks, you need a carefully designed system if you are going to get results.

Here, step by step, is the system I use. I didn't pay for it in blood, but I certainly paid my share in tears and mental anguish over years of figuring it out.

Follow these five steps again and again to come up with your own strategy for leveraging your centers of influence and turbocharging your business.

Step 1: Make a Smart List of COIs

Like any proven prospect strategy, they only succeed if you work them right and long enough. Odds are your first few COIs, maybe even your first dozen, will never send you a referral. As such, you need to be ready to meet with all of the ones in your area. Yes, this will take time and money, which is why so few people end up successful.

The easiest place to start is with all the CPAs, tax preparers, bookkeepers, attorneys, and business bankers in your area or who specialize in your niche. I have the best luck with independent/solo professionals and those who are part of small firms. That said, I've gotten several referrals from attorneys at large law firms. Either way, the key is to focus on specific individuals.

Once you have your list of at least a dozen names—and now's not the time to be picky about this list, at least not until you've met them in person—it's on to the next step!

COI MEETING: WORTH THE HOURLY RATE?

Now, I know some of you are still hung up on the idea of paying for these meetings, so let's dive deeper. How much is a CPA going to charge you? Two, three, five hundred bucks? Depends on your market. Whatever it is, believe me: it's going to be the best marketing money you've ever spent. Way better than giving an expensive, empty seminar, I promise you that.

Even if it takes a dozen paid meetings before you start getting referrals (and it probably will take a dozen), once this gets going, it's the golden goose.

And it's not just a marketing scheme. By investing this time and money in getting to know all the COIs in your area, you are also putting yourself in a perfect position to Deliver Massive Value to your clients!

Step 2: Fine-Tune Your Approach

Part of providing a fantastic client experience is always being prepared to respond in different situations. When you have a solid list of good, trustworthy people you'd like to cultivate as COIs, give them a call and say,

---

"Lots of my clients ask me for an introduction to a CPA, so I'm
interviewing CPAs in the area. I can't promise to send you any
referrals because I don't know if you're going to be a good fit,
but I want to pay for an hour of your time to find out."

The next time your client expresses a need that has you thinking of your COI, try this:

> "Ms. Client, it looks like you need a new CPA for XYZ. I've done paid interviews with most of the CPAs in the area and the best one in your situation will likely be XYZ."

What about the COIs you already know in your community/market?

> "I'm in the process of making several changes to my practice, and I value your feedback. I'd like to pay for an hour of your time to get your thoughts."

Whatever you say, like all successful marketing, needs to be done with sincerity, so really approach it from a place of wanting to learn from this COI.

It is possible that the COI will offer some pushback. The more experienced (read: jaded) ones might respond with "Let's just talk now on the phone" or "I already refer all my clients to someone else." If you're approaching them carefully and respectfully, you shouldn't have this problem, but don't let it surprise you when it happens.

How do you respond to this pushback? Try this:

> "It's really important to me that I refer my clients to the CPA best suited to their situation, and I've found the best way to do this is for me to pay for an hour of your time to learn which of my clients are the best fit for your services."

You will still have some COIs who won't play along. Great—one less person to weed out. As Nick Murray would say: "NEXT!"

Step 3: Do Your Research

Before you go and see anyone you're considering as a COI, make it your business to learn everything you possibly can about them. Scour LinkedIn, google their name— anything you can think of to learn more about them. You want to know where they went to college, if they're on the board of Junior Achievement, if they're a Rotarian.

It helps to imagine you are going to introduce them at a very important event. For example, I want to know where they went to college, the organizations they support, and any awards or recognition they've received. Like all things, this requires balance and discretion. Hiring a private detective to follow them around would *not* be a good idea, but being able to walk into the meeting asking about their recent recognition for supporting the Boys and Girls Club takes your credibility to an entirely new level.

You might say something like this:

> "When I was googling how to get here, I saw that you are on the
> Chamber of Commerce Board. How long have you been doing that?"

It's a small thing, but it makes a huge impact as it shows you cared enough to actually learn something about them. After all, what usually happens when a vendor, wholesaler, or anybody else who isn't a client comes into your office? What do they talk about? Themselves and their product. Not you.

You want to walk in, demonstrate that you care about forming an actual relationship, and have a really good discussion. Even if nothing ever comes of your efforts, you'll at least have had a good conversation.

Step 4: Nail the Meeting

When it's time for your meeting with the COI, you will walk into their office exactly ten minutes early. With a smile, you will walk confidently up to the front desk, explain that you have an appointment with the COI, but you're a few minutes early. While you wait, could they please tell you to whom the check for the COI's time should be paid?

Then, when you sit down with the COI, before you say a thing, set the check on their desk and say, "Thank you for this time. Here's my check."[1] This tells them from the moment you walk in that you're serious and not just talk.

> "As I explained when scheduling this meeting, my clients
> often ask for a referral and so I'm interviewing COIs to make
> sure I can match clients with the COI best suited to their unique
> situation. If you don't mind, I have a list of questions I'd like
> to ask. Is that OK with you?"

---

1 This is such an effective strategy that some COIs may actually give you the check back. They're just honored that you would really offer to pay for their time. Of course, you're not playing a game; if they take the check, great. It shows that you both respect the value of time, and it's still the best marketing money you've ever spent.

Don't be surprised if the COI is stunned by all of this, as it's likely something they've never experienced. Once they agree to continue, open your portfolio to the list of questions you've printed in advance. Here's the list I use to interview my COIs:

www.ThePerfectRIA.com

As you can see from this list, the questions have been carefully designed to show the CPA that I'm more than just some idiot paying for their time. I'm asking questions I know CPAs struggle with (for example, "How do you decide which clients get put on extension?"), and I'm humble enough to ask what advisors like me do that really makes their life difficult.

ASK THE RIGHT QUESTIONS!

You may have paid for their time, but you still owe it to them to come prepared to use it well. I like to prepare an interview questionnaire ahead of time. I say something like this:

```
"Like I mentioned, my clients ask me for introductions to CPAs
 or attorneys. I have a handful of questions that will help me
 understand what you do."
```

Then, ask your questions:
- Who goes on extension and who gets filed on time?
- Where did financial advisors help you the most?
- Where do they annoy you the most?
- When do you recommend a will versus a trust?
- Who do you recommend they name as executor if they don't have any trusted family members?

The whole time they're talking, I'm writing down all their answers, right in front of them where they can see, even the ones I already know the answer to. I want them to see that I'm serious and that I respect their time. Then, just like any meeting, I record a memo after my COI meeting, especially any action items for prompt follow-up.

Step 5: Deliver Massive Value (Of Course!)

Now that you've paid them and paid attention to them—and carefully timed them out—it's your turn to shine. Believe me, you'll have a receptive audience.

Whatever the final questions on your list, they should take no more than half of the hour for which you've paid. When you get to the end of this list, explain:

> "That was all the questions I have for you, and your answers were very helpful. Since we still have a few minutes, do you have any questions for me? Otherwise, I'd like to take just a minute to share how we help potential clients make an educated and informed decision about our firm. Is that OK with you?"

Then, spend the next twenty minutes walking them through the prospect process that you so carefully created in Chapter 10. You can even give them one or two examples of a one-page financial plan.

Approximately ten minutes before your time is up, thank them for their time, ask if they have any other questions, and then stand up to leave. Explain how much you enjoyed speaking with them and that you hope to be able to refer clients their way in the near future, then ask, "Would it be possible in the future for me to pay for another hour of your time, or at least buy you lunch, to get your feedback on cases/clients?" This further flatters the CPA and opens the door for future calls.

I can do this because I know that their biggest concern when they refer a client or a friend somewhere is that the client or friend is going to have a bad experience, and their friend is going to ask them why they sent them to a jerk who gave them a hard sell.

At no point should you *ever* ask for referrals, discuss investments, or talk about your "proprietary fee–only strategies." Doing so immediately makes you a salesperson, which will destroy all of your carefully planned efforts. This is especially important when sharing your prospect process. It must be strictly educational, never "who do you know who will benefit from this process?"

Why? Because they know you want referrals. You don't need to tell them that. You want them to think of you and say, "Wow, if I ever see someone who needs a financial planner, this is the advisor I'm going to call."

Try to meet with your COIs twice a year. Put them in your database as both an A-level client and as a prospect. Invite them to your client events, your marketing events. Send them generic copies of your value-adds, just to keep them informed … and of course, because you respect their time, offer to pay for their time if they have any feedback on your cases or clients. Then, continue to be unlike any advisor they've ever seen.

Action Steps

Having a reliable stream of new clients from COI referrals may not be a strategy that works for most people, but that doesn't mean it can't work for you. As with everything you do to elevate your business and Deliver Massive Value, you just have to be smart about your strategy and do the legwork to make it happen.

Keep these action steps in mind as you grow your network of COIs, do the work, and then watch the referrals come streaming in!

- ○ Make a list of all the people in your area who can most benefit your business and who tend to form long-term relationships with their clients. Learn everything you can about them.
- ○ Always offer to pay for their time. It shows them you respect their time, and it keeps you top-of-mind whenever anyone in your space is looking for services like yours.
- ○ Keep your COIs engaged, and follow up with them regularly so they never forget the value you can offer their clients (and themselves).

Bonus content available for this chapter at ThePerfectRIA.com/BookBonus:
→ Webinar recording with CPA Steven Jarvis on actually getting referrals
→ PDF with questions to ask every CPA
→ The email I send for a CPA introduction

Actually Getting Client Referrals

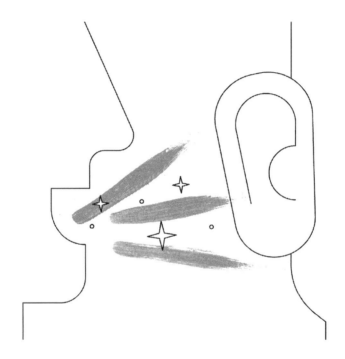

"Surge meetings have changed my whole business.

It's been incredible. Yes, we learned a few lessons and had to make some adjustments along the way, but it gives my practice a streamlined process and a clear path when we are off surge. Wish I had done this years ago!"

Justin Long, CFP
Henderson, NV
Diazo Wealth Group

Each year, roughly a third of my new client assets come from referrals from existing clients. While this is a major driver of new business for my company, I was hesitant to include a chapter on this for two reasons:

1. For smaller practices with ambitious growth goals, referrals are rarely a viable strategy.
2. You can only do so much to effectively drive referrals (all of which we will cover in this chapter).

The problem is, while giving a referral seems like a logistically easy thing to do, the reality is that giving a referral is *emotionally* difficult. After all, the person doing the referring—ideally, your client—is taking a big risk by recommending that their friend talk with you. As such, we need to do everything we possibly can to make it easy for other people to send you potential clients.

That said, it makes a huge difference to my own business, and I know it can work for yours too. In this chapter, I'm going to outline the key tenets of client referrals so that you can put systems in place that will have all your happy clients bringing in more of the same.

Bad Referral Habits to Break

If your referral strategy isn't working, I can almost guarantee you it's because somewhere along the way, you've acquired some bad habits that are bringing down your success rate. If you recognize any of these habits in your own practice, it's time to reexamine your methods.

You're Too Picky

As outlined in Chapter 13, you need to have a solid niche. That said, it should not be your client's responsibility to decide if their friend is a good fit for your niche. This is especially true if you have requirements related to age (e.g., retirees) and/or assets (e.g., $1 million-plus). Especially with assets, clients don't always know their friends' financial situation and they don't want their friends to know their own finances. As such, when you tell them, "We only work with people with $1 million-plus in assets," you've basically guaranteed yourself no referrals.

Instead, I tell clients:

> "While we work primarily with people just like you, one of the benefits of being a client is that we are glad to talk with any of your family and friends who have any kind of financial questions. Even if what they need is not a fit for our specialty, we will still give them great advice and get them introduced to someone who is a fit for their needs."

This approach isn't without downsides. Roughly half of the referrals I get from clients are way outside our niche. While this takes time from my team, it is still a win, as it Delivers Massive Value to the client, who is now happy that they (via an introduction to me) were able to help their friend.

You Make It Awkward to Give Referrals

We've all been told by "experts" truly awful strategies for getting referrals, including pure garbage like this:

- "I get paid in three ways ... including your referrals."
- "The highest compliment you can give me is a referral."
- "I see you know [name]—can you introduce me?"
- "To whom should we be sending our newsletter?"

Seriously, who wants to hear any of that crap? Instead, rely on a much more passive (but far more successful) referral awareness that I use in most of our meetings.

For example, any time a client asks how business is going, I nearly always respond with the following:

> "Thanks to all the great referrals we get from clients like you, we continue to grow."

It's simple, it's powerful, and it puts the idea in the client's head just as certainly as if you'd asked for it. No awkwardness required.

You Feel Entitled to Referrals

Let's get really clear: *nobody* owes you a referral. At the end of the day, if you're not getting the referrals you want, it's because *you* are not doing a good enough job Delivering Massive Value to the client.

For example, have you ever given a referral to your power company? No? Why not? The power comes on almost every time you turn on the light switch, exactly as they promised. As such, don't you owe them a referral? Nope, because the power company did exactly what they said and in no way did they blow your mind or even exceed your expectations. The same is true for your clients. If you are doing exactly what they expect, there is no reason to give you a referral. On the other hand, if you are constantly exceeding their expectations, they will be far more likely to send you referrals because they can safely assume that you will also exceed their friends' expectations.

In other words: if you want more referrals, deliver more value!

You're Being Lazy

In survey after survey (all of which are crap, but hang with me) advisors consistently report that referrals are their top source of marketing/new clients. However, when pressed on what they do to get referrals, they can't articulate an actual strategy. If you want to consistently get referrals, you need to treat it like any other marketing strategy by committing to taking action.

As you learned in Chapter 14, the referral strategy we actively employ in my office includes client education events three to four times a year. These events are purely educational, they're never sponsored, and we never discuss products. Instead, we have a fun time—complete with dinner and live music—discussing relevant topics like identity theft, staying out of nursing homes, retirement income, and long-term economic updates. On rare occasions we do have guest speakers, but these are very, very carefully vetted. With each event we physically mail clients a second invitation with a note that says, "Please feel free to have a friend join us for dinner and a fun evening."

I've been doing these events for years, and we consistently have forty to fifty clients in attendance. Each event will also have one or two friends (read: prospects). While some advisors might call this a terrible ratio, for me it's awesome, because it's another opportunity to Deliver Massive Value to my clients. Having the friends attend is a bonus that often turns into new clients. Given my average client revenue of $10,000 annually, if I average just one new client a year from these events, it's still a positive ROI—and if these events help me keep just one client a year, that's also a win.

To up-level your events, have your team call everyone who was invited to confirm if they are coming, and ask if they'd like you to save a couple of seats for a friend or two who might enjoy the evening.

"If you want more referrals, deliver more value!"

How to Get More Referrals

In so many cases, the reason advisors fail at getting referrals is because they've put up roadblocks to their own success. Now that you know what you've been doing wrong, how do you fix it?

It's time to smooth out those wrinkles that hold your process back so you can clear the way for referral success. Here's how.

Engage the Prospect Process

The first step in making it easier is making sure you have a consistent, reliable prospect process for helping people make an educated and informed decision. As covered in Chapter 10, this process should be clearly documented on your website.

In every other client meeting and at least annually in our client newsletter (which we mail), we outline to clients what happens when they send us a referral. Clearly documenting this process and regularly reminding clients what happens when they send a referral will make it far more likely that you will receive referrals *and* that both the client and their friend will be happy with the process.

Know How to Handle Referrals That Are Not a Good Fit

As outlined in Chapter 13, a good niche excludes nearly everyone, which means fielding a large number of referrals you receive. These referrals should be viewed as an opportunity to improve your skills and Deliver Massive Value to your client. However, just because someone is referred by your best client does *not* mean that you bend or break your rules. Instead you spend fifteen to sixty minutes, depending on the referral source, giving this person the best advice you can regarding their situation, but then explain:

> "Just like you wouldn't go to a heart surgeon if you needed a knee replacement, my expertise doesn't fit your needs. But great news, I know someone who specializes in exactly your situation and I'd be glad to make the introduction."

This approach, while powerful, does require you to maintain a network of people to whom you can refer clients who do not fit your niche. Personally I know several of the advisors in my area who can serve these prospects far better than I, if only because their fees are a fraction of mine. I also regularly refer prospects to Vanguard's "dial-a-CFP" program. XYPN is also a great resource for referring out small clients who need minimal advice/service and/or whose needs would be best served by an hourly type relationship.

Add a Personal Touch to Every Contact

As you know, a big reason clients want to pay you top dollar is the experience you're providing them, and that goes beyond just the office.

It doesn't have to be a huge inconvenience or expense; look for any opportunity to include that extra something to show your clients they're valued.

• Proper birthday gift
• Family holiday card
• Quarterly client newsletter
• Quarterly check-in call
• Surprise and delight with every response

It's very easy to respond to a client comment or request with exactly what they asked while using the experience as an opportunity to add that personal touch that will set you apart. For example, imagine a client emails asking the Roth contribution limit for the current year. An average advisor will quickly respond with the answer, which, while helpful, puts you on the same level as Google (which, by the way, never gets referrals either): it's just an answer to a question.

Instead, your office's email to a typical client inquiry might look like this:

Mrs. Client,

Always great to hear from you! The quick answer to your question is that the limit for Roth contributions this year ranges from zero to $$$, but for most people under the age of fifty, it's $$$ and above fifty it's $$$.

In your situation, the limit is $$$$, which we plan on contributing in January each year in an effort to get the maximum tax benefit. This is what we did in years XXXX and XXXX.

My favorite educational piece of Roth IRA contributions can be found at [link].

If you have any questions or concerns about this topic (or any other), I'm always glad to schedule a call or meeting.

—Your Advisor
P.S. In our last meeting you mentioned XYZ—any updates?

Yes, a response like this takes time—which is why so few advisors have amazing practices. But when you take the time to make every client feel personally appreciated, and you're Delivering Massive Value at every turn, you'll launch your business into the next level.

Life's four rules were best articulated to me by a legendary financial planner (and Micah's father), Floyd Shilanski:

1. Be on time.
2. Do what you said you were going to do.
3. Say please and thank you.
4. Finish what you started.

When I have an appointment with a client or prospect, especially a phone appointment, their phone rings at exactly the appointed time. Not a minute before and certainly not a minute after. This can seem like a small thing, but I routinely get compliments from clients and prospects for being so punctual. In order to do this, at least five minutes before the appointment I stop everything else (and I've already turned off all alerts and distractions). I have their number typed into my phone and my finger is hovering above the dial button waiting for the clock to turn. By being exactly punctual I stand out from nearly every other product or service in the client's mind.

What's more, it shows that even in the little things, I follow rule #2 and do exactly what I say I will. If you said you would call a client at 9:00 a.m., then you do what you said by calling them at exactly 9:00 a.m. If you promised to email them a follow-up or do any other task, you do that task.

A key element here is being very clear about what you say you are going to do. In every client meeting I keep a list in front of the client of promised action items, who on my team is going to do them, and by when the activity will be completed. This level of clarity both holds me accountable and allows me to do what I said vs. what the client imagined I meant by "I'll send you an email."

Give Clear Advice

Any question or scenario presented by a client needs to be answered with a clear recommendation by you, even if both options are perfectly equal. Telling a client, "Well, you've got three options here, and you'll have to decide" is a chickenshit move that is not Delivering Massive Value. Clients come to you for advice, not information (the latter of which Google has in endless supply). In this example where both options seem identical, you present them as follows:

"Mrs. Client, we have two ways of accomplishing your goal of XYZ. Both options are great, and I can fully support either one, but ultimately my recommendation is option ABC, and here's why."

Always Do What's Right for the Client

Last but certainly not least, I learned one of the most important lessons about being a successful financial advisor from my father, Nathaniel Jarvis: always do what's right for the client.

Yes, I know this is cliché, and every advisor's marketing claims to do this, but it's not just a wasted marketing line. It is critical to the integrity, and therefore the long-term success, of your business.

Action Steps

Your happy clients could be your number-one cheerleaders—if you let them. If you're committed to growing your business through client referrals, you *need* to examine and improve your process so that you can remove any roadblocks standing in the way and encourage them to refer you all on their own.

If you want your top clients to bring more of the same your way, keep these action steps in mind to develop a rockstar client referral system that works seamlessly to keep the prospects rolling in.

○ Kick the bad habits! Examine your current client referral system, and if you spot any ways you're sabotaging your own success, stop what you're doing and build a better way.
○ Ask for referrals without ever needing to ask! By just mentioning that other clients refer business to you, you'll put the idea in your clients' heads in a way that keeps the pressure off and leaves them feeling in charge of the situation.

Remember life's four rules:
○ Be on time.
○ Do what you said you were going to do.
○ Say please and thank you.
○ Finish what you started.

They're the keys to a successful business *and* a successful life.

Bonus content available for this chapter at ThePerfectRIA.com/BookBonus:
→ PDF of our most popular client gifts that lead to referrals
→ PDF of our client newsletter "asking" for referrals
→ A demonstration of my script for "asking" for referrals

The One-Page Financial Plan

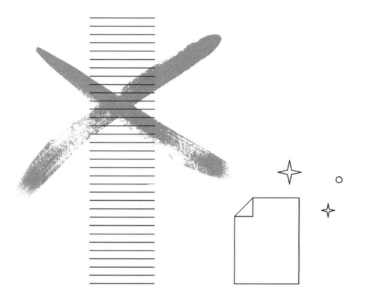

"Jarvis takes a no-nonsense approach to the reality that adding huge value to clients takes a ton of hard work, strength, and discipline.

If you are looking for a quick fix and an easy answer to what is plaguing your practice, be assured—this book is *not* that! A heavy dose of tough love from Jarvis about how to get rid of your head trash and get tough with yourself is what it takes if you want to have the practice of your dreams. This is not theory!"

Mark Walhout, CFP
Ontario, Canada
Walhout Financial

For some reason, most financial planners seem to think the only "proper" financial plan is a fancy, intimidating, hundred-page, spiral-bound document that clients will never read. As long as you *can* run all those projections, you probably should, right? If one projection is good, then fifty are better, and surely five hundred are even better than that ...

I've talked a lot about the One-Page Financial Plan as a key component of my prospect process so far, but when people first hear of my One-Page Financial Plan (or OPP), their first reaction is that I must be full of shit. You might even be a little skeptical yourself.

"Come on, Matt," you're thinking. "I've spent an entire meeting pumping clients for information. How can I possibly distill all of my recommendations down to a single page? Is that even real financial advice?"

If you've ever questioned the value of your financial plan, wondered how long it should be, or carefully considered how many Monte Carlo simulations it needs—only to have a prospect or client stare blankly at you when you try to explain—this chapter is for you. I'm going to walk you through exactly how I put together and deliver my OPPs to clients so that you can create and use them for your own business. It allows you to give clients personal, actionable advice *without* requiring them to do a bunch of work upfront. It's the culmination of your carefully designed prospect process. And most importantly, it's the perfect way to Deliver Massive Value.

Why a One-Page Financial Plan

Whether you're filling one page or one hundred, any effective financial plan should have two main goals:

1. Deliver personal, actionable advice.
2. Save the client time.

To accomplish this, every single inch of that plan needs to be personalized and save time for the client. That's why they're here talking to you and not browsing Google.

If you're giving them two hundred pages of the same generic printouts that fifty thousand other advisors are giving out, you are neither giving them personalized advice nor saving them time. They'll ignore your carefully calculated plan, throw it in a drawer, and never look at it again, and they'll have an even harder time approaching a financial planner in the future. And if the client is too daunted to look at the plan ever again, you're really giving them *nothing*.

What does this mean to you and your firm? Your client doesn't want to look at a bunch of charts to discover that they're supposed to convert $47,000 into a Roth IRA; they just want to know that's what they're supposed to do. Let's look at how an OPP helps you accomplish that.

It was legendary financial planner Tom Gau (rest in peace) who first introduced me to the idea of doing a One-Page Financial Plan (which Gau called a Financial Action Checklist). This chapter wouldn't be complete without giving them a healthy shout-out for changing my financial outlook—and thus, by extension, yours—forever.

Friendly reminder: while self-proclaimed experts love to talk and write about this concept, whenever possible, learn from people who are actually doing it. As the old saying goes, those who can't do, teach.

Gives Clients What They Really Want

Clients aren't paying you by the page, and they sure aren't paying you to show off your work. They're paying you to understand their situation, use your expertise to measure it against the overall financial landscape, and tell them what to do with their money to best accomplish their goals. Do you really need more than a page to deliver that information?

Let's use your car as an example. When you consult a professional for help, you don't want to read a twenty-page report on everything that went through the mechanic's mind while they looked at your car; you just want to know that you need new brakes and it'll cost you four hundred bucks. You don't walk into a hospital hoping a doctor will hand you a medical journal; you want your prognosis.

Ditch that head trash! There's nothing lazy about giving clients a One-Page Financial Plan. In fact, the opposite is true. I'm not just giving clients a stack of papers and inviting them to get to work; I'm actually doing the work for them by analyzing their situation ahead of time.

I would dare any person doing a fifty-page financial plan to boil that down to one page and tell me if it took them more or less effort. After all, how much work does it really take to plug some numbers into whatever software you're using, check a bunch of boxes, and print some paper? If this is your process, what are you really trying to prove?

Short, Powerful, and Scalable

When I give talks, I encounter two groups of people. The first group is full of people who want to learn. The second group is made up of the skeptics who think a One-Page Financial Plan is fine for lazy financial planners with average clients but could never address the need of someone with serious wealth.

Let me tell you a story about how my OPP beat out billion-dollar RIAs to land my biggest client ever.

I had the opportunity to meet with a gentleman whose portfolio topped out at around $70 million. When I admitted that my largest client was $12 million, he was ready to walk, feeling that his net worth was way out of my league.

Maybe he was just humoring me. Maybe it was my rugged good looks and winning personality. Whatever it was (honestly, it was probably my rugged good looks and winning personality[1]), he agreed to meet with me before heading to Seattle the very next day to meet with the top financial investment firms in the state. I told him, "I think you'll agree that you're probably not the right fit for our firm, but since you're here, let me create a One-Page Financial Plan that you can use to evaluate other firms." He agreed and said that I could email him the OPP (the only time I've ever not presented the plan in person). To be honest, I didn't expect he would even read it, and I had no hope whatsoever that my OPP could compete with the top RIA firms in Seattle.

Three weeks later, I received the most shocking phone call of my professional life. It was the gentleman with the $70 million portfolio—and he wanted to work with *me*!

Why, with billions of dollars and tons of expensive and robust software, could none of these major financial players land this client? He explained, "I couldn't understand what any of them were telling me. Your financial plan was the only one that made any sense."

I picked myself up off the floor and tried to sound casual, but I soon realized I shouldn't have been so surprised. You wouldn't look for information in an academic report or a scientific study without reading the abstract first, would you? The OPP serves the same function: it saves clients time by letting them know everything they *really* need to know at a glance, and it shows them exactly what to dig into or what questions to ask if they decide more information would be valuable.

I'm honestly surprised more advisors haven't adopted this approach. Maybe they will after enough of their clients leave to work with me.

In fact, lots of people at all levels of wealth are overwhelmed by finance management. Your goal as their advisor isn't to make your clients drown under enough paperwork to make you feel like you've earned your fee. It's to *actually deliver value*. Making this information easier to digest isn't cheating, and it isn't slacking. It's giving your clients exactly what they need—sound, personalized, actionable advice— and showing them a pathway to continue going down if they choose to work with you.

Say goodbye to those hefty spiral-bound reports. After I landed that $70 million portfolio, I never looked back. You won't either.

---

1 For the record, I find myself neither charming nor handsome, and any level of either I currently possess is strictly the result of a ton of hard work and practice. In other words: what's your excuse?

Questions to Ask While Building OPP

Name Surname XX/XX/XXXX

THE **PERFECT** RIA

Primary Goals

Using as many of their own words as possible, restate their goals as gathered from the first meeting. In other words, why did they come and see us?
I always like to add "never run out of money" and "don't leave the IRS a tip."

Retirement Income

How specifically would we help them accomplish their retirement goals?

- How much money can their portfolio generate? What are their other incomes sources? Net of taxes, how much income will they have? How does this compare to their current lifestyle expenses?
- What advice can we offer and/or recommendations can we implement to improve their retirement income?

Risk Management—Asset Protection

- Are their estate documents current? How would they handle LTC? What other risks are they facing?
- What advice can we offer and/or recommendations can we implement to improve their ability to avoid risks in retirement?

Income Taxes

- How can they pay less in taxes? Roth conversion? Capital gains? Enhanced charitable giving? Asset location optimization?
- What advice can we offer and/or recommendations can we implement to reduce their income tax bill?

Investment Portfolio

- Can they consolidate? Can they pay less in fees? How should their portfolio be changed to generate income? Where can their portfolio be improved? What asset allocation do we recommend? Do they have a war chest?
- What advice can we offer and/or recommendations can we implement to improve their portfolio, specifically as it relates to income?

Laser-Focused on What Really Matters

One of the biggest problems with traditional financial plans—and the reason it's so easy for clients to go home and forget about them—is the *huge* disconnect between this dense and intimidating stack of pages and the client's actual life. This makes complete sense: unless you, the financial planner, draw real connections between the information and the actual lived experience of your client, that document is destined for that special filing cabinet under the desk, every time.

I know it's scary. When I first presented someone with a One-Page Financial Plan, I was absolutely sure that they were going to walk. But they said yes.

Still skeptical? Try the "highlighter trick": go through your next long-form financial plan and highlight every line you can find that is actually *personal, actionable,* and *saves the client time.* (Don't worry about running out of ink!) Those highlighted portions are the pieces of the plan that actually matter to the client. Go ahead and guess how many pages it will take to fit it all.

And what about all the junk that's left over? If it doesn't help your client, they don't need it. The unbelievable part is that other advisors hand out all this useless stuff at all.

REMINDER: KEEP SETTING EXPECTATIONS

The OPP is many things, but it's not magic, and it doesn't work all on its own. There's a reason most firms hide behind traditional plans. For the one-page plan to really do its job, it must be part of a carefully designed prospect process that manages client expectations.

As we covered in Chapter 10, you must set and manage these expectations *before* presenting a One-Page Financial Plan, or you risk the prospect being insulted that you "did so little work." Here's how I prepare my client to appreciate the type of value I plan to deliver with my OPP:

"I used to create these really long and elaborate financial plans, but nobody liked to read them except me. With your permission, I'll create a one-page executive summary for you so you know exactly what action needs to be taken without having to read an entire book. Is that OK with you?"

Remember, by asking clients questions you already know the answers to, you can easily get them on the same page and eager to accept your recommendations— especially when they can see those recommendations are designed to make their lives easier.

Anatomy of a One-Page Financial Plan

We've all seen a client's eyes glaze over when we give them far too much information. But as soon as you pass them that OPP, you're going to see something magical happen. Rather than cringe and turn away from the report, your client is going to lean forward, intrigued. Interested. Engaged.

By a financial document.

I know.

What's really happening here? Your client is skimming their one-page plan and doing their own highlighter test, pulling out what's truly personal and relevant to them—and that's *all of it*. (Sure, some of your engineer-brained clients might actually want to see the longer version, and that's fine—but expect that most of your clients will be relieved not to have to.) This is where all that behind-the-scenes work and careful expectation management really pays off: every single word delivers personalized, actionable advice.

In this section, I'm going to show you exactly how to structure your OPP to maximize the space available and hit all the main points a twenty- or fifty-page report would (only better, because your client is actually looking at them).

Primary Goals

I could write an entire book just on the topic of creating an OPP, but it would likely speak to only *one* of the countless niches you could be serving. Instead, what follows is a framework of the questions you should be asking yourself when building the OPP.

Before you can get to the business of helping your clients grow their wealth and achieve their goals, you have to understand what those goals are—and you have to present them in a way that truly matters to the client. Since you've been talking with your clients, you should be able to anticipate their primary goal and help them articulate it. That said, as much as possible, use the client's exact words. If they want to "quit at age 62," that is exactly what you write down. Whatever it is, add it as a "Primary Goal."

Then, after your client's listed goal, add two additional bullet points: "Maintain Dignity and Independence in Retirement" and "Minimize Lifetime Tax Bill." These aren't always top of mind for clients, but I have yet to meet a client who argued with me about including them.

Retirement Income

From here on out, everything in your OPP is listed as a recommendation, and every single word of your document delivers actionable advice. Even so, this section is what will intrigue clients the most: everyone wants to know they'll have enough money when they retire. (If your niche is not retirees, adjust this to whatever speaks most to your niche.)

If the client needs to make changes, start by stating the net monthly income their current portfolio and situation could generate, then make specific recommendations to achieve that. These recommendations might be "Pay off tuition expenses before retiring" or "Confirm pension vs. lump sum options."

Or, if a client is already on track, you may have fewer recommendations to offer. In this case, list out their monthly Social Security benefits and portfolio-generated income so they can review their situation at a glance.

"As soon as you pass them that OPP, you're going to see something magical happen. Rather than cringe and turn away from the report, your client is going to lean forward, intrigued. Interested. Engaged."

Risk Management—Asset Protection

Back in our initial meeting with prospective clients, we played a little coy with clients and talked about "managing risk" to get them thinking about their insurance and long-term-care plans in ways that weren't driven by emotion. This part of the OPP is really just an opportunity to look for holes in their existing plan. (Hint: those clients who provided vague answers to your "What is your strategy for ..." questions will have more recommendations listed here than others.)

Depending on the situation, you might recommend the prospect review their estate documents to make sure they reflect their desires and current laws and update them as necessary. You might recommend they review P&C insurance. You might even recommend that they look at home equity as a quasi-long-term-care policy. Whatever your recommendation, this is where you do that "real financial planning" your client will actually be interested in and benefit from.

Income Taxes

Lots of aging people don't consider the ramifications of unchecked income taxes. Poorly managed, up to 80 percent or even 90 percent of someone's wealth could be lost to the government. I like to tell my clients,

"Don't leave the IRS a tip!"

This is about protecting yourself, but it's also about protecting your wealth so that you can pass it on to loved ones. One recommendation might be to evaluate strategic Roth IRA conversions after retirement. You might recommend that they begin gifting some of that wealth now, while they're around to enjoy the results. Writing checks to family members or picking up a loved one's tuition bill are all ways to accomplish this.

Investment Portfolio

This is the nuts and bolts of the financial plan. With all the data we've collected, we are now able to make recommendations that can dramatically change our client's financial picture. Start with overall recommendations, then get specific with how they should reallocate their investments in order to accomplish the goals listed at the top of the page (their personal, top-of-mind goals, plus the goals you added for them).

For example, a recommendation to a person near retirement age might be to roll other retirement accounts into an IRA to increase flexibility and investment options, simplify tracking, and potentially reduce investment expenses. For a younger person, you might recommend building up their portfolio through more aggressive means. Whatever it is, also include an initial (but specific) plan for reallocating funds. These recommendations might look something like this:

- 35% US Large Companies
- 20% US Small Companies
- 5% US Commercial Real Estate
- 10% International Companies
- 30% Cash and Bonds as "War Chest"

And that's it! With this single page of information, you can arm your potential client with everything they need to take control of their financial life, while sparing them the heavy emotional drain of digging through spreadsheets and following complex information.

"Lots of aging people don't consider the ramifications of unchecked income taxes."

Mr & Mrs Prospect
February 20XX

Primary Goals:
- *Minimize lifetime tax liability*
- *Maintain dignity and independence in retirement*

Retirement Income
Using today's numbers once all income sources are "on" at age 62 (portfolio, pension, Social Security, ex-rental, & ABC share sales), your maximum monthly before-tax income will be approximately $14,000 a month
- Properly structured, your portfolio of approximately $2,200,000 can generate a dynamic income of up to $10,000 in monthly income before taxes
  - Excludes potential additions of ABC ownership sale
- Prioritize retirement, rental, second home, lifestyle, and legacy goals
- Be prepared and plan for the cost of health insurance before and during Medicare
- Estimate tax bracket in retirement and create a forward-looking tax strategy
  - Depreciated rental property
  - Stock ownership sale
  - Roth contributions/conversions

Income Taxes
- In 2021, you paid approximately $170k in taxes to the federal government
- Evaluate restructuring retirement plans for maximum potential tax savings
  - SEP, Solo 401(k), employer contributions, Defined Benefit Plan
- Reprioritize retirement contributions to minimize self-employment taxes
- Evaluate pros and cons of establishing a Donor Advised Fund for charitable gifting
- Review K-1 from ABC company for charitable contributions
- Review tax return for additional potential business deductions and expenses

Risk Management—Asset Protection
- Review estate planning documents
- Review amount of insurance necessary for retirement
- Evaluate payoff of mortgages in retirement

Investment Portfolio
- Review investments within Roth accounts for tax efficiency
- Review use of target date funds for desired goals
- Build a simplified portfolio designed to support long-term income needs in retirement
- Maintain 5–10 years of portfolio income inside of a "war chest"

Supporting Documentation

I've hinted before that a One-Page Financial Plan is really more than a single page. You wouldn't hand someone an executive summary or abstract of a report they couldn't access if they wanted to, and you wouldn't leave a client hanging either.

What you'll include here is up to you, the client, and your firm's compliance requirements. (In any case, be sure to save detailed copies of any projections you ran or information you collected.) Remember to include just the most relevant (and required) information. For more visual learners, you might also have one of your talented support staff create a pie chart of your asset allocation recommendations to include as the second page.

After that, it's all up to you. Just keep the highlighter test in mind, and make sure everything you hand your client is designed to Deliver Massive Value.

TIME TO STOP ASKING—ASSUME!

Remember back at the beginning of this chapter, when we carefully asked clients whether giving them just the salient information about their financial plan was OK with them? (See page 209.) We already knew the answer to the question—"Of *course* I want you to make my finances easy for me to understand!"—but we still asked it in good faith.

But now that it's time to actually show them the OPP, we're no longer asking. At this stage, simply remind them that it's a One-Page Financial Plan. They aren't expecting a hundred-page document, because you've been managing their expectations from the very beginning, and they know exactly what to expect (or, more importantly, what not to expect). At this point, you can safely assume they're on board and present the OPP with the confidence it deserves. Your clients will *love* it.

Action Steps

Whittling a long, overblown document into its most important points isn't just good for your clients; it's a valuable exercise to help you cut through the noise so you can give your clients only what they need. By following these steps, you'll learn to focus solely on the ways you can be most impactful.

- ○ Take your last five financial plans and highlight only those lines that provide specific, personalized, actionable advice. Whatever's left over isn't important enough to bother your clients with.
- ○ Anytime you present a financial plan to a client, ask them which pages they would like to keep and which they'd like you to recycle. (Note what they're actually interested in. Could you fit it on a single page?)
- ○ If you're not ready to let go of your giant financial plans, at least commit to including a one-page executive summary. You just may find that your clients think it's the most valuable part of your presentation.
- ○ Whatever the style or length of your plans, remember to manage expectations every step of the way so you never present your clients with a nasty surprise.

Bonus content available for this chapter at ThePerfectRIA.com/BookBonus:

→ PDF packet of my last two prospects who became clients
→ Access to a recording of my process for creating OPPs
→ Template for creating your own OPPS

CHAPTER 19

Delivering Massive Value in Every Client Meeting

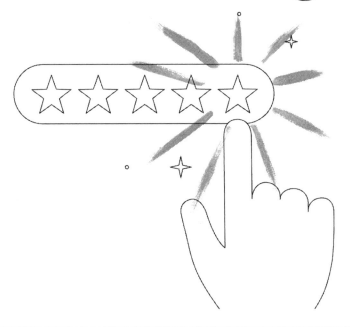

PROFILE OF SUCCESS

"That feeling when a new client brings *all* of the documents you requested ... and it's well organized.

Thank you, Jarvis, for so beautifully laying out your meeting flow and teaching how to value your time and run a practice.

#DeliveringMassiveValue"

Nick Covyeau, CFP
Newport Beach, CA
Swell Financial

I still vividly remember having one of my best clients sitting in my lobby, waiting to meet with me, while I scrambled around in my office gathering information and desperately trying to figure out how I was going to justify my fees. Once I finally sat down with the client—who, by the way, had scheduled this meeting weeks ago—I was frantic and disorganized, and I had to leave the room several times to "get something I left on my desk" (read: to run out and hurl illogical demands at my team to put together last-minute materials and paperwork … which were, unsurprisingly, full of errors).

Ultimately, this led to a terrible experience for both the client and me. Did I learn my lesson? I did eventually, but I'm embarrassed to admit that for the first many years of my career, this was the rule, not the exception. The meetings often ran late, and I rarely Delivered Massive Value. Sound familiar?

Thankfully, after years of trial, error, and learning from some of the most successful advisors in the industry, I've perfected a process for Delivering Massive Value in every single client meeting. In this chapter, I'll walk you through my process for holding highly systematized client meetings that still make every client feel like a VIP.

How to Clear Your Head Trash

Before we dig in, I want to focus on one important point. The *only* way to consistently Deliver Massive Value in client meetings, especially in a surge meeting format (Chapter 2), is by streamlining and systematizing your meeting prep, meeting follow-up, and the meeting itself. In fact, if you sat in on the process in my office, you'd discover that more than 90 percent of every client meeting is exactly the same.

If this idea doesn't sit quite right with you, you're not alone. This idea typically leads to one of two negative responses from struggling advisors:

"But all my clients are unique."

First of all, this head trash screams *victim mindset*, as it focuses you on things outside of your control: the client. At a minimum, flip your mindset to look for similarities between your clients and the ways you interact with them. You don't repaint your conference room and bring in new furniture between each meeting, do you? Of course not—you are already streamlining a large portion of your client meetings. We just want to up the ante. As you study this chapter, instead of focusing on the things you *can't* change, look instead for things that are within your power to implement. For the average advisor, saving just ten minutes per client meeting will result in nearly a week of saved time each year.

To cite more specific examples, we know that every client will need advice in the areas of risk management, cash flow, estate planning, retirement planning, and other common areas. Especially for advisors with a niche, much of what you're already doing can be significantly streamlined. For me and my niche of retirees, I know that every client will need to review their guardrails (Chapter 20) and whatever recent value-add we've completed (Chapter 23). What do the majority of your clients need?

"I want each of my clients to have a unique experience."

I get where you're coming from, I really do. But consider whether the "unique experience" they need is really the one you have in mind.

Imagine getting on an airplane and hearing the pilot announce that she wants you to have a unique experience, and therefore she will not be following her regular checklists and has told air traffic control to leave her alone. Would you be excited or terrified? Imagine your doctor explaining that he's bored with the standard procedure for knee surgery, and for you he's going to try something completely different. Again, would you be excited or terrified?

While we want both pilots and doctors to follow carefully designed proven processes, we also want them to be agile and able to adapt to unique circumstances. Even so, the systems behind 99 percent of their activity are what allows them to Deliver Massive Value when needed. Even in war, as described by Navy SEAL Jocko Willink—where every mission is extremely varied and unpredictable, to say nothing of literal life-and-death consequences—the special ops team streamlines and systematizes everything possible, from how they load their gear to how they talk on the radio, so that as much of their attention and brain power as possible can be focused on dealing with the things they can't control.

Your practice needs to function the same way. Streamline everything possible so that you and your team can Deliver Massive Value where it's needed most. After all, would a client rather you spent your time manually calculating a Roth conversion or listening carefully to their goals, fears, and dreams?

Now, with that head trash out of the way, let's jump into the systems and processes required to Deliver Massive Value in every client meeting, especially during surge weeks.

"For the average advisor, saving just ten minutes per client meeting will result in nearly a week of saved time each year."

Every now and then, a client will say, "Wait—I've got to wait three months to see you? Isn't there any kind of outlet?" I've been preaching the importance of surges for years, but our office still struggles with this. It's so easy to say, "Sure, we can squeeze you in." That's why you need firm structure for your outside-of-surge time, because you *will* receive requests like this.

One word of warning: Don't just break the system; that way lies madness.[23] Instead, create a new system to supplement: block out time every month or so for "mini surges" so that your staff knows to route any appointments outside of surge week to those times.

If you need to, you can also schedule a two- to three-hour block of time (say, Wednesday mornings) for quick phone calls. For example, in my office, we schedule a two-day block (typically Wednesday and Thursday) each month for meetings outside of surge. Unless I'm on vacation, we also leave time open Wednesday afternoon for current clients and Thursday afternoon for calls/meetings with potential clients.

How to Structure Your Client Meetings

Sometimes, the best way to learn is by example. Let's start with a detailed breakdown of how I conduct the meeting itself, and then we'll dive into some of the best practices that will get you there.

Before the Meeting

In my office, when a client walks in, they are always greeted by someone from my team, who offers them a beverage and seats them in our conference room. Unless a client comes unusually early to their meeting, we *never* keep them waiting. During this greeting/seating/beverage process, the relationship manager (RM) is making personal small talk based on what we know about the clients as recorded in our customer relationship manager (CRM) system.

Far from idle chit-chat, this is designed to give the client the feeling that we know them personally (as opposed to many other professionals, for whom they are just a number). I also need the client to have a solid relationship with the RM so

---

1 On very, very rare occasions, a client will have a legitimately urgent, time-sensitive issue (or they will at least *think* they have an urgent, time-sensitive issue) and will insist on a meeting ASAP. In that situation, my team will schedule a time that day or the next morning where I can call the client from wherever I am in the world. This *might* happen once or twice a year, tops—but when an emergency arises, at the end of the day, we can always find a solution.

that they are comfortable going to them with questions and trusting that the RM's recommendations match mine.

Then, at exactly the time of their meeting and not a second later, I walk into the room with a big smile and a very warm greeting. We shake hands, I express how it's always great to see them, and I sit down across from them at the table, subtly matching their body language. Similar to the greeting they received from my team, this is designed to create the experience that I am excited to see them and that I know them personally.

Then, with the clock on the wall behind their head helping me keep on schedule, the meeting proceeds as follows.

Minute 0 to 10: Building Rapport (a.k.a., "Small Talk")

During these first few minutes of our meeting, I ask about their family, recent travels, health, and any other follow-up questions I have from our rapport-building during our last meeting. For example, during our fall meetings, I might ask how they enjoyed the summer and if they have any big plans for the upcoming holidays, followed by a question or two about known hobbies, health issues, and/or family situations. I'm very careful not to pry, and all of my questions come from my sincere interest in their well-being.

Why is this important? While this time does serve the purpose of building rapport, it also gives me as a financial planner valuable insight into their goals and personal situation. After all, if they've always wanted to take a big expensive trip or they've got serious medical issues, this factors into my planning.

Note that in this portion of the meeting, as with all of the meeting, it's critical that you steer clear of politics or any other potentially polarizing topics. Why? Even if you both agree on the issues, nearly all political discussions are negative, and your office is a place of positivity. Even in sad situations (e.g., terminal illness, family death, etc.), stay focused on the positive, and avoid complaining, criticizing, or otherwise dwelling on things no one can control.

If asked—and only if asked—I will spend a few minutes talking about my life and family. This, however, stays very brief, as this is not a social setting where stories are exchanged in a balanced fashion. Instead, *you* are the one being paid to have this conversation; as much as possible, keep the focus on your client.

Rookie advisors (a.k.a., me early in my career) will think this rapport-building time is a waste. "After all," I used to think, "they are coming to me for financial advice, not friendship." This attitude is a mistake. Your clients and prospects are trusting you with their financial future—with all their hopes and dreams—and when the world goes crazy, at the end of the day, they are trusting your advice almost entirely based on the relationship capital you've established. Don't skip it!

Minute 10 to 15: *Their* Questions and Concerns

As soon as the small talk is wrapped up, I always begin every single client meeting with this line:

> "I've got several things for us to cover today, but first, what questions or concerns do you have?"[2]

This is critical, because if a client does have an urgent question, they will almost certainly ignore everything you say until that issue is addressed. To pick an extreme example from my own practice, I recently had a client pause dramatically in response to this question and sit quietly, contemplating her answer. Fighting my urge to keep talking, I sat quietly waiting for her to answer. After what seemed like an eternity, she explained that she had just been diagnosed with stage 4 cancer, but she hadn't planned on telling anyone, even me.

Setting aside the major financial planning implications of this life event, imagine how our meeting would have gone had I not given her the opportunity to lead with her questions and concerns. While I waxed lyrical about long-term planning and guardrails, she likely would be totally focused on her very short life expectancy and wouldn't hear a word I said.

Certainly, not all of your clients will have a bomb of this magnitude to drop. A more common occurrence is that a client, feeling the need to be polite, will ask that you go first, and they will ask their remaining questions at the end. When this happens to me, I like to gently counter that I always like them to go first so that I can incorporate the answers into anything else we are discussing.

Whatever the outcome of this question—whether it's a confession of a major life event like stage 4 cancer or a simple "I just want to make sure everything is OK"— by simply asking the question, you're Delivering Massive Value. Where else in the client's professional (or even personal) life does someone take a genuine interest in their questions and concerns? This is especially true for your more senior clients, who remember a more personal era and who now see doctors who treat them like just another cog in the machine to be processed as quickly as possible.

Start by acknowledging that we've heard them, we value their question, and answering it is our top priority. Some questions require just a simple answer, others

---

2 Notice that I didn't say, "Do you have any questions?" That question would be too easy to answer with a "no." It's difficult to overstate the value and importance of this question, along with its follow-up question: "What else?" Why is this? The client is here for their own reasons, which includes anything that is on their mind. They did not come for you, your agenda, or whatever is important to you (at least not until their needs have been met). By leading with this question, I'm inviting the client to share what is on their mind.

can be jotted down and answered when you get to that part of the meeting, and others—like the cancer diagnosis—mean throwing everything you had previously planned out the window. The one other type of response/question are those that you can't answer during this meeting, questions that require you to do some research. In that case, I use this simple script:

> "That's a great question, and while I could come up with a back-of-the-napkin answer, I'd like to crunch some more numbers first. I've written down your question, and would it be OK if I got you the answer by [date/time]?"

"Start by acknowledging that we've heard them, we value their question, and answering it is our top priority"

Minute 15 to 30: Add Value

Once all their questions have been answered, scheduled, and/or deferred, we can launch into the next portion of our meeting.

As discussed in Chapter 11, each calendar quarter, we proactively send a value-add to every client that focuses on some aspect of the financial planning process. In addition to setting us apart from other advisors, it also gives us a talking point during our meeting, especially if we discover something that needs review. To pick just one example, perhaps we had just sent out a value-add reviewing their strategy for long-term care. In that case, during the meeting, I would pull out a printed copy of what we had sent them and walk through it together, highlighting areas where they had done well and areas where improvements could be made.

By doing quarterly value-adds, we can streamline this area of the financial planning process, constantly Deliver Massive Value, and always have something valuable to discuss during the client's meeting.

While I always have this quarter's value-add ready to present, if the client has other concerns and/or some significant life event, I always have the option to table the value-add until we've solved the time-sensitive issue at hand, as well as any highly customized issues that don't fit the standardized value-add process.

Whatever the topic, by the bottom of the hour, we've gotten through it and have recorded any related action items.

Minute 30 to 40: Guardrails

As will be discussed in Chapter 20, guardrails are one of the most valuable tools in my practice, as they show clients in very easy-to-understand terms how much they can safely take from their nest egg. Because this is such an important tool, and because it requires the client to be willing to take pay cuts in down markets, I make sure to review it in every meeting.

If your clients are not retirement-focused, or if you are not a fan of guardrails, you need something equally easy to understand that benchmarks their progress toward their goals. Whatever the tool, we spend five to ten minutes reviewing their status.

Minute 40 to 50: Portfolio Review

Once we've reviewed the value-add and the guardrails, now (and only now) we'll do a review of their nest egg. For most of my clients, this is a quick review of how much money they are up or down this past year and since inception. (Remember to talk about this in dollars, never percentages.) We also take a look at how much money (cash/fixed income) is in their war chest, translated into years of income.

> "Ms. Client, as you can see here, we've got some $400,000 in the war chest, which would cover your monthly income for about five years. In other words, should the market take a big hit, we'd have five years to ride it out."

Then, at *exactly* minute 50, my RM gently knocks on the door, cracks it open, and smiles at me. I respond with a big smile and say, "Thank you for keeping me on track." This gentle reminder helps both me and the client know that it's time to wrap up our discussion.

Minute 50 to 60: Questions and Expectations

Just after the reminder from my RM, I wrap up my current thought and then—as at the beginning of our meeting—I ask, "What other questions or concerns did you have?" I also take a minute to review with them my written action items, along with who is going to complete them and by when. I also take a moment to set expectations for when we will meet again.

Then, wherever the meeting takes us, I always end with, "Odds are as soon as you leave you'll think of a question or concern you forgot to mention. When that happens, be sure to call or email our office."

Tips for Surge Success

Make no mistake: flipping your entire client calendar on its head can be overwhelming—but the benefits you'll reap are worth the effort. With this framework for conducting your client meetings, you'll be well on your way to streamlining your conversation topics and value-adds.

As you put it all together, keep these tips in mind for avoiding common pitfalls, and maximizing your efficiency, and making every client feel like you're doing it all just for them.

Set Good Expectations

Keeping meetings focused on the topic means continuing to set expectations—and this starts well before your client ever walks in the door.

Three weeks before your client review meetings, start to assemble your plan to contact all of your clients based on client level. Then, two weeks out, send an email to invite your clients to their review meeting. For ideas, look at this example of the letter we send our clients:

> Dear Client,
>
> We hope this email finds you well and [something specific to the time of the year]. [Your advisor] will be doing client review meetings next month, and we would like to schedule some time to talk with you to get an update on your life, goals, and dreams, as well as give you some updates on how we are keeping your nest egg hard at work for you and review your plans for [quarterly value-add topic].
>
> To schedule a meeting in our office, a video meeting over the internet, or simply a phone call, please respond to this email or click on the link below to directly access our calendar. We look forward to seeing you soon.
>
> —Your team at Jarvis Financial
>
> P.S. If you haven't yet, please check out our upcoming event on [topic] and be sure to RSVP.

This email sets the tone for what you'll be discussing, and it's a good opportunity to remind clients of whatever you've got going on in your marketing calendar.

Never Be Late

There is never an excuse to be late to a client meeting. *Never.*

Yes, I know traffic was bad (not an excuse), your family was sick (not an excuse), and you got an urgent phone call (still not an excuse), but you told the client you would meet at a specific time. Either do what it takes to be on time, or in very, very rare scenarios—I'm talking once a year, *maybe*—notify the client the second you realize you might be late and try to reschedule.

Any time you are late, it is because you did not respect the person's time. As soon as you start running late, it burns up your buffer time—or worse, forces the next client to wait past their allotted start time. To prevent this from happening, make sure there's a wall clock somewhere in your conference room positioned somewhere you can see without actually looking at it. In other words, the client shouldn't be able to notice you looking at the clock.

Better yet, organize your life so you are never late. For example, my goal is to be at the office thirty minutes before my first meeting, thus giving me plenty of buffer time. I also stop looking at emails, answering phone calls, or engaging in any other distractions at least five minutes before the meeting. For phone calls, two minutes before the meeting, I have their number typed into my phone so their phone rings at *exactly* the scheduled time.

Never Go Over Time

No matter how urgent the topics that come up in the meeting, we never go over the time allotted for the meeting.

Why? Lots of reasons. The first is that you likely have another meeting after this one, and by running late in one meeting, you risk making all of your clients late too. More importantly, the client likely has other plans for their day, and by allowing the meeting to run late (even at the client's request), you are setting them up to run late all day. Perhaps most importantly, research shows that longer meetings are less effective: there is a limit on how long you and the client can stay engaged in the meeting, and that margin of diminishing returns hits very quickly. I recommend scheduling meetings for no more than an hour. Be concise, get to the point, and move on.

If we start using up the allocated ten minutes, I'll begin shifting the discussion back to the agenda with comments such as "We've got several topics to cover today, so we'd better jump in to make sure we get you out of here on time."

If a topic comes up that is truly too much to handle in one meeting, don't be afraid to schedule another one. Simply say, "It looks like we need to schedule a second meeting to finish this discussion. My team can get that scheduled for you before you leave." It works like a charm!

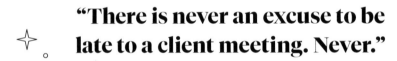

"There is never an excuse to be late to a client meeting. Never."

Make Every Meeting Your Best Performance

You may be walking into your fifteenth meeting of the week or your fiftieth meeting of the surge cycle, but for your client, it's their first and only meeting with you. Just because you gave an amazing performance in all your other meetings that week, that does not mean you can slack off in this one.

Here are a handful of things you and your rockstar team can do to stay at the top of your game:

• **Have a rescue plan.** Approximately ten minutes before the end of each meeting, have someone from your team knock gently on the door, crack it open, and smile at you. This is a signal, both to you and the client, that it's time to wrap up. To ensure the client notices the signal, respond to the door opening with "Thanks for keeping me on schedule."

- **Use your buffer time to recharge.** It can be tempting to come out of one meeting, run around putting out fires, and then jump into the next meeting. While it sounds nice to chalk this up to extreme productivity, odds are you'll burn out. Instead, get a drink (of water), use the bathroom, walk outside, review notes for your next meeting, and then get after it.

- **Have your personal life in order, at least during surge.** Prior to surge weeks, make sure all your suits and shirts have been dry-cleaned, your shoes polished, and anything else is in order for the week. This way, each morning, all you need to do is grab the next outfit on the shelf and you're good to go for another great day of client meetings.

- **Keep your evenings light and get to bed early.** During surge weeks, your only scheduled non-work activity is working out and vegging with loved ones—period. No dinners out, no social activities, nothing complicated.

- **Stay nourished.** During surge, make sure to eat great meals, which includes bringing in food for your team each day. Consider sandwiches or something equally easy.

DON'T BE REACTIVE: FLIP THE SCRIPT!

We've talked before about why it's so important to schedule calls ahead of time—but when push comes to shove, do you and your team have what it takes to stick to your guns?

"I need to talk with ..."

The most common request your team receives is likely a request or demand to see the principal service provider—you. In most offices, the team will respond to this request with something like this:

"Let me put you on hold to see if the advisor is available."

Never do this. Never. Never. Never! Here's what your team is really telling your clients: "Let me check whether you are important enough for the advisor to talk with."

And that's not the only pitfall you're likely to encounter when you allow yourself to react to the whim of your clients. When you decide to pick up the phone, you've interrupted your flow (strike one). You were not expecting the call, so you're likely a bit flustered (strike two). And because you're unprepared, you're scrambling to find the information you need to answer the client's request (strike three!). Even worse, nine times out of ten, the client wants or needs something that your team could have handled without your involvement.

Let's look at how the scenario might unfold if your team had responded a little bit differently:

> Client: "Hello. Can I speak with [Advisor]?"
> Rockstar Team: "Hello Mr./Mrs. Client! [Advisor] would love to speak with you, but he/she is not available at this moment. Is there something I can help you with?"
> Client: "I don't think you can help. When can I talk with [Advisor]?"
> Rockstar Team: "[Advisor]'s next client meeting days are [date] and [date], but if this is time sensitive, I can have him/her give you a call on [date later that week, if possible]."
> Client: "Great. Please schedule the call."
> Rockstar Team: "Perfect! So that [Advisor] can be best prepared for your meeting, what can I tell him/her it is regarding?"
>
> Compared to the first scenario, this one produces an infinitely better client experience.
>
> Further, when the client explains why they need to talk with you, it will very likely turn out to be something your team can handle. For example:
>
> Client: "I have a new bank account and need to change the link on my Fidelity accounts."
> Rockstar Team: "Great news! I can take care of that for you right now. [Solves the problem.] Now, would you still like to meet with the advisor?"
>
> Typically, if your rockstar team really can solve their problem, the client won't need to see you at all. And if the team really can't handle the request, I can go into the scheduled meeting totally prepared to Deliver Massive Value to the client and potentially solve any issues before the meeting even starts.

With all these behind-the-scenes details in order and everyone in their places, your rockstar team will be prepared to crush every single surge meeting while making every client feel like a rockstar too.

Check In and Fine-Tune

As with every other strategy for Delivering Massive Value, surge meetings work only if you take the time to implement them—but they *improve* only if you *take the time to improve them.*

When you wrap up a surge week, quarterly value-add, or any other process, don't just file it away for next time. Systems improve by feedback loops, so it's important to review with the team what worked and what didn't so the next surge can be even more effective. After each surge week, hold a meeting to discuss the following questions about how you did and what changes you'll make next time:

- What systems worked?
- What systems failed?

- What did we learn for next time?
- How could we improve the client experience?
- How will we celebrate?

Remind yourself of your goals and objectives, and look closely at how close you came to achieving them. What roadblocks stood in your way? What didn't flow as smoothly during that client meeting? What slide in the presentation didn't seem to connect? Take the time to reflect on these major experiences and draw specific lessons that you can apply to your business.

Trust the System

With the One-Page Financial Plan making all the action steps really easy, that means that each quarter, you're free to tackle a new subject for all of your clients. You never have to wonder, "When was the last time I looked at a Roth conversion for Client X?" The answer is the same as for any other client: whether it's beneficiaries, estate documents, or a lot of tax planning, you're doing it for everybody.

Whatever it is, by systematizing our information and sending the same thing out to all our clients, we can say, "Hey, if you have concerns about this, give us a call. Come in during the next meeting surge." But we're doing the same topic across the board, which always keeps us on task and delivering the highest possible value.

Action Steps

You've spent almost an entire book setting good expectations and preparing your staff and clients to Deliver Massive Value during surge week. Now it's time to set it all in motion. Follow these steps and you'll be well on your way to surge success!

○ If you haven't done it already, implement surge week! This will bring all your clients to your office during the same short time span, so you don't have to spend every day preparing for meetings.

○ And if you haven't done *this* already, develop your marketing calendar! This will get all your clients on the same information rotation, so you always know when you last covered any given topic.

○ Put together a welcome pack for every client meeting. With a marketing calendar tied closely to your goals for meeting surges, this welcome pack is perfectly targeted to every client and perfectly in line with your goals for your business and your client's portfolio.

Bonus content available for this chapter at ThePerfectRIA.com/BookBonus:
→ PDF of our email invites to schedule meetings
→ PDF of our most recent client meeting agenda
→ Access to recorded training on client meetings

CHAPTER 20

Staying on Track with Retirement Guardrails

PROFILE OF SUCCESS

"This is the best FA practice management book I've ever read or listened to, and I've listened to a lot over the years.

It certainly delivered massive value for me and my practice. I've been in the business for sixteen years, and it took me years of missteps to learn some of the lessons you clearly articulated in your book. We're implementing some client pruning and moving toward a surge meeting schedule now and look forward to the freedom it yields. Thanks for sharing your wisdom and being so straight-up about everything."

Ryan Kittredge, CFP
Northborough, MA
Clear Path Financial Partners

I f you're like me, you've spent large portions of your career obsessing over the dark arts of financial planning software.

I used to spend hours carefully massaging the inputs until the magic eight-ball of my software would display "86 percent probability of success"—never mind that with enough tampering, you could get any output you wanted. It would (eventually) look something like this:

But I soon realized that telling a client they have an 86 percent probability of funding their goals wasn't helping them, and I wasn't at all confident in the "recommendations" being presented by the software. For years, I tried out almost every financial planning software in our industry looking for a tool that would clearly tell the client how much they could take out in retirement, how they could respond to good or bad markets, exactly where they stood in retirement, and if they could take out that extra $100,000 to buy a fancy RV. Not being able to answer these questions with confidence really bothered me, so I kept searching for a better method. This search eventually led me to create my retirement income guardrails.

When I look back on my journey from failure to success, it's easy to get hung up on the hundreds of mistakes that fill my heart with regret, shame, and a general feeling of "what an idiot." However, I now realize that from the ashes of these mistakes came one of the most important discoveries of my career. Second only to the One-Page Financial Plan from Chapter 18, retirement income guardrails are the most important prospecting and client tool in my practice. (My good friend Micah Shilanski and I like to debate which is more important, guardrails or income buckets, but I remain convinced that guardrails are the single best retirement income tool in our industry. I only wish I had discovered them sooner!)

In this chapter, I'll show you how to develop, implement, and bring your client onboard with the retirement income guardrails that will keep their investments on track and moving forward for years to come.

Probabilities Suck

While the particular financial planning software you are using may produce a slightly different version of this report, they all fail to answer the single biggest question every client is asking when they approach retirement:

"Will I run out of money and die?"

This isn't just fruitless worrying on the client's part. Humans have been around for something like four hundred generations, and only in the past three of those—the past hundred years or so—have the majority of humans even *considered* retirement. For pretty much all of human history, when you stop working, *you die.* In other words, when a client retires, all of their biological programs start screaming that their time is up. It's no wonder that even the wealthiest clients get nervous about retirement.

You might think that the more informed a client is, the more comfortable they'll feel—but is a chart like the one shown above really imparting useful information to your client?

Given this emotional state, there is almost zero chance that the client will understand a graphic containing hundreds of squiggly lines, let alone take comfort in it. Even if the client could block out these emotions, what exactly are they supposed to learn from the dozens of different assumptions in this chart—that they'll run out of money in less than ten years, or that at age 127 they'll still have $10,000,000 in assets? Not super helpful.

Worse yet, the computer-generated "86 percent probability of success" tells them nothing about how much they can safely take from their nest egg each month, what to do when the markets go down, or what they can do during bull markets. It certainly does not answer their core question/fear about running out of money in retirement. There had to be a better way.

Monte Carlos and Marshmallows

The Monte Carlo simulation may be the sacred cow of our industry, but I always cringed at presenting complex Monte Carlo–based financial plans to answer a client's question. Instead of allowing both the advisor and the client to focus on the real goal, I found these meetings got way too in the weeds, and the client's concerns became fragmented into questions that really didn't help us get a grasp on the larger plan.

For example, if a client asks me about taking out a hundred thousand dollars to buy an RV, we might find that the Monte Carlo simulation moves them from 86 percent to 74 percent—but what does that mean? If 74 is too low, what's the right number? For all its strengths, the simulation doesn't help me answer the questions the client is really asking:

- "Why 74 percent? I want to be 100 percent!"
- "What about that line showing me running out of money in fifteen years? I don't want that!"
- "Can't we just take this top line that shows me with ten million dollars?"
- "Can I or can't I take out that money?"

The thing is, all this talk about "Monte Carlo illustrations" and "probability of success" is fine for us financial advisors, who know how to use the simulation and place the data in their proper contexts—but these phrases mean *nothing* to a client. To be clear, I'm not disrespecting clients or their ability to follow an explanation. The fact is that they hired *us* to do that thinking. They paid us to manage their money, not distill all our training and experience into one meeting (an impossible task).

You might as well substitute all those phrases—along with all your other industry jargon, including "percentage," "rate of return," "alpha," "standard deviation," and even "diversification"—with the word "marshmallow." Why? Because saying "marshmallow" again and again would be just as useful as trying to force-feed clients a bunch of jargon they don't understand.

Stop talking to your clients like they're trained business advisors! They'll never measure up, and they won't enjoy the feeling. Instead, start looking for ways to speak their language.

A Better Way

Inspired by Jonathan Guyton's work on dynamic distribution rates, I realized that while the strategy I developed is far from perfect, it clearly articulates to the client how much money they can safely take from their next egg, what happens when the markets go down, and how much room they have for extra distributions before causing a problem. In other words, it clearly answers the client's core question.

This chapter isn't intended to be a primer on distribution rates or how guardrails work; a quick Google or Kitces.com search for "dynamic distribution rates" or "Guyton" will give you all the technical data you need. Instead, this chapter focuses on implementing these guardrails in real life and how to communicate that plan to your clients.

> **"Stop talking to your clients like they're trained business advisors! They'll never measure up, and they won't enjoy the feeling. Instead, start looking for ways to speak their language."**

So, if we're taking all the industry jargon and marshmallow fluff out of play, how do you actually answer your client's question? Here's how I like to explain guardrails to my clients:

"Mr. & Mrs. Client, when it comes to retirement, running out of money is never an option. That said, leaving behind a mattress stuffed full of money is also not winning the game. As such, we need a strategy that keeps us somewhere between the two, no matter what. However, there are two major unknowns that make this very tricky.

First, we don't have any idea how long you will be retired, which is a nice way of saying we don't know how long you will live. If we did know, this would be easy, and we could bounce the last check on your way out the door. However, to be safe, we plan for you to spend thirty to forty years in retirement.

Second, we don't know what the markets will do. All we know is that at times, they will go way up, and at other times, they will go way down. It's a little like starting a car trip without knowing the distance to our destination and with no map on how to get there.

Since we don't know the length of your retirement or how the markets will respond, we've devised a strategy, similar to driving on a winding mountain road, which we like to call "guardrails."

[Here's where you'll show them your printed guardrails report.]

With your nest egg of $1,000,000, we will start retirement by taking $4,500 of income each month. This income will continue so long as your nest egg stays between $800,000 and $1,200,000. If we drop below $800,000, either because of bad markets or because you decide to take a big distribution—let's say, to buy a $100,000 RV—we will plan to temporarily reduce your income to $4,000 until your nest egg recovers.

By being willing to tighten our belts during the bad times, we can safely take a lot more income during the good times. Is this OK with you?"

Most clients love this explanation, and they love the illustration.

Sure, a few will push back, asking about things like the 4 percent rule or assumed rates of returns. Most of these concerns can be addressed with the following explanation:

> "When asked the worst time in modern history to retire,
> most people think of the Great Depression. As bad as things
> were in the Great Depression, the worst time to retire in modern
> history was actually 1972. Not only did you have the bear market of
> '73–'74, when the markets fell 50 percent, but it was followed by more
> than a decade of extreme inflation. The guardrails worked in this
> period and every other period we've seen. While this is certainly
> no guarantee that it will work in every future scenario, based on
> everything we know and can control, guardrails are our best strategy."

If the client continues to press you about the 4 percent rule or any other fixed distribution rate, you might use the following explanation (and if you know the client's nest egg, do the math and incorporate the numbers as you explain):

> "Generally speaking, the 4 percent rule tells you to take
> out 4 percent of your current nest egg balance every year,
> no matter what. With that strategy, whether the markets do really
> good or really bad, you're still taking out the same amount. Using
> guardrails allows us to take out more when times are good, in
> exchange for being willing to tighten our belts when times are bad."

If the client/prospect has already agreed to hiring you, excellent—but if they are still on the fence even after they've bought into your guardrails strategy, outline why they need your team to implement it. Here's the script I use for this:

> "One of the reasons most firms and individuals use the 4
> percent rule is that it's very easy to implement. Just do the
> math once, set up the monthly distribution, and you're on
> autopilot for the rest of your life (or until you run out of
> money). On the other hand, for guardrails to work, we need
> to constantly monitor and adjust your portfolio, including
> maintaining a 'war chest' of cash and bonds, strategically
> rebalancing for income, and adjusting course when you hit a
> guardrail. That's what my team is prepared to do for you."

Who could say no to that?

The "War Chest"

As discussed elsewhere in this book, jargon has no place in client communication, and one of the more powerful examples of this is telling a client they have "30 percent in fixed income."

Almost no one can easily do percentages in their head, and if asked to articulate the benefits and costs of fixed income, at best they would give you a mumbled response. Knowing this and knowing the alternatives is one of the many seemingly little things that separates truly exceptional advisors from the merely above-average advisors.

In my office, we almost never use the term "fixed income"; instead, as you saw in the script above, we use the concept of a "war chest." When we explain the war chest to our clients, it goes something like this:

"Mr. & Mrs. Client, while we can't predict when or where the next bad market will hit, we can say with total confidence that it will hit during your retirement, likely several times. In fact, Murphy's law says that the moment you quit your job, the markets will go down, a lot. As such, we need to be prepared with a five-year war chest of cash, bonds, and other really safe, really stable investments. This way, when—not if—the markets go down, we have five years to ride it out before needing to sell anything at a loss.

To give you an example of this, let's say you retired in 2007 just before the 2008–2009 financial crisis hit. As you watched the value of your investments get cut in half, we would have had five years of protection from our war chest. In other words, 2008, 2009, 2010, 2011, and 2012 would have all been covered. While a five-year buffer didn't get us totally back to all-time market highs, it did give us five years of safety through the worst of the decline.

What this looks like behind the scenes is that every calendar quarter, if the markets are up, we will top off your war chest. When—not if—the markets are down, we'll use your war chest until the markets are up again. Is this OK with you?"

Educate Yourself First

Before you go running out to clients telling them about guardrails and war chests, make sure *you* totally understand how this strategy works during good times and bad, and have systems for implementing this approach. For example, most asset managers and portfolio management systems will arbitrarily make cash proportional across all the investments in a client's account, which often means selling equities at a loss (rather than taking it strictly from fixed income) when the markets are down.

In our office, we run this process manually, and I recommend you do the same. That doesn't mean the process shouldn't be systematized; as I type this, *The Perfect RIA* is rolling out a platform for guardrails. But either way, it's on you to make sure you can actually implement any system you adopt.

WHEN TO ADJUST

I recommend treating your guardrails document as a static document, either a PDF or a printed page, while reviewing it with clients. But what if you end up wanting to make changes to your guardrails?

If the client asks you for a variation, simply do some back-of-the-napkin calculations for now, and tell them you'll follow up with an adjusted guardrail document soon. You should never actually work on tweaking your guardrails in real time with the client; you don't want to take up their time, and you certainly don't want to pull away the curtain to reveal all the magic behind what you're doing.

Why Use Guardrails?

It's shocking but true: not every financial advisor uses the guardrail system. But you and I aren't *every financial advisor;* we're totally committed to giving our clients the most reliable advice possible. Based on my own experience, guardrails are the most useful, easy-to-explain tools by which any financial advisor can keep their client on track.

So why does implementing guardrails have such an incredible impact on the value you can deliver?

Makes It Virtually Impossible to Run Out of Money

The biggest benefit to using guardrails is that they *work*. No one can guarantee 100 percent success, of course—but that's not what I'm promising. Instead, I can promise exactly what I'm offering: the *highest chance* of success. If anything, this strategy is more likely to err on the side of paying clients an income they don't need than to leave them high and dry.

Of course, as one of my audience members once pointed out, a higher probability of success can equal a higher probability of *excess*—and we definitely don't want to leave clients with a mattress full of money. That's why having these projections outlined in terms of upper and lower guardrails lets us see at a glance when we're approaching that upper limit, and we can periodically reallocate that extra amount in other ways.

Makes My Job Easier

One of the things I love about the guardrail is that it works for me. Whatever happens to the client, in their lives or in their finances, I just look at it as a matter of math.

Remember the two main issues with addressing the client's wealth after retirement: we don't know how long their retirement will last, and we don't know what the markets will do. Now, because we always want to be somewhere in between these guardrails, I know exactly how to pivot for any scenario, and I know exactly how to articulate that to the client.

When they say, "Hey, I want to pull out X amount of money," I can say,

> "Well, let's pull out the guardrails and look at what that scenario would mean."

(I always have it handy.)

If it looks like the change is going to keep the client within that buffer, I'll say,

> "Great news! We're still above the lower guardrail. Go ahead and take the money—just be warned that we've used up a lot of that buffer, and it won't take much of a market downturn for that to have to be reset."

If it looks like we're approaching (or blowing through) the lower guardrail, I'll say this:

> "To respond to these new conditions, we'll temporarily reduce your pay until the markets come back up."

Sometimes I'll even suggest that clients tighten their belts: another great way to visualize what's needed without getting stuck in numbers or wrapped up in fear. However you put it, if you've been setting good expectations, none of this will be unexpected news to your clients.

Works for Almost Every Situation

A market downturn isn't the only event that can threaten to derail your carefully laid financial plans. Lots of things could happen in a client's life that might be disruptive to their finances, both expected and unexpected:

- Divorce
- Illness
- Death in the family
- Foreclosure

Whatever happens to make a client blow through their lower guardrail, you have powerful systems in place to handle 80 percent to 90 percent of the scenarios that come up—and when you need to whip out the guardrails and readjust, your client is right there with you. You, as the advisor, haven't become their spouse or their parents, saying, "Hey, you can't spend that money!" You're a trusted partner in their life planning.

Before I had figured out guardrails, we'd run the numbers that would take the client from an 83 percent probability of success to a 79 percent probability of success ... whatever *that* means. With guardrails, I always have a clear explanation of what we're doing. Whatever situation your client will face, you'll be able to meet it together as a team.

The #1 Key to Guardrail Success

For any of your guardrail strategies to really work to take your clients through the tighter times, clients have to actually be willing to take a reduced income. And just because they agreed to your strategy once, that doesn't mean they'll always act consistently with the theoretical agreement they made several years ago.

That's why, with *every* client meeting, you *must* reiterate the guardrail plan. You have to be talking about what the client might change in their lifestyle to accommodate that reduction, so that when—not if!—they have to move to that reduced income, they know exactly what that looks like for them and exactly what to expect.

Action Steps

It should be clear by now that guardrails are the best way to keep both you and your client on track with their financial goals, regardless of the client's current concerns or what's going on in the news. Just follow these steps to implement guardrails in your own practice.

○ Ditch the Monte Carlo—and ditch the lingo. You know what really matters to your clients, so cut everything that doesn't out of your client communication. (In other words: Stop feeding your clients marshmallows. They deserve better.)

○ Keep learning. Yes, guardrails are a system—but this system works best when it's carefully monitored and manually adjusted, and that means honing your investment knowledge and staying up to date so you can deliver the value your clients expect. No slacking!

○ Keep setting expectations with clients that dealing with uncertain times means tightening their belt. Don't just have this conversation in a single meeting; have it in *every single meeting*.

> **HOW DID I SCREW THIS UP?!?**
> Not sure how I wrote an entire chapter on guardrails without a single sample! On page 282 you can see a sample and there are multiple samples in the chapter bonuses.

Bonus content available for this chapter at ThePerfectRIA.com/BookBonus:
→ PDF samples of our guardrails reports
→ Links to the technical background of guardrails
→ Recording of me presenting guardrails to a clients

CHAPTER 21

Tax Planning

PROFILE OF SUCCESS

"Every day I talk with advisors who have exponentially increased their value to clients by providing tax planning.

At almost the same frequency, I hear from consumers asking to be referred to advisors who actually *do* tax-planning. And yes, I am the better looking brother :)"

Steven Jarvis, CPA
Spokane, WA
Retirement Tax Services

I have to admit, tax planning is one of my favorite topics. I *love* to nerd out about it. But it's not just a hobby (and it's not because I'm eying a career change either!). In fact, I believe this obsession has given me an almost unfair advantage over many other financial planners.

Here's what I mean. I had a new prospect come in recently who opened by saying, "Matthew, I just want you to know I'm comparing you with other planners."

Now, I don't know if he was trying to intimidate me or just being honest, but I said, "That's perfect! In fact, you can use the One-Page Financial Plan I'll assemble for you as a guide for evaluating all the other planners you may be considering."

Then, this client dropped the name of the firm they were comparing me to, which happened to be headquartered not far from my office. (I won't name them, because I don't need enemies there; suffice it to say they're one of the largest RIA firms in the country.)

Challenge accepted.

I smiled and said to the prospect, "That's really great. Just curious: what did they say when they reviewed your tax return?"

He gave me a funny look and said, "Well, they didn't look at my tax return. In fact, I was going to ask you why you wanted a copy of it."

As a financial advisor yourself, by now you're probably wondering the same thing: why is your client's tax return any of *your* business?

In this chapter, you'll learn why your client's tax life is *totally* your business—and how you can take this opportunity to help your client save money wherever you can, look like an absolute hero to your clients, and make your reputation soar.

Why Taxes Matter

Just to be clear, in almost no case does it make sense for a financial advisor to get into the business of *preparing* tax returns. In most cases, tax preparation is a purely commoditized, low-margin business where very few tax preparers earn any kind of ROI for the expertise required to do this right. However, tax *planning* is a totally different ball game—one that you can, with some effort, win almost every time.

So why is tax planning so effective at making you stand out?

Nobody Else Is Doing It

At least for now, most of the major investment firms steer away from any kind of tax planning. There are some legal/compliance reasons for this, but part of it is simply a lack of expertise. Especially for the big firms, they already have all the AUM they want, so there's no real incentive for them to add another layer of complexity or liability. Don't be discouraged; the big dogs' lack of interest in tax planning is a *huge* potential windfall for you, as I'm guessing the fact that you're reading this book indicates that you are still looking to take on more clients.

In addition to giving you an advantage over so many other firms, odds are that even the client's tax preparer (including nearly every CPA and EA) is focusing all of their attention on reporting what happened last year, and *maybe* they're spending a few minutes trying to reduce this year's tax liability. As part of my COI marketing strategy and in my work with advisors around the country, I've talked with hundreds of tax preparers, and I've found maybe a handful who do meaningful tax planning. (Somewhere, someone reading this is a CPA and is screaming at the book that they do meaningful tax planning—to which I gladly say: good for you!)

So what does all of this mean to you? Not only will tax planning differentiate you from the competition, but you will also be providing a service to the client that they are in all likelihood getting nowhere else. How's that for Delivering Massive Value?

Taxes Move the Emotional Needle

At least in America—though I suspect it is a universal part of human nature—we all abhor paying taxes. Put more precisely, we all abhor the idea that we are paying *too much* in taxes. As such, when you can show clients how to reduce their tax bill, even by a relatively insignificant amount, you quickly become their hero.

Let me give you an example. Several years ago, I met with a prospect who worked with a very respected (and expensive) CPA. Like most higher income earners, this prospect—we'll call her Jane—complained about having to pay too much in taxes. Her biggest gripe? The Medicare premium surcharge for those making "too much" income. Now, keep in mind that relative to her approximately $10 million net worth, the combined $800 a month in premiums for her and her husband were, relatively speaking, a rounding error, but they really upset her.

In reviewing her tax return, I discovered that by changing her small business retirement plan (and later through QCDs), we could pull her income just below the highest limit, thus saving her a few thousand a year in Medicare premiums. I almost didn't share this strategy with her at all, as the benefit seemed so small compared to her assets/income. However, when I did mention it, she was ecstatic and hired me immediately, and she was furious with her CPA for not pointing out the strategy. (I later learned that the CPA had considered this strategy but didn't bother sharing it because she thought it wasn't material.)

"Not only will tax planning differentiate you from the competition, but you will also be providing a service to the client that they are in all likelihood getting nowhere else."

Taxes Are an Easily Quantifiable Benefit

As I shared in Chapter 10, I tell every prospect,

> "It only makes sense to hire an advisor if the value they provide is worth some multiple of the fee they charge."

Tax planning is a very clean way to demonstrate this value. For example, if I map out for a prospect how much they will be paying in taxes over the next several years, and then show how working together can reduce that amount by $$$, I've gone a long way toward creating an ROI on my fee. The emotional value of tax planning tends to be significantly higher than the emotional value of almost anything else related to finances.

My friend and brilliant advisor in his own right, Sten Morgan of Nashville, Tennessee (www.Kitces.com/210), takes this one step further by doing a quick calculation of the lifetime benefit of his recommendations, which, like me, he gives before charging a fee. To pick a simple example, he might advise a prospect to start making backdoor Roth contributions, which at $12,000 annually for a married couple could quickly become tens if not hundreds of thousands of tax savings over their lifetime. This is a powerful strategy for closing prospects and demonstrating value to clients.

Taxes Happen Every Year

Think about it: your clients and prospects are forced to think about taxes at least annually, when they do their yearly tax filing. This, along with the constantly changing tax code, gives ample opportunity to make tax planning an integrated part of your financial planning process. In fact—as outlined in Chapter 23 on value-adds—taxes play such an outsized role in our clients' lives that in my office, *two* of our four value-adds each year are focused on taxes and tax planning.

> "The emotional value of tax planning tends to be significantly higher than the emotional value of almost anything else related to finances."

Early in my career I had read dozens of books on tax planning, taken hundreds of hours of CE on tax planning, attended multiple tax planning workshops, and even studied all of the IRS publications related to my niche of retirees (e.g., Publication 590). However, despite all the technical knowledge, I didn't understand how to translate it into actionable advice (a.k.a., Massive Value) for prospects and clients.

In what would be a sliding door moment in my life, legendary financial planner Tom Gau spent thirty minutes with me going through a tax return for one of my real prospects. This prospect, a C-level executive for a publicly traded company and a former CPA, was well, well above average when it came to tax knowledge. However, in just a few minutes of looking at the return, Tom was able to spot multiple tax planning opportunities the prospect had never considered. When added to my One-Page Financial Plan (another tool learned from Tom), the prospect almost immediately agreed to become a client, one of my biggest at that time.

What Tom demonstrated to me, and I hope this book demonstrates to you, is that technical knowledge, while important, is of no value unless you can communicate it effectively to prospects and clients. That said, while tax planning is useless without communication skills, you still must walk-the-talk by either having technical skills yourself *or* having the ability to leverage someone else's tax skills.

Unfortunately, Tom has since passed away, but your clients still need you to be, or have access to, technical and practical tax knowledge. Here are the top resources I recommend every advisor study:

- **Kitces.com** – While Michael's voluminous work goes far beyond my niche of retirees, I still scan at least the summary of every article he publishes. From those summaries, I can decide which are relevant to my niche, at which point I'll read the entire piece. (Remind you of anything ... like a One-Page Financial Plan?) This is also the first place I go anytime I have a technical question. You are, however, still left with needing to translate the technical into client actionable advice.
- **Life and Death Planning for Retirement Benefits by Natalie Choate** – This is the technical tax bible of retirement benefits. Every time a new edition comes out, I immediately buy it and read it cover to cover. While it can be very dry, it's invaluable. Choate is also a brilliant speaker, and I never miss a chance to hear her present.
- **Retirement Tax Services Desktop Guide** – You will always find a laminated copy of this tax guide on my desk, as well as within arm's reach during every client meeting. It shows the key points of the federal and state tax numbers. Having this resource allows me, at a glance, to know in round numbers the impact of various financial decisions. You can get a free copy of this guide by visiting www.RetirementTaxServices.com

Speaking of Retirement Tax Services (RTS), it is *the* single best resource for real-world, in the trenches tax planning. The monthly tax newsletters, written by CPA Steven Jarvis and his team of rockstar financial advisors (including yours truly) provide both the technical and the real-world application of the most widely applicable tax strategies.

As you might have guessed from the shared last name, Steven is my brother, which does make me a bit biased (though if you have siblings you know that can cut both ways). Family ties aside, Steven's partnership with financial advisors to Deliver Massive Value to their clients is unmatched anywhere in the industry.

To cite just one example of this, many of us have clients or we talk with prospects who are required to make estimated payments. Not only are estimated payments a painful reminder of the "pound of flesh" taken by the IRS, they are often the result of poor planning, and nearly every tax preparer recommends the downright terrible strategy of making payments via a check put in the US mail.

Why is this such a terrible idea? Setting aside that your client's check has their account number proudly displayed for the entire world to steal, the IRS is also notorious for losing and/or misprocessing mail. Knowing this mess, Steven and his team at Retirement Tax Services created a one-page client guide for making electronic estimated payments, which includes several tips for dramatically reducing errors with the IRS.

This guide, which I give to all my clients making estimated payments *and* to all my COIs is a simple but effective way to Deliver Massive Value to clients, even *if* your compliance department mistakenly tells you not to provide tax "advice."

In addition, while I have devoted hundreds of hours and tens of thousands of dollars to developing a deep tax knowledge for my niche, other rockstar advisors, like my good friend Ben Brandt, CFP, instead leverage RTS to provide a similar level of tax expertise, without needing to become experts themselves.

This of course leads us to the second most common question asked of Steven: how does RTS compare to Ed Slott and/or Holistiplan. Short answer: it doesn't. Slott is great with the technical stuff and Holistiplan is great with the calculations. Where Steven is head and shoulders above everyone else is in his ability to translate technical subjects into actionable advice for advisors and their clients.

Reading back on this excerpt, I realize that it is really starting to sound like a sales pitch, but here's the thing: if one of your clients or prospects meets me and you're *not* doing top-level tax planning, that person is going to become my client. This isn't a hypothetical as it happens again and again. Become a tax strategy expert.

To help you on that path, visit www.RetirementTaxServices.com/Brothers to download the desktop tax guide and the estimated payment guide, with a quick video tutorial on how to use them.

How to Get Prospects and Clients to Give You Their Tax Returns

Sure, *you* know how valuable tax records can be in putting a financial plan together, but how do you convince your new prospects and existing clients to hand over the goods?

As you've learned throughout this book, the best way to bring your clients and prospects along with you on any plan or strategy is to set good expectations from the very beginning. Here are a few scripts you can use to break down the barriers and encourage cooperation from current and future clients alike.

Getting Tax Returns from Prospects

As detailed in Chapter 10 about the prospect process, during my initial screening call, I explain that my relationship manager (RM) will be sending them a list of documents to bring to our first meeting together. My explanation sounds something like this:

> "Mr. & Mrs. Prospect, so that we can make the best use of our time together, my RM is going to send you a list of documents to bring, including investment statements, Social Security and pension details, estate documents (like a will or trust), and your past two year's tax returns."

For most every prospect, this request, plus the follow-up by the RM, is more than enough to get them to bring their tax documents. On very rare occasions I'll get some pushback, including things like "But my tax return is so long" or "I have a CPA who does my taxes." I respond like this:

> "I totally understand. In my experience working almost entirely with clients just like you, their single biggest expense in retirement is taxes. In addition, the IRS is not so patiently waiting to take somewhere between 0 percent and 90 percent of your retirement accounts. As such, tax planning is a critical piece of what we do."

In the very, very rare case they continue to push back, I'll explain:

> "I can only do my best work with all the information about
> your finances, and I insist on only doing my best work. Let's
> do this, please bring your tax documents and we'll review them
> together only if you are comfortable doing so."

If that doesn't work, I wish them all the best and explain that there are lots of other advisors in the world who can help them, but I'm not one of them. (And as we hang up, I'm thinking, "Good luck not getting killed in taxes ...")

Getting Tax Returns from Clients

If you have not yet been consistently getting tax returns from clients, I suggest the following approach (which works nicely for any changes you make to your practice):

> "Mr. & Mrs. Client, as you know, I'm always looking for ways
> to deliver even more value to your family. In fact I spend
> hundreds of hours each year improving my skills so that you can
> spend that time enjoying your retirement. This year, I've focused
> much of my training on learning strategies to help my clients not
> overpay the IRS. In order to see if any of these strategies make
> sense in your situation, I'll need to review your most recent tax
> returns. Please bring them with you to our next meeting or send
> them to the office, whichever method is easiest for you."

Now, just because you've mentioned it once, that does not mean the client is going to automatically give you their tax return every year. Taxes aren't pleasant for anyone, so it's not something clients will easily remember. In addition, many tax preparers are reluctant to share copies of the client's tax returns, partly due to privacy issues and mostly due to ego.

To keep clients on track and onboard with your plan, this *must* become a constant topic of discussion in meetings, appointment confirmations, newsletters, value-adds, and every other point of contact. Most advisors have to follow the system of asking again and again for tax documents; the trick is doing this in a way that is empowering, not annoying, to the client.

The silver bullet for getting tax documents is having each client complete an IRS Form 8821 that gives you access directly to the IRS's tax transcripts for the client.

While far from a perfect system—for example, it can take weeks for the authorization to process and months before the most recent year's tax return is in their computers—once set up it puts you head and shoulders above every other advisor. In addition to giving me access to all of the client's tax data, by having a Form 8821 on file, I also get notified of any notices the client is receiving from the IRS, which is a huge value-add as I can proactively contact the client, explain what the letter means and how, with the cooperation of their tax preparer if needed, we are going to fix the issue.

Now, while having access to the Form 8821 has the potential to change your practice, due to the IRS's concerns about data security and privacy, it is *not* easy to get approval to the digital system (which is the only scalable way to make this work). You can learn all about this process from the IRS's website, but in short, you must:

- Apply to become an IRS approved e-filer (which requires being fingerprinted, completing a lengthy application, and waiting weeks or months for approval).
- Once approved, figure out how to work the IRS's confusing e-filer website and work your way through being assigned a CAF number (typically after you submit your first Form 8821).
- Here's the real kicker: to be approved for online access to the transcript system, and to keep your approval, you have to e-file at least five tax returns annually.

As you can imagine, this process takes months to complete, and the filing of tax returns each year opens up all sorts of compliance issues, including some that your firm simply won't allow. One alternative is to find someone who has a CAF number with whom you can partner. This, of course, is no small task and it comes with lots of logistical issues to solve.

Looking for an Easy Button to get client tax data directly from the IRS? CPA Steven Jarvis of Retirement Tax Services (RTS) partners with advisors to do just that. Learn more at www.RetirementTaxServices.com.

My Most Common Tax Recommendations

Now that we've tracked down tax information, let's take a look at my most common recommendations. The following four examples have been taken from One-Page Financial Plans I've actually prepared for clients.

Example 1:

Create a ten-year tax strategy incorporating inherited accounts, trust distributions, Social Security, gifting to children, and gifting to charity.

· Utilize cash to potentially repay 401(k) distributions (Timing? How much?)
· Max fund Roth contributions annually ($13,000)
· Max fund 401(k) plan to offset inheritance money ($26,000)
· Review PPP loan options

Example 2:

Create a ten-year tax strategy incorporating inherited accounts, trust distributions, Social Security, gifting to children, and gifting to charity.

· Prepare to convert non-deductible IRA contributions into Roth accounts ($60,000-plus)
· Max fund non-deductible 401(k) contributions for Roth conversions ($70,000-plus)
· Evaluate pension plan for increased tax deductions (company census required)
· Establish Donor Advised Fund to leverage charitable giving

Example 3:

Create a ten-year tax strategy incorporating inherited accounts, trust distributions, Social Security, Roth conversions, state of residency, gifting to children, and gifting to charity.

· Be prepared to lose health insurance credit due to trust distributions
· Make gifts to children in-kind to reduce your tax burden
· Leverage tax benefits/costs of current and/or future state of residency

Example 4:

Create a ten-year tax strategy incorporating inherited accounts, trust distributions, Social Security, gifting to children, and gifting to charity.

· Maximize tax benefits of any planned gifts to children and charity
· Begin making back-door Roth contributions
· Consider tax benefits of max funding 401(k) plans to offset inheritance income taxes

You'll notice that the examples above are taken from One-Page Financial Plans, which everyone seems to talk about but almost no one actually shares.

Roth Conversions

For retirees, I'm a big fan of Roth conversions. Endless technical analysis has been done on the pros and cons of Roth conversions, so I'll leave that debate for someone else. Instead, I'll focus on how we communicate this to clients and why it needs to be part of every client and prospect's financial plan.

Here's the script we use to explain this strategy:

"Mr. & Mrs. Client, I want to congratulate you on having saved up [$$$] in your retirement accounts! This represents a lifetime of diligent savings and discipline. Well done. Unfortunately, the IRS is not-so-patiently waiting for you to pay taxes on this money. While the IRS will get paid eventually, how much they get paid will depend a lot on you, and in your situation it can range from 10 percent to 90 percent. If it's OK with you, I want you and your family to keep as much of that money as possible.

The IRS makes the most money whenever you take a bunch of money from your IRA all at once. Hopefully this is for something fun, like buying an RV and traveling the country, but maybe it will be for something not so fun, like paying for long-term care. Either way, if you pulled out $100,000 all at once, your tax rate would spike, and the IRS would get a lot more money than they would otherwise.

Instead, I recommend that each year, we calculate how much money you can pull out of your IRA without causing your tax rate to go up. This amount—and for discussion, let's say it's $15,000—will be subject to taxes now, but all its growth from here on out will be tax free. Not only does this give you a bucket of tax-free money from which to pull lump sums of money in the future, but it also protects you from future tax rate increases. Does this all sound OK to you?"

Then, each year, we calculate how much room is left in their current tax bracket, round it down to the nearest thousand, and convert that amount to a Roth IRA account. We typically wait until October/November to do these conversions to minimize the risk of unexpected income throwing off our calculations.

When doing Roth conversions (or any kind of tax planning), it is essential to manage expectations, especially around paying taxes. On paper, when doing a Roth conversion, the client would have no taxes withheld, so the entire IRA withdrawal is converted and the taxes paid from a non-qualified account when the tax return is filed. However, anyone who works with real clients immediately recognizes the error of this approach: when the client has to write a big check in April (typically accompanied by their CPA throwing you under the bus), they will be upset or even furious.

The experienced advisor knows that behavior and emotion always trump logic and numbers. This means that at the time of the conversion, taxes are either withheld from the conversion, paid out of pocket with an estimated payment, or set aside in a designated account. Whatever the situation, it's important to explain to the client:

> "The one disadvantage of Roth conversions is that it requires 'paying the devil we know' now. While this is painful today, long-term we will be paying much less now than we would in the future."

You'll also want to remind the client about the Roth conversion, the taxes paid (or due), and the benefits of the conversion again at the end of the year, in February when they start getting tax documents, and again in March, when they are doing their tax return. This is especially important if they are going to wait until April to pay.

Charitable Giving

At the risk of this book becoming outdated when tax laws change, I want to tread carefully here. As with everything else in this book, but especially with taxes, you alone are responsible for the recommendations you give to a client. That said, many clients and prospects give money to charity but are unable to realize any tax benefits due to the rules and limits on standard vs. itemized deductions. Because of this, the client could be making regular charitable contributions, and the advisor would never know unless she asks.

> "Mr. & Mrs. Client, are there any charitable organizations you support, like the Red Cross or your local church? The reason I ask is that the IRS has a soft spot for charitable gifts, and with careful planning we can get some tax benefits for the money you are already giving."

If they are giving funds, we can look at things like establishing a Donor Advised Fund to donate appreciated securities and/or "front-load" five to ten years of donations before they retire. For those clients over age 70.5, we can also look at Qualified Charitable Distributions (QCDs) from IRA accounts.

Make sure you specifically ask your clients about their charitable giving. If you wait for them to offer information they might not see as important to the discussion, you may miss out on important tax benefits.

"Deliver at *least* one massive-value tax item on your calendar every year to keep clients in the right tax mindset for overall financial success."

Communicating Tax Strategy to Your Clients

You don't have to be a tax professional to recognize the important role you play in your clients' tax lives. There are a ton of reasons to make the effort.

Micah Shilanski sums it up perfectly: "If you want to grow your practice, if you want to increase your client base, if you want to make your clients happier—bring up taxes on a frequent basis, and at least once a year, do a massive value item with taxes." It takes only a bit of planning to launch you into the stratosphere as the best financial advisor the client has ever seen.

Remember that marketing calendar? Now's the time to add "tax strategy" to the information cycle you're working every one of your clients through. Deliver at *least* one massive-value tax item on your calendar every year to keep clients in the right tax mindset for overall financial success.

Ahead of tax time, I recommend sending every client a checklist with personalized tax information. This helps to supplement what they're learning from their tax professional by giving them important insight and recommendations only their financial advisor can provide.

On the next page is an example of a tax planning value-add we use every few years to remind clients of all the tax strategies we consider on their behalf. Following that is the tax-guide I keep laminated on my desk at all times.

TAX CHECKLIST

"You must pay taxes. But there's no law that says you gotta leave a tip."

RETIREMENT
TAX SERVICES

–Morgan Stanley advertisement

Tax analysis prepared for [   ]

Based on your [YEAR] tax return your income tax bill was $ [   ]

Your marginal Federal Ordinary Income Tax bracket was [   ] %

Your marginal Federal Long Term Capital Gains Tax bracket was [   ] %

and your effective rate was [   ] %

The following is a list of our 19 most effective strategies for reducing your lifetime tax bill. I have marked the strategies I would like to discuss during our next meeting:

Discussion Needed	Complete for [YEAR]	Not Applicable	
			IRA/Roth IRA contributions (annual limit of $6,000/$7,000 with catch-up)
			Nondeductible IRA contributions/cost basis
			Roth IRA conversion up to $
			Optimize investment accounts for tax efficiency
			Utilizing tax-free money to pay investment fees
			Evaluate tax free investment options (e.g., Muni Bonds)
			Non-cash charitable contributions
			Required Minimum Distributions (RMD)
			Utilizing RMD for charitable contributions
			72(t) periodic IRA distributions
			Family gifting (annual limit of $15,000 per beneficiary)
			Medicare means-testing strategies
			Medicare 3.8% surtax strategies
			Leveraging income tax brackets
			Harvesting capital gains/losses
			Annual withholdings/estimated payments
			Mitigating deferred tax liabilities
			529 accounts
			Estate planning and beneficiary listings
			OTHER:

RETIREMENT TAX SERVICES

RETIREMENT
TAX SERVICES

Ordinary Income Tax

	If taxable income						
	Is over		**But not over**		**The marginal tax rate is**		
	2021	2022	2021	2022	2021	2022	2026*
Married filing jointly and qualifying widow(er)s			$19,900	$20,550	10%	10%	10%
	$19,900	$20,550	$81,050	$83,550	12%	12%	15%
	$80,250	$83,550	$172,750	$178,150	22%	22%	25%
	$172,750	$178,150	$329,850	$340,100	24%	24%	28%
	$329,850	$340,100	$418,850	$431,900	32%	32%	32%
	$418,850	$431,900	$628,300	$647,850	35%	35%	35%
	$628,300	$647,850	-	-	37%	37%	37%
Single	-	-	$9,950	$10,275	10%	10%	10%
	$9,950	$10,275	$40,525	$41,775	12%	12%	15%
	$40,525	$41,775	$86,375	$89,075	22%	22%	25%
	$86,375	$89,075	$164,925	$170,050	24%	24%	28%
	$164,925	$170,050	$209,425	$215,950	32%	32%	32%
	$209,425	$215,950	$523,600	$539,900	35%	35%	35%
	$523,600	$539,900	-	-	37%	37%	37%

*Brackets will be indexed for inflation; rates are set to increase in 2026 with the expiration of the rate cuts in the Tax Cuts and Jobs Act (TCJA)

2022 State Income Taxes

RETIREMENT
TAX SERVICES

	Tax Rate Range	Top Bracket	Standard Deduction
Alabama	2%–5%	$6,000	$7,500
Alaska	**None**	-	-
Arizona	2.59%–4.5%	$333,684	$25,900
Arkansas	2%–5.5%	$8,500	$4,400
California	1%–13.3%	$1,250,738	$9,202
Colorado	4.55%	-	$25,100
Connecticut	3%–6.99%	$1,000,000	-
Delaware	2.2%–6.6%	$60,000	$6,500
Florida	**None**	-	-
Georgia	1%–5.75%	$10,000	$6,000
Hawaii	1.4%–11%	$400,000	$4,400
Idaho	1%–6%	$15,878	$25,900
Illinois	4.95%	-	-
Indiana	3.23%	-	-
Iowa	0.33%–8.53%	$78,435	$5,240
Kansas	3.1%–5.7%	$60,000	$7,500
Kentucky	5%	-	$5,380
Louisiana	1.85%–3.5%	$25,000	-
Maine	5.8%–7.15%	$108,900	$25,100
Maryland	2%–5.75%	$300,000	$4,650
Massachusetts	5%	-	-
Michigan	4.25%	-	-
Minnesota	5.35%–9.85%	$284,810	$25,050
Mississippi	4%–5%	$10,000	$4,600
Missouri	1.5%–5.4%	$8,704	$25,900
Montana	1%–6.75%	$18,800	$9,660
Nebraska	2.46%-6.84%	$66,360	$14,700
Nevada	**None**	-	-
New Hampshire	5% on dividends	-	-
New Jersey	1.4%–10.75%	$1,000,000	-
New Mexico	1.7%–5.9%	$315,000	$25,900
New York	4%–10.9%	$25,000,000	$16,050
North Carolina	5.25%	-	$25,500
North Dakota	1.1%–2.9%	$445,000	$25,900
Ohio	2.76%–3.9%	$110,650	-
Oklahoma	0.25%–4.75%	$12,200	$12,700
Oregon	4.75%–9.9%	$250,000	$4,840
Pennsylvania	3.07%	-	-
Rhode Island	3.75%–5.99%	$155,050	$18,600
South Carolina	0%–7%	$16,040	$25,900
South Dakota	**None**	-	-
Tennessee	**None**	-	-
Texas	**None**	-	-
Utah	4.95%	-	$1,554 (credit)
Vermont	3.35%–8.75%	$251,950	$12,700
Virginia	2%–5.75%	$17,000	$9,000
Washington	**None (ongoing legal challenge to capital gains tax)**		
West Virginia	3%–6.5%	$60,000	-
Wisconsin	3.54%–7.65%	$374,600	$21,820
Wyoming	**None**	-	-
D.C.	4%–10.75%	$1,000,000	$25,900

Tax Planning: One More Way to Deliver Massive Value

If all of this tax planning stuff sounds like a lot for a financial planner to worry about, that's because it is! That's why there's so much potential for you to be wildly successful with it: you'll be offering something other financial advisors just aren't bothering with.

As with every aspect of the prospect process and Delivering Massive Value to clients, tax planning must be done as part of an intentional process that leaves the client/prospect thinking, "Wow, this advisor is really smart—I don't know what I would do without them!" What are you waiting for?

Action Steps

Now that you see how tax planning can help you add value to your client's life, it's time to make it happen! Integrating tax planning into your business isn't easy, but if you can manage it, you'll be poised to launch your business into a whole new playing field.

If you're ready to make the move, follow these steps to tax planning success, and watch the clients come pouring in for that special insight only you can provide.

○ Whether it's a QCD review, a Roth conversion review, or just a note to say, "Are you on track for this year's taxes?" plan to check in with your clients every year on their taxes, and make that part of the plan for this and every year of your business.

○ Time to up your tax game. I don't care what level you're at right now; make it your business to climb up another level or two this calendar year. You can do it!

○ Keep speaking the client's language. You're there to support them, not to confuse them.

Bonus content available for this chapter at ThePerfectRIA.com/BookBonus:

→ PDF of the samples in this chapter

→ Access to a recording of one of our most popular tax webinars

→ A sample of the IRS 8821 Tax Transcript

Responsive, Not Reactive

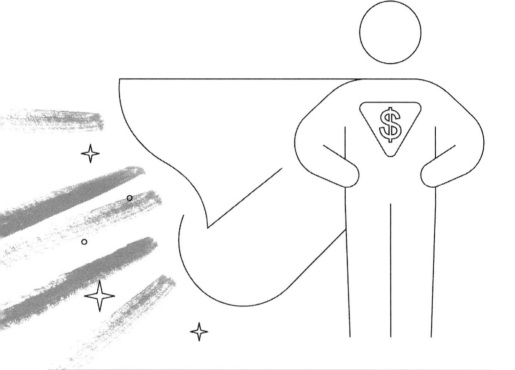

"I would rather copy genius than invent mediocrity.

Jarvis has figured out how to build a hyper-efficient, highly profitable practice. Don't reinvent the wheel!"

Michael Henley, CFP
Kennett Square, PA
Brandywine Oak Private Wealth

Much of what we've talked about in this section has been focused on proactively Delivering Massive Value to clients. One reason for this is that clients need to see that we are working on their behalf, so that when they see our fee, it's easy to connect the value we provide to the fee we charge (more on that in the next chapter). I like to compare this to the old adage, "If a tree falls in the forest and nobody is there to hear it, does it still make a sound?" The corollary for our industry: "If you provide value to a client, but they don't know it, does it still count?"

The second reason for delivering all this value is to help clients build up their defenses against what Nick Murray calls "The Big Mistakes" (*Simple Wealth, Inevitable Wealth* by Nick Murray). These excuses are too many to list. Sometimes it can even seem like clients are using personal or world events as an excuse to sabotage their financial plan. At some point in every client's relationship with you, they will be tempted at least once to engage in one or more of these mistakes.[1]

It goes like this: Whenever some particularly worrisome piece of financial news hits the headlines and stays there, clients understandably start to worry. They automatically think that because something has changed, there's some action that they need to take to stay on top of it. "What should we do?" they ask us earnestly.

But we know that as financial advisors, being reactive is one of the worst things we can do. Our job is to pick a winning strategy, then have the commitment to stick to it over the long haul. So what should you do when clients vent their frustrations and want to react?

Helping Clients Respond, Not React

It's true that much about the future seems uncertain, and it's no wonder that those general feelings of disquiet and concern bleed into our clients' financial lives. This is just human nature.

When this happens—assuming you've built up enough relationship capital through proactively Delivering Massive Value—you have an opportunity to earn your fee for the remainder of the client's lifetime. After all, if you can keep them from selling low, buying a fad, or blowing up their tax strategy, that one mistake *you* helped them avoid could potentially be the difference between their financial success or failure. How's *that* for value?

The following three steps will help you and the client succeed even when it appears that all hope of avoiding the big mistakes is lost.

---

1 Whatever the client's reason, chances are it's some version of "This time is different, so our plan needs to change." Even so, I strongly recommend that you never, *ever* respond to a client's claims that "this time is different" with the quote from Sir John Templeton, "The four most dangerous words in investing are 'this time is different.' " Don't insult your client's intelligence; answer their real questions by addressing their fears.

Step #1: Be Prepared

Perhaps the most important step you can take in helping clients avoid the big mistakes is by always taking on this challenge on your terms. As we talked about extensively in Chapter 2, time-blocking and surge meetings are the foundation of any successful practice.[2] Yes, time-blocking will dramatically improve your productivity, but it will also allow you to work with clients on your own terms.

It's vital that you use your structured time with clients wisely. In the most common scenario, a client calls with some article they read and wants to advise you on how to change their investments. This dynamic will continue until both of you are frustrated: your client will lose respect for you because they are actually the one financial planning, and you will not be confident about the investments because you're being reactive to their every whim. You must work to make financial discussions and decisions on your terms, not your client's. Otherwise, while you think you are giving great customer support by talking to them every time they want to talk, you're actually doing more harm than good. Let's look at how you should handle these situations by confining these discussions to structured time where you can prepare yourself rather than be caught off guard.

SCENARIO: THE PROACTIVE, ACTUALLY HELPFUL ADVISOR

[phone rings]

Relationship Manager (RM): "Thank you for calling Awesome Advisors. How can I help you?"

Your Best Client (YBC): "I need to talk to [Advisor], is she available?"

RM [regardless of what the advisor is currently doing]: "She's helping another client right now, but I know she is always excited to talk with you. Is there something I can help you with?"

YBC: "I don't think you can help me. I really need to talk with [Advisor]."

RM: "Perfect. Is this something you would like to talk with her about as soon as possible, or shall I add it to the agenda for your next meeting?"

YBC: "It's time sensitive, so I'd like to talk with her as soon as possible."

RM: "No problem. I can send you a link to her calendar via email, or if you have your calendar handy, she has time Tuesday at 2 p.m. and 3:30 p.m. Will either of those work for you? Of course, if this is very urgent I can probably get her later today."

---

2 I'm writing this book in the depths of the 2020/2021 COVID-19 crisis, riots, political turmoil, predictions of severe inflation and tax increases as well as a dozen other seemingly catastrophic events, so these scenarios are more panic focused. However, the exact same approach works when the client is overly optimistic about buying Tesla stock or Bitcoin. It's all about coming up with a smart plan for the worst-case scenario, then sticking to it.

```
YBC: "Tuesday at 3:30 p.m. works for me."
RM: "Great. So that [Advisor] can be prepared for your discussion,
what can I tell her this meeting is regarding?"
YBC: "I just saw a headline about [Bitcoin/COVID/taxes/ politics],
and I think we need to make changes to our portfolio."
RM: "That sounds serious. I'll be sure [Advisor] is ready to discuss
[Bitcoin/COVID/taxes/politics] Tuesday at 3:30 p.m. What else
should I have her ready to discuss?"
YBC: "That's it, I just want to hear what she thinks we should do
about this issue."
RM: "Perfect. Advisor will call you Tuesday at 3:30 p.m. to discuss
[Bitcoin/COVID/taxes/politics]. What else can I help you with today?"
YBC: "That's it. Thank you."
```

Then, at exactly the scheduled time—when the advisor's head is in the game, when all the case prep is ready, and when the advisor feels confident in the topic being discussed—she calls the client and is in the best position possible to give her recommendations.

The outcome of these two scenarios will be night and day. In the first scenario, the advisor is totally reactive, trying to respond to being blindsided (not to mention now having totally lost focus on whatever other project she was trying to finish). In the second, the advisor can be totally prepared and focused for the discussion. As an added benefit, having slightly restricted access to the advisor creates a sense for the client that the advisor is busy (read: successful), which is great social proof. Wouldn't we all rather work with someone who is successful?

"If you can keep them from selling low, buying a fad, or blowing up their tax strategy, that one mistake you helped them avoid could potentially be the difference between their financial success or failure."

Step #2: Validate the Client's Concerns

Let me tell you about a recent conversation I had with a client. (I've intentionally left out the subject of her concern, as this same process works for *every* concern). The conversation started like this:

"Hey Matthew, I don't want to hear that this is just another bump in the road. This is really unprecedented, and it could really cause disruptions to the supply chain that could have a trickle effect throughout the economy."

Now, this particular client—we'll call her Sue—wasn't a panicky, flighty person prone to fantasies of financial ruin. This is a very intelligent woman: she was a high-level consultant in her career, and she has a good head on her shoulders. I've never seen her rattled by the markets before. But here she was, trying to swallow her panic and clearly hoping I'd say something to calm her fears.

I said,

> "Sue, you know what, I can't argue with that. It definitely could
> cause disruptions to the supply chain and have serious negative
> impacts on the economy. I don't think there's a high probability of
> that, but it definitely could."

I could tell by her brief pause that this wasn't at all what she expected to hear. Then, she said, "Well, Matthew, what should we *do*?"

Before we jump into the answer to her question, I want to make sure you noticed a couple of critical things:

I listened

As soon as Sue started describing her apocalypse du jour, I was tempted to launch into some kind of rebuttal. Instead, I listened to her concern. Additional strategies for really listening would include

> "I agree, that sounds really concerning. What else about this
> situation concerns you?" or even something as simple as
> "Please tell me more about this."

I'm intently listening for several reasons: This client is paying me a lot of money, and the least I can do is give them the respect of listening to their concerns. Because so few people really listen, this small act stands out in the client's mind. Further, the client's stated concern is rarely the real issue and listening is my best way of getting to the core issue. Maybe the client just needs to talk it out. Many a client has talked themselves out of a big mistake just by having somewhere to talk it through.

I validated her concern

No matter how outlandish a client's concern may sound, if it is their concern, it's a valid concern. However, approach this cautiously, as you don't want to cross the line into agreeing with, supporting, or—worse yet—encouraging their concern. Try to strike a note that says, "I hear you, and I understand/agree that if things go as you describe, the effects could be devastating." This is why being a good financial advisor means expressing empathy by validating the client's concerns, whatever they are.

I didn't argue

Clients sometimes call with wild, unfounded theories we may find it difficult to believe *they* actually believe. They also call about very real concerns. Whatever your perspective on the thing they fear, remember that fear is always very real to the person experiencing it. The last thing they want to feel on top of that fear is patronized or dismissed, and the second you begin to argue with a client (or anyone), you become their enemy. Being "right" about an issue is irrelevant, especially when nobody can predict the future. Instead, agree with the client as much as possible, so long as it doesn't compromise your core financial beliefs or the client's financial plan.

Whatever the client's fear, it's important that you take the time to really listen. At worst, you'll alleviate their anxiety and make them feel heard and respected—and at best, you'll uncover important and relevant information that will enable you to deliver even more value.

> # "Many a client has talked themselves out of a big mistake just by having somewhere to talk it through."

Step #3: Uncover the Real Issue

While it is tempting to think we've heard the client's concern and now it's time to respond, the truth is we are nowhere close to the client's real concern, as we've not yet hit an emotional response. Even your most intelligent, successful, and seemingly logical clients are still human, and at the core, all of their money decisions are emotional. Until we get to that emotional concern, any attempts at solving the issue being presented would be fighting the proverbial wrong dragon.

To illustrate this, take a look at how the rest of my conversation with Sue went.

> Me: "Like you, I can't predict the future, but just looking at where we are at today, it feels like we've been through worse. Maybe this one will be the worst ever, but either way, how long do you think it could take to recover from this crisis?"
> Sue: "I don't know, maybe years."
> Me: "We currently have some $300,000 in your war chest, which at your spending level represents more than five years of income. Do you think that will be enough time?"
> Sue: "I don't have that long to wait."

At this point in this real client exchange, I was tempted to argue with Sue, to explain that she is just sixty-three and has decades left of life. Plus, her son was her only beneficiary, and he had decades more of life after that. Thankfully, I remembered to listen and dig deeper until I hit the real emotional concern.

> Me: "Tell me more about not having enough time to wait this out."
> Sue: [with some emotion] "I was just diagnosed with cancer again, and it doesn't look good. I'm not sure how long I'll live."
> Me: "Sue, I'm so sorry to hear that. I totally understand why you are concerned about not having enough time to ride this out. What would you like to do?"

This is now a bit tricky; we are balancing keeping the client from panicking based on market conditions, but her cancer diagnosis does change her financial situation. As Murphy's law would have it, these both happened at the same time.

> Sue: "I want to move everything to cash."
>
> Me: "Tell me more about that. What is your goal of moving to cash?"
>
> Sue: [again with some emotion] "I want to make sure my two granddaughters have all the money they need to go to college, and I want to leave plenty of money to my son."

Aha! Now we've found the real issue. What started as a concern about politics really boiled down to wanting to financially support her son and granddaughters. This is what we wanted to find out all along.

> Me: "Sue, that is an awesome plan. I totally agree that no matter what, we need to have money set aside for your granddaughters and for your son. How much money do you want to set aside for your granddaughters' education?"
>
> Sue: "$200,000 each so they can go to any school they want."
>
> Me: "So $400,000 total? Perfect. We already have $300,000 in your war chest; with your permission, we will add another $100,000 to the war chest and move all $400,000 into a designated account for their education. Is that OK with you?"
>
> Sue: "Yes. That would be perfect."
>
> Me: "Great. My team will make that happen by next week, and we will send you confirmation once it's complete. Now, let's talk about your son. If, heaven forbid, you were to pass away when the markets are down, would he sell at a loss or wait for them to come back?"
>
> Sue: "He's a smart guy, very responsible with money. He would certainly wait for the markets to come back."
>
> Me: "Perfect. So if we set aside the $400,000 for your granddaughters and left the rest invested, knowing that hopefully you, but certainly your son, will wait out the market recovery, would that be OK with you?"
>
> Sue: "That is exactly what I want. Thanks."

In this lengthy but illuminating exchange, you can see where so many advisors—like me in my early career—fall into the trap of thinking, "The client said XYZ, and I need to rebut that belief," when in reality, what you really need to do is uncover the real issue.

Be warned that you won't always be able to uncover the real issue, as the client may not always know it themselves. In those cases, you need to stick to the plan, no matter what.

Tips for Helping Clients Respond (Not React)

As we all continue into the uncharted territory that began in early 2020 and goes on to this day, we financial advisors are bound to receive more calls expressing concern about the long-term stability of their finances. Your clients don't have "the last pandemic" to refer to, so it's no wonder they're going to feel like they're out on a limb. They want to feel like they're taking action, like they're doing everything they can to prepare for the changing markets. They want to *react*.

That's why it's so important for clients to keep trusting the plan—to stick to the process—through the coronavirus panic and beyond. Here are a few tips for talking even the most upset and concerned client down from their worry and reminding them that everything is going according to plan.

Be Prepared

By now, you've learned tons of reasons you shouldn't be answering the phone on the fly. Here's a very good example of why waiting until a scheduled time to discuss sensitive information benefits not just you but your client as well.

If I had answered Sue's call when it first came in, I wouldn't have known ahead of time what she was calling about, and I would have been scrambling. I would have been trying to pull an answer out of thin air, and my own feeling of discomfort would have fed her own. I would only have exacerbated her fears.

But because I scheduled the call ahead of time (or, rather, my team did), I was able to gather my thoughts and look at my notes. I went back and saw that we had met some time ago, when Sue was concerned about the trade war with China, and we had agreed at that time to not go a more conservative route.

Because I had done that research, I was able to say, "Hey, do you remember when we met back in May of last year? We talked about moving money to cash, but we agreed to stay invested. Because we agreed to stay in the market, we're up $100,000." That was certainly welcome news to Sue, who wasn't prepared to hear that things were actually going well.

Put Things in Perspective

One of the most awful things we as financial advisors do is ask our customers to fill out those terrible risk assessment questionnaires. We usually do this right after we tell them how financial management shouldn't be an emotional choice. But isn't asking them "What would you do if your portfolio were cut in half?" really just conditioning them to make an emotional choice when things change?

"Scenario role-playing" like this, which the client has undoubtedly encountered at some point along their financial journey, even if it wasn't at your office, sets people up to look at things the wrong way. It's up to you to help them zoom out and look at the bigger picture.

And so the first thing I did with Sue—the first thing I do with any client—was say, "Well, first I want to provide some perspective. All this craziness the last couple of weeks has set the market back four months—just four months. In fact, over our relationship, we're still up $700,000 of growth. We gave back $70,000 of that. I just want to put that in perspective before we go any further."

Helping clients understand their overall progress over time can go a long way toward quelling any panic about the immediate future.

Use Real-World Terms

We know it's important to speak in terms the client is comfortable with, and this is especially the case during conversations where emotions are high. Don't talk in fancy projections; instead, turn the conversation into something the client is in control of, and use language they're familiar with.

Say, "How long do you think it will take for this issue [the coronavirus, the political administration, interest rates, whatever it is] to resolve itself?"

They say a number: "I think it will take two years to resolve itself."

"OK, perfect. Great news—we have five years of income in that war chest."

Then, go on to translate that into real-world terms that matter to your client's life: "Hey, of your $1.5 million portfolio, about $400,000 of that is totally protected from the markets and stock markets. Is that a big enough buffer for you?"

I find that clients usually say something like, "Actually, I forgot about that. That's a great buffer actually."

> "Perfect! That's why we're here." ▤

Project Good Energy

One thing Micah Shilanski warns our podcast listeners about is to always be mindful that clients will react the way *you* react. Are you anxious? Are you watching the markets and reacting to them, or are you having a nice calm conversation?

Your clients think they're calling so you can tell them what action you should take, but that's not what they really want; what they really want is to be told that everything is OK. If you're all riled up from binging on CNN and you're feeling reactive yourself, clients will never believe you when you say that everything will be OK.

It's important to do whatever mental and emotional preparation you need to in order to project a quiet confidence and help clients temper their emotional energy so that they feel equipped to weather the storm ahead, whether real or perceived. To help them calm down, you need to be calm. Micah's summary: "You need to be the fixed point in the crisis to help those clients get through it."

Client-Facing Communication Policy

We believe that communication should be consistent, clear, and effective. As a client of ours, you have unlimited access to our team. Most clients find the following guide helpful in understanding when best to call by phone and when to email our office at [insert your company client email address].

911 Priority Call Our Office	Medium Priority Call or Email	Low Priority Email Generally
You need an answer within 24 hours, or same day.	You need to visit with someone within the next 72 hours, but it is not immediate.	You want our office to be aware of something, but no immediate action is needed.
The matter IS time-sensitive.	The matter is not time-sensitive.	There are no deadlines with this matter.
The matter involves a traumatic event.	The matter cannot wait until your next appointment.	This matter can wait until your next appointment.

Email is not instant communication.
We know how reliant as a society we have become on email and oftentimes, treat it as instant communication. We want to stress that if you have a 911 priority item, please call our office so that we can give the matter the immediate attention it deserves.

What should I ask or tell you about when it comes to my finances?
We want to be your 411 and your 911 when it comes to your personal finances. You will find confidence in our team being able to handle most matters. However, if it falls outside of their areas of expertise—like providing financial advice—they will ensure it is escalated to your financial advisor and an appointment will be made.

We hope that by outlining our firm's communication policy you will find that it is consistent, clear, and an effective method of maintaining a strong and healthy relationship.

–[insert your company name]

Keep the Strategy Front of Mind

We talked about the bucket of cash reserves, or what we like to call the war chest. I know you're going to throw this book across the room if you hear me tell you one more time to manage client expectations, but bear with me, because this is where doing your homework and bringing up your war chest strategy in every meeting really matters.

When a client calls you in a panic, worried about their portfolio, you'll witness the result of your careful expectation-setting ... and if you haven't been so careful about it, you'll soon learn. As so much of this book has emphasized, we always need to be one step ahead of clients.

For my clients' sake, I wish I could tell you that Sue was an outlier, but she wasn't. During the midst of the coronavirus panic, everyone's conversation started the same way, with some version of the same question. But because I did so much careful preparation, I was able to turn each conversation into my own variation of the following:

"Mr. and Mrs. Client, guess how much money is in your war chest?"

"I don't know—probably like $10,000?"

"Great news! You actually have $700,000 in your war chest."

"Oh, wow! I forgot about the war chest!"

"Yep—and if you remember some of the guardrail conversations we had, $700,000 is more than enough to take us through five years."

More often than not, the conversation is over at that point; they say, "That's really all I wanted to talk about today." You were able to quell the client's fears while also making them feel confident about the future—not bad for a thirty-second conversation.

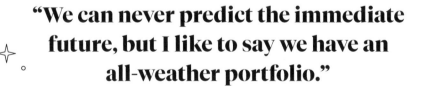

"We can never predict the immediate future, but I like to say we have an all-weather portfolio."

Anytime the markets have a substantial decline (whatever that means), you will have some clients who want to abandon your strategy and move to cash, or something worse. While their reason for making this move may sound very logical and well thought out, at the end of the day it boils down to some version of "this time is different," which will result in equities never recovering, or at least never recovering in their lifetime.

When this concern comes up, and only when it comes up, you must proceed with great caution and even greater skill.

Client: "I'm concerned that XYZ will cause the economy to collapse, therefore we must sell now while our accounts are still worth something."

Advisor: "The last time something similar to XYZ happened, the markets still recovered. What is different this time that indicates the markets will never recover?"

Client: "I heard/read that XYZ is unlike anything we've ever experienced"

Advisor: "Well, my crystal ball is as fuzzy as everyone else's, but let's walk through a scenario where the economy is so bad that equities never recover. Where will be a safe place to weather that storm?"

Client: "Gold, crypto, cash, annuities, inverse ETFs, etc."

Advisor: "I'm not sure about your grocery store, but mine only has a few days' worth of supplies and in any case, in the scenario where the economy collapses, will they accept gold, crypto, etc., for the supplies they don't have?"

Client: "I suppose not, but what's your point?"

Advisor: "In the never-before-seen scenario where the markets permanently collapse, so too will all bonds, bank deposits, and government debts, which will be the least of our problems, because if the economy collapses, farmers won't have fuel for their tractors or seeds for their fields and things will get really ugly really fast."

Client: "That sounds like the end of the world, but what does it have to do with selling stocks?"

Advisor: "If we think this time is different and things are going to be so bad they never recover, things like gold, crypto, and cash also won't do you any good, in which case, we might as well keep owning equities, just in case this time turns out like every other time the world seemed like it would end."

Client: "I guess that makes sense."

Despite what you've heard in the news, tariffs are nothing new. In fact, from 1789 to 1914, tariffs were the primary source of income for the US government. While tariffs are no longer needed to support the government, both political parties still use them to advance their respective agendas.

Setting aside the loudspeaker of Twitter, today's battles over US tariffs are no different from what we've seen for hundreds of years.

Setting aside the loudspeaker of Twitter, today's battles over US tariffs are no different from what we've seen for hundreds of years.

So what impacts will tariffs, real or threatened, have on the economy and our investments? Tariffs, like every other tax, will have disproportionate impacts largely based on political whim. Some industries, companies, and groups of consumers will benefit, and others will suffer.

One response to this disproportionate impact would be to try and buy or sell companies that one believes will most benefit or suffer. However, like all attempts at market timing, the odds of being successful with this strategy are very, very low.

A far better response would be to have ongoing faith in the brilliance and resilience of the companies we know and respect. For example, do you suppose Boeing is considering giving up on building airplanes because tariffs have driven up the cost of metal? Probably not. How about Apple? Have they scratched plans for the next iPhone? Pick any company we invest in, staffed by thousands or tens of thousands of smart people who want to keep their jobs and be successful. Is it more likely they will call it quits because of tariffs or instead find innovative ways to deliver new and exciting products and services?

So what's the best way to respond to tariffs? Turn off your TV, go outside, and enjoy life. You won't miss much; in just a few weeks, the media, in typical Chicken Little fashion, will find a new reason to claim the world will shortly end.

Taking Extreme Ownership

I want to leave you with one important note about quelling a client's fears.

Sometimes it's easy to say, "Oh, that client—they're just not very smart. They must be watching too much CNN." But that's not the way good financial advisors value their clients.

Extreme ownership means that if your clients are freaking out about their finances, somewhere along the way, you as the advisor did not properly train them and did not properly articulate the strategy. It's *your* responsibility to help your clients be ready for downturns in the market; if they're a big surprise for a client, you haven't been doing your job to prepare them.

Every time the market turns down, the ideal scenario is for your clients to turn on the news and say, "Yep, sure enough—my financial advisor told me this was going to happen." We can never predict the immediate future, but I like to say we have an all-weather portfolio: it's set up for the good times *and* the bad. We will never be surprised by the market, because we're prepared for everything. And, if we've done our jobs, so are our clients.

And if you've truly done everything you can do, but at the end of all of your efforts, you are still unable to effectively communicate consistently with that client, what then? Simple: they are not a good fit for your office. If you can't help them achieve their goals, you need to graduate them to someone else's relationship, and get back to your job of managing the rest of your clients to the best of your abilities.

Bonus content available for this chapter at ThePerfectRIA.com/BookBonus:
→ PDF of our internal communications policy with clients
→ PDF of our external communications policy with clients
→ Newsletter example of setting client expectations

Quarterly Value-Adds

Early in my career, it was decided by our Broker Dealer's compliance department that if we were doing AUM fee billing, we had to send clients a billing statement. Apparently, the B/D (who didn't like us doing our own AUM billing because they got less of the action) had decided that the line item on the client's billing statement wasn't enough, so each quarter, we would physically mail a letter that showed our fee calculation and the exact amount taken from the client's account.

Due to a lot of head trash at that time, I was convinced that if clients were so clearly reminded of my fee, they would quickly fire me. In my desperation, I decided that if the client would be reminded of my fee each quarter, I would remind them of the value I provide at the same time. So, out of head trash and desperation, the quarterly value-add system was born.

In this chapter, we'll talk about why a quarterly value-add system completes your winning strategy for leveraging all the tools you've acquired throughout the book to Deliver Massive Value to your clients. We'll learn what truly adds value to the client's life above and beyond financial management—and what's just noise. And we'll wrap up with *tons* of examples that you can use to craft your own value-adds throughout the year.

What Do Value-Adds Do?

In our office, as well as in the offices of hundreds of advisors I've mentored, we define a value-add as a personalized document or report that helps the client better understand their financial situation. As much as possible, these value-adds must be in plain English, free from jargon like percentages (or marshmallows), and it must give the client something actionable.

Before we jump deeper into what *is* a value-add, let's get really clear about what *isn't*:
- Anything that can easily be found on Google
- Any kind of short-term market commentary
- Anything generic in nature
- Anything that couldn't be understood by a twelve-year-old
- Anything generated by fancy financial planning software (which every other advisor is providing them).

At the risk of getting too theoretical (the trap of every self-proclaimed expert), let's look at why value-adds can be so powerful and how they can transform your business—*if* you get them right.

They Demonstrate Your Value

It's not just that going long stretches between seeing your clients gives them a chance to forget about you. Even with all the facetime in the world, clients aren't usually in the room when you're doing the bulk of your work on their accounts: reviewing their beneficiaries, implementing tax strategies, generating reports. *You* know you're delivering value, but if your client doesn't realize it, they can't appreciate the full scope of what you bring them.

But with a strong system for adding value at every possible juncture, you can consistently demonstrate value to clients while freeing up important time for building your practice, being with your family, and doing what you love. What's more, I have a theory that a client's memory when it comes to financial investment information is limited to ninety days, making four the ideal number of check-ins per year.

If your office is like mine, every quarter, your client will see your office's fee. That means every quarter, your client will say, "Oh, here's where my advisor's office deducted $5,000 from our account. What have they done for me this quarter?" With a value-add system, you can make sure they can always point to something specific you've done and say, "This is what my advisor has done for me this quarter. That's really cool."

This is why I recommend sending something out every single quarter. This is the frequency with which you're probably taking money out of their account for your AUM fee (if that's the way you're structuring your business).

They Deliver Value with Hyper-Efficiency

Because you're surging your meetings and building a client experience that gets everyone on the same info cycle, you're able to maximize the use of your existing data sources, minimize advisor and staff time, and practically eliminate the potential for mistakes. Not only are you Delivering Massive Value for your clients across the board; you're doing it in a way that works seamlessly with your schedule and leverages all the work you're doing all along across all the other areas of your business so that you can constantly improve your value to the client.

For example, instead of trying to track the last time you reviewed the client's beneficiaries, you can run one beneficiary value-add across your entire client base all at once. This allows you to look at everyone for planning opportunities at the same time while also easily demonstrating massive value to clients.

They Cover All Aspects of Financial Planning for All Clients

With a strategic value-add system, it doesn't matter whether you've been managing an account for two years or two decades or how long it's been since you last sat down for a face-to-face meeting. Everyone gets what they need at the same time.

When you consider everything a client needs to know across an entire calendar year, you can break down the information into four quarterly communications and get everyone on the same information cycle. This means no one misses out on any important information throughout the year, no matter how many points of face-to-face contact you have with them or how new they are, and you're never left wondering how long it's been since you took a certain action on a given client account.

When it comes to your own business, do you itemize your fees, or do you de-emphasize them wherever possible? It can be scary to think about a client focusing on how much they're paying you, but how you present the way your business makes money says a lot about your confidence in your ability to Deliver Massive Value—or at least how to articulate that value to your client.

As we discussed in Chapter 10 on the prospect process, one of my most powerful prospecting scripts is as follows:

"Mrs. Prospect, each calendar quarter my office will deduct our fee from your account. This will appear as a line item on your statement so that you and I can clearly see the fee being charged. Each quarter, both of us will look at that number and decide if the value of working with my office is worth some multiple of that fee. If the answer is yes, we continue another quarter. If the answer is ever no, we need to have a serious discussion and potentially part ways as friends. If we decide to part ways, my office will do whatever we can to make the transition as smooth as possible for you, and as a gesture of good faith, we will refund our fee for the previous quarter. Is that OK with you?"

Just how well does this script work? I've heard from other advisors who have lost clients to me that their now-lost clients have repeated this script back to them nearly word for word as they transferred accounts to my office!

Of course, while this is a powerful prospecting strategy, by using it, you're setting the expectation that every quarter you really are going to Deliver Massive Value. Are you prepared to follow through on that promise?

What *Really* Adds Value?

As we mentioned in Chapter 11, marketing is a hard game to win: your prospects have no interest in the stuff everybody else is doing, and "what everybody else is doing" isn't a game you can win anyway.

Every quarter, my team and I send out an extra value-add for our A and B level clients. It works for us—but as I've said before, you can't send stuff just to send stuff. Everyone's on guard against emails and mailers they don't want and never asked for; you *have* to cut through the noise.

If you're going to try to speak to the entire world, you've got to speak in a way that's unlike what everybody else has said. These are the requirements for a successful value-add.

Personalized to Their Situation

One of the fundamental principles of this book is that the advice you give has to be customized to the client. They can find general investment advice anywhere; they come to you based on your insight and your ability to make the best recommendations for their situation.

Never is this truer than with your quarterly value-adds. Four times a year is infrequent enough that clients won't feel inundated by your contact, so they're set up to be receptive to it. *Don't* blow this opportunity by sending them the same generic articles they can find online or information that doesn't directly tie to their situation.

Useful for Your Client

The second fundamental principle is that everything you say has to be directly useful and actionable, and quarterly value-adds are no exception. This means actionable advice in plain, understandable English that your client can understand and follow through on.

It's not that we don't want to hear from clients; we just want to be one step ahead of them so they never have to be the ones bringing anything to our attention. Whenever we can, we want to preempt whatever it is they're going to do.

Demonstrates Your Value to COIs

By telling your clients, "Please give a copy of this to your CPA," you're not just preempting a lot of calls that would otherwise come into your office and bombard your team. You're setting yourself up to look like the best advisor they've ever seen!

Think about it: every other advisor they're calling is trying to figure out which 1099 they need or not. You're doing the opposite: you're actually letting them know when the deadline is and when the 1099s will be out, which puts everyone on the same page (and makes you look awesome). Just because you're not working directly with the CPA yourself doesn't mean you each don't have a vested interest in your client's financial success and making efficient use of your time.

Streamlines the Information Cycle

When all of your clients receive the same information at the same time, you never have to wonder where you are with any individual client.

For example, many practices will do a beneficiary review as a client comes in, but from there, they lose track of the last time beneficiaries have been reviewed. To counter this tendency, tackle beneficiary reviews for the entire book of business at once and send the report out to all clients. That report becomes your focus for the next round of meetings.

That way, if anyone ever calls in with a beneficiary question, or you're in the middle of an SEC audit and someone asks, "When was the last time you did this?" you can answer right away. You know that you did it for every single client—the third quarter of the year—and since you're consistent across your entire client base, you'll know your facts are reliable.

Examples of Quarterly Value-Adds

When I give presentations or teach courses to financial advisors like you, I like to include a packet of value-adds. I figured there was no better way to end this book than by letting you see the inner workings of the value-adds we use in my office to stay top of mind and highly respected in the client's mind.

Before we jump into my most popular value-adds, a disclaimer:

Advisors often react with excitement about my value-adds, only to realize when they get a good look that they take real work to implement. Doh! As I always say, if it were easy, everyone would do it and nobody would get paid.

Feel free to customize these templates and examples for use in your own practice!

Beneficiary Review

One of the easiest things your office can do to check in regularly with your client is review their beneficiaries. Financial advisors who aren't on a value-add cycle have to keep track of where they are with every individual account. Having no review schedule can lead to important beneficiary information becoming outdated, which can mean a huge headache for the surviving family in the event of a client's death.

To prevent this, my office goes through every client's beneficiary designation and physically mails them a summary. Along with that summary, we'll include a cover letter saying, "One of our jobs is to make sure that if you're not here anymore, your money goes where you want it to go. Enclosed is a report for each of your accounts letting you know what your beneficiaries would receive today."

Now, you may be thinking, "Beneficiary review? That's hardly a value-add! The custodian sends that to them every year!" Ah, yes, but the custodian sends it as percentages (read: "marshmallows"), and as we've talked about elsewhere in the book, practically no one can do percentages in their head. Instead, our report shows them, in dollars and cents, how much each of their beneficiaries will receive from each account. (Ideally, all the beneficiary dollar amounts would be added up in a single report, but that can be a headache for most advisors. Instead, you might do it by account, which can be a simple Excel report using data from the custodian: Account Name, Number, Beneficiary Name, Percentage, and Account Value.)

Then, in the corresponding client meeting, you can explain to the client while looking at the report:

"When you pass away—and hopefully that is many, many years from now—your two kids will each get \$357,000 from your accounts, which they can take in a lump sum. Is that OK with you?"

This discussion is valuable because it's likely the first time the client has thought about this in actual dollar amounts. It can also lead to discussions about estate planning, why their NQ accounts have no beneficiaries, and any number of other topics. Or it may lead to nothing more than the client confirming, "Yep, all the money goes to my only son Dave, who is a bright guy and will do smart things with it." Perfect. Even when no additional action is needed, you still win, because you've proactively demonstrated value.

Below you'll find an example of a beneficiary review that you can modify for your own use.

Sample, Joe & Jane
XX/XX/XXXX

THE **PERFECT** RIA

Investments: Sample, Jane

Value	Account Name	Account Title	Beneficiary Type	Beneficiary Name	Beneficiary Percent	Beneficiary Receives
\$465,000	test-136	IRA	Primary	Joe Sample Jr.	100.00 %	\$465,000
			Contingent	Charity Sample	100.00 %	\$465,000
\$940,000			Primary	Joe Sample Jr.	100.00 %	\$940,000
			Contingent	Charity Sample	100.00 %	\$940,000

Investments: Sample, Jane

Value	Account Name	Account Title	Beneficiary Type	Beneficiary Name	Beneficiary Percent	Beneficiary Receives
\$214,000	test-152	Savings	Primary	Joe Sample Jr.	100.00 %	\$214,000
			Contingent	Charity Sample 2	100.00 %	\$214,000

Investments: Joe Sample and Jane Sample

Value	Account Name	Account Title	Beneficiary Type	Beneficiary Name	Beneficiary Percent	Beneficiary Receives
\$214,000	test-152	Savings	Primary	Joe Sample Jr.	100.00 %	\$214,000
			Contingent	Charity Sample 2	100.00 %	\$214,000

1099 Report

Take a look at the example on the opposite page of a value-add we send out to clients every year in January to kick off Q1. This brief report simply lets them know which accounts will receive a 1099 and which won't.

Now, you might think that's a pretty obvious thing. But how many of you have had a client who called and said, "Mrs. Advisor, how come I didn't get a 1099 account from my IRA?" And you say, "Well, you didn't take a distribution." "I know, but I got one last year." "Well, you took a distribution last year, you didn't take one this year." "Sure, but why didn't my CPA want the 1099 for this year?"

Don't get me wrong; I mean no disrespect to any clients. It's just reality. The average client truly doesn't understand this stuff—that's why they're clients. We're here to make their lives easier; they came to us because they want a professional to deal with these things. If they wanted to do it themselves, they would be doing it themselves.

To preempt these unnecessary calls and questions—as so much of this book is focused on doing—we send our clients this report every January that lets them know the 1099s they can expect for the accounts held through our office.

In a perfect practice, this 1099 report is run seamlessly through your CRM platform. Prior to having that level of technology in our office, running this report was far more labor-intensive, but it ended up being worth the effort. Because every office runs their technology differently, this process would be difficult to describe in a book, and even if we could, it would be immediately outdated. Instead, let me briefly describe the logic your tech stack should provide:

1. Create a list of all client accounts by type (e.g., IRA, Roth, NQ).
2. Autotag all NQ accounts as getting a 1099 (assuming they had at least one penny of activity).
3. Review all IRA and Roth accounts for distributions and/or conversions. As appropriate, tag as getting (or not) a 1099.
4. Review all accounts for any specific activity that would aid the tax preparer (e.g., conversions, QCD, gifts, etc.).
5. Find some kind of Excel wiz on Upwork who can merge this report (or contact *The Perfect RIA* to be considered for licensing our software).

Jarvis Financial
20XX Tax Information

Sample, Jane

The following is a list of your accounts held through Jarvis Financial and the respective tax forms that you will need from each account to complete your 20XX tax return. Please note that we only have tax information through our office.

Account Name	Account Number	Tax Form	Special Notes
Brighthouse Financial (MetLife)	11223344	1099	NONE
Fidelity – Individual, Jane	555-666777	Tax Report/1099	NONE
Fidelity – IRA, Jane	111-122333	1099	RMD to Charity/QCD
John Hancock – 403(b), Jane	23456	NONE	NONE
John Hancock – IRA, Jane	78989	NONE	NONE
John Hancock – IRA, Jane	34567	NONE	NONE
National Western – 403(b), Jane	345678	1099	NONE

Please remember the following:

- The deadline for companies to make all form 1099s available is February 15th. Different types of accounts (e.g., IRA, Joint, etc.) are generated at different times and may arrive separately.
- In an effort to save trees (and money), many companies are no longer mailing 1099s and are instead posting them online.
- All traditional IRA, Roller IRA, and Roth IRA accounts will generate a form 5498, which is not typically needed for tax preparation.

If you are missing a 1099 or if you have any questions or concerns regarding your accounts through our office, please contact us at clients@jarvisfinancial.com. Once your 20XX tax return is complete, please send Dee a copy so that we can continue providing you with the best possible tax strategies.

> **Scam alert** – Please assume that every email or phone call you receive is a scam until proven otherwise. The FTC estimates that $17 million was lost to IRS scams and another $19 million to Social Security scams. Don't be the next scam victim! When in doubt, call our office.

Our attorneys would like us to remind you that this report is provided as a courtesy and is for informational purposes only. Only the tax information you receive directly from your investment companies should be considered official. This guide is not a replacement for having a licensed professional complete your tax return.

On the following pages you will find three additional value-add examples (plus a second version of my Retirement Income Guardrails™). Instead of trying to fully detail them in this book, included in the bonuses for this chapter are videos of me explaining each one.

Guardrails V1 Value-Add

As discussed in Chapter 20, Retirement Income Guardrails™ is the foundation to my approach for financial planning. I use guardrails in every client meeting and in addition send it out to clients once a year as a value-add. The example on page 282 is my original version, of which you can find an Excel copy at Kitces.com/7 and in the chapter bonuses. No macros, moving pieces, or dynamic images, but it works and is widely copied throughout the industry.

Guardrails V2 Value-Add

Because Excel can be so temperamental, and because I wanted a dynamic illustration, and because half the industry was asking for it, Micah, our dev partner Orion Matthews, and myself invested several hundred thousand dollars (thankfully, the tool does all our value-adds and not just guardrails) to create a fully web-based version, which you can see on page 283.

Paying for the Unexpected Value-Add

This value-add worksheet was used in our office to transfer credibility to my new advisor. It gave him an easy piece to work through with clients that was very well received. It is scheduled in our rotation to pre-fill and send to clients, but not until next year (the goal is always to be one year ahead on value-adds).

Estate Documents vs. Beneficiary Value-Add

This tool requires you to have all of your clients' estate documents (which is table stakes for premium advisors), and it allows you to illustrate for clients which of their assets are governed by their will vs. beneficiary agreements. Great example of a simple-to-use value-add.

Notice at the top of this report, we remind clients to provide a copy to their tax preparer. Having the client give this information to their tax preparer reduces the risk of errors on the tax return, but it also lets me demonstrate massive value to their COI. As discussed in Chapter 16, this is one of the many documents I would share with tax preparers to distinguish myself from every other advisor begging them for referrals.

Guardrails

In Chapter 20, I explained how to establish guardrails for your clients, allowing them to better conceptualize how different actions and events affect their nest egg and the personal choices they'll need to make to keep themselves within the guardrails. Several years ago, I'd help my clients visualize guardrails in an Excel sheet like this:

Retirement Income Guardrails™

In Good Times/Upper Guardrail

THE **PERFECT** RIA

If portfolio grows above:	$1,410,000	
Income increases 10% to:	$66,900	$5,575

Plus inflation in growth years

Upper Guardrail—not leaving a mattress stuffed full of money

Portfolio value

Lower Guardrail—not running out of money in retirement

Portfolio Income Potential:

Income Baseline:	$1,129,000	
Distribution Rate:	5.40%	
Available Income:	$60,900	$5,075
	Annually	Monthly

In Bad Times/Lower Guardrail

If portfolio falls below:	$940,000	
Income decreases 10% to:	$54,800	$4,567
	Annually	Monthly

Plus inflation in growth years

To Be Successful:

- War Chest of Cash and Bonds
- Strategic Rebalancing
- Careful Diversification
- Tax Efficiency
- Discipline

All numbers are based on Portfolio values as of   DATE

This strategy is designed to give you the highest possible monthly income, without jeopardizing your portfolio when (not if) the markets decline.

Our attorneys would like us to remind you that this report is provided as a courtesy and is for informational purposes only. Only the statements you receive directly from the investment companies (e.g., Fidelity) should be considered official. While we spend a great deal of time and money ensuring the accuracy of this report, mistakes can happen. Thanks.

Retirement Income Guardrails™

THE **PERFECT** RIA

This strategy is designed to give you the highest possible monthly income, without jeopardizing your portfolio when (not if) the markets decline. It relies upon five key philosophies:

- War chest of cash and bonds
- Strategic rebalancing
- Careful diversification
- Tax efficiency
- Discipline

	Maximum available	Current***
Dynamic Distribution Rate	5.40%	0.00%
Before-Tax Monthly Income	$7,380	N/A

Upper Guardrail/Pay Raise—not leaving a mattress stuffed full of money

Upper Guardrail Portfolio val: $2,049,000 / Available Inc: $8,110

Current Bal: $1,639,000

Lower Guardrail Portfolio Val: $1,366,000 / Available Inc: $6,640

Lower Guardrail/Pay Cut—not running out of money in retirement

***All figures referred to as "current" were last updated DATE

THIS REPORT IS NOT COMPLETE WITHOUT ALL ACCOMPANYING DISCLAIMERS!

Paying for the Unexpected

THE **PERFECT** RIA

Client Name: _____

Current Balance	Account Source	How Much	Liquidity Need	Unexpected Example	Needs Attention?
$ _____	Cash	$1K–$2K per Person	Emergency Expenses	Power Outage/ Lost Wallet/ Snowstorm	_____
$ _____	Checking/ Savings	3–6 Months Expenses or SWAN	Large "Planned" Expenses	Last-Minute Vacation/ Hot Water Tank Goes Out/Car	_____
$ _____	Lines of Credit (i.e., home equity, credit cards, etc.)	Next-Day Availability, $50K– $100K+	Sudden Unplanned Major Expenses	Fun Item on the Bucket List/ Long-Term Care	_____
$ _____	War Chest	3-5 Years Portfolio Income	Economic Decline	Bear Market (2020, 2008, 2000, 1987)	_____

Notes/Actions:

_____

_____

_____

_____

Luck favors the prepared ... even in death.

For the record, we are holding out hope that you will be the first to stay forever young and healthy. But just in case your retirement ends like every other human's, we want you to be prepared, at least financially, so that when the time comes, we can work with your beneficiaries to ensure your wishes are fulfilled. Below you will find how your assets will be directed after your passing. This is something we will review together during our next meeting, but please don't hesitate to call or email with any questions, concerns, and/or changes.

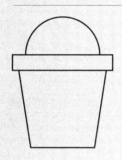

Distributed according to your estate documents:

- Real estate (including home)
- Vehicles
- Personal belongings
- Most bank accounts
- Non-retirement investment accounts
- Anything that does not have a listed beneficiary

According to our records, this bucket will be distributed based on your will/ trust last updated:

Per your beneficiary agreements

- IRA accounts
- Roth IRA accounts
- Life insurance
- Annuities
- Transfer on Death (TOD)
- Anything that has a listed beneficiary

This bucket will be distributed based on the beneficiaries listed on each account (e.g., Fidelity).

During our next meeting we can walk through this together.

*This information is for illustration only. Estate planning is complicated and should involve your attorney and accountant.

"How the hell do you get these out the door?!?"

This is the most common question I get once advisors take a look at my quarterly value-adds. I'll confess this can be a lot of work, but that's why I call it "Massive" value.* The key is to establish what data you can get (and from where), how to gather it most efficiently (para-planner) and then get it into a system that will generate your reports. Historically we used Excel for this, but as noted previously, Micah and I have custom built a web-based value-add generator that syncs directly with our custom CRM "Infinity" as well as Redtail.

"My compliance department says..."

You have two options when it comes to compliance: #1, work with them to find a variation of these value-adds that do pass their arbitrary standards *or* #2, find a new compliance department. Neither option is easy, but before you give up, know that even our friends at Edward Jones have, with great effort, found value-add work-arounds, including a version of the RTS 1099-Letter that has been blessed by compliance. As always, if it were easy (like generating a fifty-page financial plan), everyone would do it.

*When I decided to go with the phrase "Deliver Massive Value," I was worried that the acronym of DMV would have too much of a negative connotation. However, Delivering Massive Value has now become an industry standard. I do, however, get a great laugh at the two industry "experts" who have been ripping off this expression with "Deliver Deep Value" (which somehow sounds dirty to me) and "Deliver Exceptional Value."

Your graphic doesn't have to look just like ours; as long as your report is easy for clients to understand and clearly illustrates their upper and lower limits, you're on the right track.

Income Strategy

This strategy is designed to give you the highest possible monthly income, without jeopardizing your portfolio when (not if) the markets decline. It relies upon five key philosophies:

- War chest of cash and bonds
- Strategic rebalancing
- Careful diversification
- Tax efficiency
- Discipline

Current Balance: $17,762,000
Upper Guardrail Portfolio Value: $5,581,000 / Available Including: $22,000
Lower Guardrail Portfolio Value: $3,692,000 / Available Including: $18,000

Joe & Jane	Available	Current***
Portfolio Value	$17,762,000	$17,762,000
Dynamic Distribution Rate	5.40%	1.35%
Upper Guardrail	$22,203,000	$5,581,000
Lower Guardrail	$14,802,000	$3,692,000
Baseline	$17,762,000	$4,444,000
Monthly Income	$79,930	$20,000
Upper Income	$87,920	$22,000
Lower Income	$71,940	$18,000

***The figures referred to as "current" have been adjusted to reflect accounts not held at Fidelity as of 03/31/20XX. This report is not complete without all accompanying disclaimers! Our attorneys would like us to remind you that this report is provided as a courtesy and is for informational purposes only. Only the statements you receive directly from the investment companies (e.g., Fidelity) should be considered official. While we spend a great deal of time and money ensuring the accuracy of this report, mistakes can happen. Thanks.

Long-Term Care

This is a great tool if you work with retirees, like I do. (If you work with a different niche, you can still benefit from this value-add, but consider framing it in a more appropriate way for your clients: "What if you died?")

On the following pages, you'll find an example of the long-term-care value-add my office sends all our A- and B-level clients.

Long-Term Care Strategy

JARVIS
FINANCIAL

As part of our commitment to your ongoing financial success, we have
created the following guide that details our strategy should you find yourself
in need of long-term care. It is our hope that you will never need to use this
strategy, but as the old saying goes, "Luck favors the prepared."

PLEASE review this strategy carefully, noting any areas where you have
questions, concerns, and/or would like more information. We can discuss
these items together in our next meeting.

Being Prepared

If due to physical illness and/or diminished capacity you were unable to make
your own financial decisions, your power of attorney document provides legal
authority for someone else to act on your behalf. Without this document, the
courts would appoint a guardian.

Based on our records, your power of attorney documents are as follows:

	Joe	Jane
Year Created:		
Primary:		
Contingent:		

Recommended Action:

Consider inviting the individuals you have designated to dinner to thank them
in advance for their future assistance and to explain that our office is standing
by to assist them in caring for you when the time comes.

Fidelity's Trusted Contact:

By now you've likely received several letters/emails from Fidelity asking you to
establish a "trusted contact" on your accounts. This program, mandated by the
federal government, gives Fidelity someone to contact if they have questions
or concerns about your health or welfare.

While our office is your "trusted advisor," we cannot be named as your "trusted
contact." As such, we recommend that you name as your "trusted contact" the
same person(s) you have designated in your power of attorney estate documents.

> ### Recommended Action:
> Enclosed with this report is the Fidelity form to establish your "trusted
> contact." Please fill in highlighted areas in section 2, sign, date, and return
> the form to our office in the envelope provided.

Paying for Care

"Best Case" Scenario

Approximately 7 out of 10 retirees will spend LESS than $50,000 on long-term care per person. If you need care at this level, your total lifetime long-term care expenses would be less than $50,000 per person.

While $50,000 is very real money, your investment accounts along with your home equity could easily cover this expense. It would, however, reduce your legacy goals.

Because your assets could easily cover this "best case" scenario, we recommend focusing your attention on reducing the risks of needing higher levels of care. Specifically:

• Where in our home can we reduce the risks of tripping and/or falling (leading cause of LTC)?
• If we were unable to continuing driving, how/who would run essential errands?
• What can we do in our lifestyle to "stay young," both physically and mentally?

"Bad" Scenario

Approximately 2 out of 10 retirees will spend between $50,000 and $250,000 on long-term care per person. While this is a staggering number, it is important to remember that the expense would likely be spread over multiple years AND it would take the place of essentially all of your other lifestyle expenses.

Source: Department of Health and Human Services

In Your Situation:

As with the "best case" scenario, this IS real money, but your assets WOULD be able to cover this expense without significant disruption to your finances or legacy goals, keeping in mind that it would be largely offset by lifestyle changes (e.g., selling your car).

Recommended Action:

The most important action at this time would be selecting a future care provider, ideally something in your local area. Whatever your choice, make sure the person who will be assisting you (i.e., your power of attorney) has this information in writing.

"Worst Case" Scenario

Approximately 1 out of 10 retirees will have the misfortune of spending more than $250,000 on long-term care per person. This tragic scenario would most likely be the result of severe dementia, requiring many years of intense care.

In Your Situation:

Even this worst case scenario will not "sink" your retirement. It will, however, put a sizable dent in your legacy goals.

Recommended Action:

If you are concerned about the potential impact this scenario could have on your legacy goals, we can meet to discuss tools for ensuring your goals are met. As with the other scenarios, it is important that you create detailed instructions for your standards of care.

Putting It All Together

I've included enough examples to get you through a good portion of your information cycle, at which point you can begin repeating your value-adds with slight variations. (Your clients won't remember.) Some of these examples may be a little dated by the time you read this or may otherwise be irrelevant, but you can still use them as the foundation for new and improved value-adds.

Here's a solid value-add calendar cycle to get you started:

Q1—1099 Tax Letter

Q1.5—RMD Letter

Q2—Rotating Value-Add (or guardrails)

Q3—Rotating Value-Add

Q4—Year-End Tax Report

With quarterly value-adds as the final piece of your information cycle, your business can finally become the value-adding machine you've always known it could be.

Action Steps

Marketing works only if you put in the time and effort—but if you streamline those efforts, you can truly begin to Deliver Massive Value.

Now that you have the tools and knowledge to take your business to the next level, implement these final action steps to launch your business to new heights.

- ○ Build your value-add timeline: design the system, gather data, generate reports, and make quality control a continual priority.
- ○ Build the output first, then determine the most efficient and accurate method of compiling data.
- ○ Measure actual time required to complete the first ten items on your list. Also measure accuracy.
- ○ Allow ample buffer time before, during, and after the value-add to make sure your results are accurate.

Bonus content available for this chapter at ThePerfectRIA.com/BookBonus:

→ PDF of the samples in this chapter
→ My twelve-month value-add calendar
→ Access to training on value-adds

How to Transition Clients to a Junior Advisor

Every time I talk with Michael Kitces, he loves to remind me that in our first interview together in 2017 (kitces.com/7), I shared that my practice was "just right" and that I had no interest in growing it and certainly no interest in hiring another advisor. Less than five years later, I had doubled my revenue, which, along with some extreme accountability, led me to hire a new lead advisor for my team. Over the following twelve months, I successfully transitioned 90 percent of my client relationships to this advisor, with almost no client pushback.

Below is a basic timeline of this transition, but because the messaging on this transition is so important, on the book bonus website you will find the exact letters I sent to clients, as well as videos of my scripts making the transition. You will also find the value-add worksheet we used to transfer credibility from me to my new advisor.

- **Five Months Prior to Hire:** Retained a top-notch recruiting agency to help with the selection process. Also retained industry consultant Austin Velarde (of APFA fame) to help with final screening.
- **Three Months Prior to Hire:** Client newsletter article about the growth of our practice and that we've started on a search for a world-class advisor to join our team.
- **One Month Prior to Hire:** Client newsletter article highlighting the qualifications of our new team member and addressing potential concerns (e.g., "Will I have to work with the B-team?").
- **First Six Months of Hire:** Every client communication created credibility for the new advisor.
- **First Surge Cycle:** Advisor joined me in virtually every client meeting to "help provide a fresh set of eyes" and to specifically walk the client through our cash-management value-add.
- **Second Surge Cycle:** Depending on the client relationship, either the new advisor and I split the agenda items equally or a complete handoff was made (see next step).
- **Third Surge Cycle:** For virtually every relationship (except the twenty or so where I was remaining as lead): "Mr. & Mrs. Client, today I'm going to have Alex meet with you, for two reasons. The first is that I want him to provide a fresh perspective on your situation without my interference. The second, and this is where I need a favor from you, is to see how he does when I'm not in the room ..."

For full scripts and additional insights on this transition, check out ThePerfectRIA.com/bookbonus.

Will This Year Be Your "Best Year Ever"

and Will Next Year Be Even Better?!?

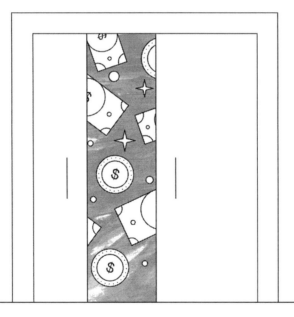

From the start of my career in 2003 until 2010, from a business, financial, stress, and work-life balance perspective, every year was my "Worst Year Ever." What made these soul-crushing years even worse was that I couldn't figure out what had to change, only that something had to. I desperately wanted to have a seven-figure practice (what I imagined at that time to be a "successful" practice). I desperately wanted a work-life balance with my young family. I desperately wanted to be confident in my ability to Deliver Massive Value.

All this changed when I invested $10,000-plus to join Tom Gau's group coaching program. Being able to "Rip-and-Deploy" exactly the way Tom communicated with prospects, exactly how he Delivered Massive Value to clients, and exactly how he managed his practice transformed my practice and my life.

Since then, every year has been an all-new "Best Year Ever" and while Tom laid the foundation of my success, to this day I invest roughly 10 percent of my income each year (which now is more annually than I earned in my first five years, combined) into personal development so that next year will again be my Best Year Ever.

What about you and your practice, and your prospects, and your clients, and your work-life balance? What will it take to make you even more successful in each of these areas so that you too can enjoy year after year of "Best Year Ever"?

Having been blessed to see firsthand the transformation of hundreds of practices, I can promise you that the key going from year to year of "Best Year Ever" is to be surrounded and coached by advisors who have already achieved your next level of success and who can get you to TAKE ACTION!

Together with my closest friend and business partner, Micah Shilanski, we have created a system for advisors like you to be trained, motivated, inspired, mentored, coached, and high-fived by some of the most successful advisors in the industry (including yours truly):

INVICTUS by The Perfect RIA

In my (not so humble and admittedly biased opinion), INVICTUS is the single best advisor coaching program in the industry. How can I make such a claim?

Every step of the program is based on exactly what Micah and I are doing in our respective practices RIGHT NOW.

- You can Rip-and-Deploy every script, system and process we have used to build a $5 million-plus and $2 million-plus practice, respectively.
- You have access (albeit via a surge schedule) to Micah and myself to assist with whatever questions, concerns, issues, and/or opportunities are facing your practice.
- At least twice a year you will be invited to spend multiple days with Micah and me as you learn firsthand what it takes to build a "highly profitable, hyper-efficient, lifestyle practice."

- MORE IMPORTANTLY, you will have the opportunity to transform your practice through our exclusive extreme accountability system.
- EVEN MORE IMPORTANTLY, during these events you will be surrounded by other rockstar advisors with whom you can collaborate for best practices.
- MOST IMPORTANTLY, each calendar quarter you will receive a white-labeled version of *all* the client and prospect communication being used by Micah and me, including value-adds, client newsletters, and education event packets.
- Plus dozens of hours of training, including team training, directly from Micah, myself, and our respective teams.
- And because we are always improving our practices, you'll also receive regular webinars with our latest and greatest tools, techniques, and processes.
- And so much more!

When you are ready to join us on the path of "Best Year Ever," mention to our team the code word "Guardrails Beat Buckets" and they will add a special bonus to your membership.

Even if INVICTUS is not right for you, in my heart of hearts I truly hope that this year and next and the one after that are your personal "Best Year Ever"!

Happy Planning!

P.S. Recently I spoke with a team of advisors who had joined Tom Gau's coaching program the same year as me. Despite having started with a bigger team, more assets, and decades of additional experience, today my practice is more than double theirs (four times if you measure revenue per hour worked). HOW IS THIS POSSIBLE? Action. When I joined Tom's program, I committed myself so completely that even if he had told me to wear purple suits and pink underwear, I would have done exactly what he said (otherwise why be in his program?). If you want my level of success (or Micah's, whose numbers are roughly double mine), you have to take action.

Please note that just as we do in our practices, Micah and I are constantly making adjustments on our journey to the "perfect" practice. As such, please speak with our team about the most current features and benefits before signing up.

Matthew Jarvis

Twelve Books Every Advisor Must Read

Years ago I lost track of the exact count of the hundreds of books I've studied that in some way are related to the art and science of financial planning. The list that follows are the books that had the biggest impact on my career and are books that I routinely revisit.

The War of Art by Steven Pressfield

Financial planning is really, really hard. While Pressfield talks specifically about the creative process, the force of "resistance" is a real threat in all endeavors. I reread this book at least annually and often give it out as a gift.

Behavioral Investment Counseling by Nick Murray

Nick Murray is the godfather of behavioral financial planning. All of his books are pure gold (and currently priced accordingly). It's nearly impossible to find in print, but you can find a digital copy on his website. I've reread my copy so many times that the pages have started falling out. His scripts in this book (and in his newsletter) kept me going during the dark days of the financial crisis.

Extreme Ownership by Jocko Willink and Leif Babin

As financial advisors, there are plenty of things to blame when we fail to achieve our BHAGs. The markets, clients who don't understand, prospects who were taken by "bad" competitors, team members who don't deliver, etc. While not specific to financial advisors, Jocko and Leif lay it out in plain terms that *everything* is ours to own and fix.

The Ultimate Sales Machine by Chet Holmes

I know, I know. You're not in "sales," you're in financial planning, but if you can't "sell" someone on the plan you created, or why they should work with you, "selling" will be the least of your concerns. Chet Holmes is absolutely brilliant and if you ever stop by my office I'll show you the twenty-DVD training series I purchased from him years ago.

The 4-Hour Workweek by Timothy Ferriss

As of this printing, the only three-star review on Amazon for my own book claims: *"Tales of working very little while making a fortune smack of smug Tim Ferriss who the author seems to idolize."* Not sure I would consider Ferriss my "idol," but I am for sure a Tim Ferriss fanboy. While his book is a bit dated, it's still pure gold, even if it did earn me my only three-star review.

Influence by Robert Cialdini

This book (and his others) are *scary* good. So much so that before you read it I ask that you promise yourself to only use these skills for good. That said, if in your heart of hearts you want what is best for clients, this book will make you a master communicator.

Solve for Happy by Mo Gawdat

Depending on where you are in your career, the following will sound either completely accurate or totally insane: Success is a false summit. If you think that "when I get to X, then I'll be/do Y," you won't. Sure, success eliminates some pressures, but they are replaced by all new ones that feel even more painful. This book helps.

So Good They Can't Ignore You by Cal Newport

I enjoy all of Cal Newport's books, but if I had to pick one, this would be it. Be the very best financial advisor you can be and everything else will fall in line. However, being the best should not be confused with playing office under the guise of "studying," "research," or any other avoidance behavior.

Never Split the Difference by Chris Voss

Strongly recommend listening to this one, as much of it reads like a crime novel. Voss is a brilliant negotiator and his techniques can be easily implemented by everyone.

Life and Death Planning for Retirement Benefits by Natalie Choate

Had to slip in at least one hard-to-read technical resource. Choate is a brilliant technician and while her book is dense, it is one of the best reference guides on retirement benefits.

A Random Walk Down Wall Street by Burton Malkiel

This book is so popular that I'm surprised how many people have not read it. More than anything, it serves as an antidote to the latest get-rich-quick investment scheme.

Basic Economics by Thomas Sowell

Every other economic textbook in the world should be burned at the altar of Sowell's work. Understanding how the economy really works makes it much easier to help clients understand why we don't panic and/or get greedy.

LAST PAGE, I PROMISE

I invested hundreds of hours and close to six figures to get this book and all its bonuses into your hands. *If* my investment, combined with your commitment to take action, saves you from just *one* of the painful mistakes I made and/or it allows you to Deliver Massive Value to just *one* more client, then it was a total success worth every penny.

That said, I hope that my journey to transforming the industry has only just begun. As such, if this book in any way helped you and your practice, I would greatly appreciate if you would help spread the word by doing one or more of the following:

1. Post to your social media (LinkedIn) a picture of yourself with the book and a quick blurb about how it helped you Deliver Massive Value to clients. Please also tag me, Matthew Jarvis, and The Perfect RIA in your post.
2. Copy your post and paste it into a five-star review on Amazon.com and your favorite podcast platform.
3. When our paths cross at a TPR event and/or an industry conference, give me a high five and let me buy you a drink.

Thank you so much!

In Memory of Tom Gau

Tom Gau was in my mind the greatest financial advisor of all time. In addition to the multiple top-tier practices he personally built and the coaching he did, he was responsible for hundreds of rockstar practices that collectively represent tens of billions in assets. His mastery of communication was documented in an entire chapter of Malcolm Gladwell's *The Tipping Point* (which is how I discovered Gau).

Without Tom's coaching of me, this book, The Perfect RIA, and even my practice would not exist today.

I was personally blessed to work with Tom for seven years as part of the Million Dollar Producer (now APFA) coaching program and I was honored beyond belief when he called me last year asking that we partner to coach advisors, a partnership that was tragically cut short by Tom's passing in August 2022.

Just a few months before his passing, I had the opportunity to take Tom to dinner to thank him for all he had done for me and the industry. At that dinner, Tom was as full of life and energy as ever, and true to form, he gave me even more great strategies for my practice (and a few more classic Tom jokes not appropriate for print).

While he is no longer with us, I am reminded of one of Tom's favorite sayings: "GREAT NEWS!" Shortly before his passing, we partnered to record a day of his coaching program held in Las Vegas. In his honor, we have made this recording available for the entire industry, which you can watch by visiting www.ThePerfectRIA.com/BookBonus. You can also hear Tom in action with Michael Kitces at Kitces.com/240.

Rest in Peace, Tom.

Notes

Delivering Massive Value

6462d6cb-992d-4fc7-b54d-b6af393bdd77R01